SHOT DOWN
AND IN THE DRINK

SHOT DOWN

AND IN THE DRINK

True stories of RAF and Commonwealth aircrews saved from the sea in WWII

Graham Pitchfork

Foreword by
Flight Lieutenant
John Cruickshank VC

the national archives

First edition published in 2005
Paperback edition published in 2007 by

The National Archives
Kew, Richmond
Surrey, TW9 4DU, UK

www.nationalarchives.gov.uk

The National Archives brings together the Public Record Office,
Historical Manuscripts Commission, Office of Public Sector
Information and Her Majesty's Stationery Office.

A catalogue card for this book is available from the British Library.

ISBN 978 1 905615 05 6

Cover design by Briony Chappell
Typeset by Florence Production Ltd, Stoodleigh, Devon
Printed in Singapore by KHL Printing Co

Contents

Foreword 7

Author's note 9

Abbreviations 11

Part One: The Air Sea Rescue Organization 13

1 Background 14
2 Early Wartime Organization 19
3 Aircrew Training 25
4 Survival Equipment 38
5 Location Aids 44

Part Two: Northwest Europe 51

6 Rescue Craft 52
7 The First Three Years 86
8 Battle of the Atlantic 116
9 The Bomber Offensive 145
10 Return to Europe 169

Part Three: Mediterranean and West Africa 183

11 The Early Years 184
12 Invasion of Sicily and Italy 208
13 The Italian and Balkans Campaign 220
14 West Africa 241

Part Four: India and the Far East   **249**

15 Air Sea Rescue Organization   250
16 Rescues   255

Epilogue   272
Bibliography   274
Index   277
Author's Acknowledgements   286
Picture Acknowledgements   288

Foreword

Flight Lieutenant
John Cruickshank VC

T HE AUTHOR HAS developed a reputation in recent years for his sympathetic understanding of the human dimensions of the air war. In his last book, *Shot Down and on the Run*, he related the amazing stories of human endeavour displayed by those who were shot down over enemy-occupied territory, yet avoided capture to return home with the aid of their gallant 'helpers'. He has now turned his attention to those in an equally desperate predicament, the aircrew that came down in the sea.

At the beginning of the war, the Air Sea Rescue Service was almost non-existent, yet just six years later it could boast many specialist squadrons and hundreds of rescue launches based throughout the world wherever the RAF and Commonwealth air forces were flying. It was a remarkable transformation, yet little has been written about its organization and achievements.

Having set out in detail the background to the development of the Air Sea Rescue Services and the advances made in rescue methods and the survival aids available, the author relates some amazing accounts of the airmen forced down in the sea. He has also paid due recognition to some quite remarkable exploits of the rescuers. Men who landed their flimsy aircraft on rough seas, others who took great risks in landing their heavy flying boats on the open sea and the masters of rescue launches who often took their craft close to enemy shores and rescued men under enemy gunfire. The rescuers were a remarkable group of men whose exploits have received far too little attention and I am pleased that Air Commodore Pitchfork has located the archives to enable him to record their deeds.

Those of us who flew over the sea were always conscious of its ever-changing moods and the need to treat it with respect and to be constantly prepared for any eventuality. Weather and sea conditions were often benign, giving those in distress a good chance of survival. But the sea could also be cruel and only those with immense resolve survived. Many did, and it is testimony to their great fortitude and courage.

This book also graphically highlights the lengths that the RAF rescue services, and the men who manned the rescue machines, were prepared to go to if there was the slightest chance of finding survivors and completing a rescue. It was a great comfort to all aircrew to know that no effort would be spared to save them.

Much has been written about the air war during the Second World War, a great deal of it concentrating on the operational aspects. Little attention has been paid to many of those who supported these major operations, not least the Air Sea Rescue Service. Air Commodore Pitchfork has made a major contribution to our knowledge and understanding of this neglected subject, and the gallant activities of the men of the Royal Air Force who manned the rescue craft and aircraft at home and abroad. The episodes that he has related are remarkable and will remind future generations what the human spirit is capable of when confronted with great adversity.

A great deal of war is about taking life, but the theme of this book in the context of war revolves around the saving of life. It is a fitting tribute to those who developed the services, the rescued and the rescuers.

Author's note

I N THE YEARS immediately following the end of the Second World War, historians of the Air Ministry's Air Historical Branch (AHB) wrote a series of definitive narratives of the major air campaigns and theatre air operations. Those dealing with the Battle of Britain and Bomber Command's offensives have been published in recent years. Over the next few years, the present Head of the Air Historical Branch hopes to publish others but this will take time. Those narratives dealing with the support areas are unlikely to be published in the foreseeable future. Amongst them is the narrative dealing with 'Air Sea Rescue', which is available to the public at the National Archives as AIR 10/5553.

In discussing the idea for this book with Sebastian Cox, the Head of AHB, we agreed that it would be appropriate to use the excellent AHB narrative as the basis for a book dealing exclusively with the RAF's Air Sea Rescue Service in the Second World War. I have, therefore, drawn heavily on the original narrative, which the authors produced by referring to the many associated RAF documents, now held at Kew. I have examined these and used extracts to amplify certain aspects of the original narrative. I would not claim that this book is in any way a 'definitive' history of air sea rescue during the Second World War, but it has been written using these primary historical sources in addition to the AHB narrative.

My primary aim in writing this book has been to highlight the activities of those involved in air sea rescue, set against a backdrop of the organization of the rescue service and, in particular, the amazing deeds of those airmen who came down in the sea and their rescuers.

Therefore, I have endeavoured to expand the AHB narrative by including many accounts of actual rescues.

In selecting over 40 individual rescues, I have chosen a wide cross section in order to illustrate the many varied circumstances of those who came down in the sea, and their subsequent experiences before rescue. I have also tried to cover as many different methods of rescue as possible embracing the RAF's global activities. This has provided a surprisingly diverse cross section of amazing experiences, which highlight that the human resolve and will to survive know no boundaries when life is under great threat. In addition, they demonstrate the lengths men will go to whilst ever there is a chance to rescue a fellow in peril.

There is one other important aim that I set myself. Sadly, the generation of men who are the subject of this book are inevitably fading into the past. I believe it is most important that their gallant deeds, courage and fortitude are set out for others to admire. They are an example to future generations of just what humanity is capable of when faced by the greatest danger, and their deeds deserve to be recorded.

The book is dedicated to those who displayed those unique survival qualities, but where rescue was either unavailable or arrived too late.

Graham Pitchfork

Abbreviations

ADGB	Air Defence of Great Britain
AHB	Air Historical Branch
AOC	Air Officer Commanding
ASDIC	Allied Submarine Detection Investigation Committee
ASR	Air Sea Rescue
ASRMCU	Air Sea Rescue and Marine Craft Unit
ASRU	Air Sea Rescue Unit
ASV	Air to surface vessel
BEF	British Expeditionary Force
BEM	British Empire Medal
DC	Depth charge
DCAS	Deputy Chief of Air Staff
DF	Direction finding
DFC	Distinguished Flying Cross
DFM	Distinguished Flying Medal
DSC	Distinguished Service Cross
DSM	Distinguished Service Medal
DSO	Distinguished Service Order
GPO	General Post Office
HF	High frequency
HSL	High speed launch
IFF	Identification Friend or Foe
kc/s	Kilocycles per second
KOSB	King's Own Scottish Borderers
MBE	Member of the Order of the British Empire
MF	Medium frequency

MGB	Motor gun boat
MTB	Motor torpedo boat
OTU	Operational Training Unit
POW	Prisoner of war
RAAF	Royal Australian Air Force
RAFVR	Royal Air Force Volunteer Reserve
RCAF	Royal Canadian Air Force
RML	Rescue motor launch
RNLI	Royal National Lifeboat Institution
RNVR	Royal Navy Volunteer Reserve
RNZAF	Royal New Zealand Air Force
R/T	Radio telephony
SAAF	South African Air Force
SEAC	South East Asia Command
ST	Seaplane tender
U-boat	*Unterseeboot* (submarine)
USAAF	United States Army Air Forces
USN	United States Navy
VCAS	Vice Chief of the Air Staff
VGO	Vickers gas operated (guns)
VHF	Very high frequency
VLR	Very long range
WOP	Wireless operator
WOP/AG	Wireless operator/air gunner
W/T	Wireless telegraphy

PART ONE

The Air Sea Rescue Organization

Chapter One

Background

T HE PRIMARY DUTY of an air sea rescue organization is to rescue airmen, not aircraft, from the sea. In times of peace such an organization has two aims: the maintenance of morale, and the closely allied humanitarian impulse of saving life. In times of war a third must be added, and it is the most important of the three: the recovery of trained manpower for the furtherance of the war effort.

In the early years after the First World War little special equipment or organization was provided for the rescue of aircrew unfortunate enough to force-land or bale out over the sea. They were issued with lifebelts or flotation jackets of various types, but once in the sea they relied on passing naval or merchant ships for rescue. However, between the wars little flying by landplanes was carried out over the sea. Moreover, the increasing reliability of aircraft engines and the limited need to fly in adverse weather conditions meant that the number of forced landings at sea was small. The only Royal Air Force aircrew who were provided with any form of rescue equipment were the flying boat crews who by the nature of their work constantly operated over and alighted on the sea, and they were provided with a triangular dinghy for use as an emergency tender, which could be used for rescue purposes. There was, therefore, little need for a formal air sea rescue organization.

The introduction by the mid-1930s of longer-range aircraft and regular flights overseas created a need for more formal arrangements for air sea rescue. Larger dinghies with a greater capacity were developed, and this included dinghies stored in the wing of the aircraft that could be released in the event of a ditching. In 1935 air staff approval was given to the building of an experimental high speed launch (HSL), to be evaluated as a seagoing safety boat. If the trials were successful, it was intended to establish similar safety boats for the use of the general reconnaissance squadrons of Coastal Command whose airfields were situated on the coast.

The experimental launch (*HSL 100*) was handed over to RAF Manston in Kent in August 1936. It proved to be a success as a safety boat, capable of carrying four stretchers and putting to sea to aid crews in distress in all but the roughest weather. As a result, orders were given for a further 15 of the launches to be established on each of the 7 Coastal Command airfields and one each at Malta, Aden, Basra, Ceylon, Penang and Hong Kong. Although these craft were allocated primarily for use with aircraft from their own units, they could be called on to assist in rescue work, when the individual station commanders co-ordinated the operation.

From 1934 onwards instructions had been issued regularly to units on the steps to be taken when service aircraft were in distress or overdue when flying over the sea near the British Isles. In 1937 the first instructions were issued in which specific reference was made to these high speed launches. The procedure was as follows:

When a distress call was received or an aircraft was known to be overdue a message was broadcast to shipping from the GPO W/T (wireless telegraphy) stations, naval authorities were requested to inform HM ships in the vicinity and HM Coastguards were advised in order that they might, if necessary, call for the assistance of the Royal National Lifeboat Institution's (RNLI) lifeboats. If the missing aircraft was believed to be in the vicinity of the Croydon–Continental air routes, Croydon aerodrome was also informed in order that civil aircraft might search along the route. If the location of the aircraft in distress was believed to be more than 300 miles from the British coast an international broadcast was sent out from the GPO radio station at Portishead, in order that ships of any nationality might keep watch for possible survivors. When RAF flying boat or general reconnaissance bases were within reasonable distance, their help could also be enlisted in the search, as well as that of any rescue HSL in the area, at the discretion of the senior officer concerned.

In 1936 and 1937 the air staff considered providing flotation gear to landplanes whose primary role was overland but which might need to fly over the sea. As a result, in 1937 it was decided that Fleet Air Arm aircraft, general reconnaissance aircraft and torpedo bombers, as well as flying boats, should be provided with emergency dinghies, marine distress signals and positive buoyancy for their aircraft. Although it was agreed that new types of bombers were to include design features for an inflatable dinghy, it was felt that modifications to current types could not be justified. Accordingly, crews of existing bombers were provided with a type of flotation jacket only.

At the beginning of 1938, Bomber Command staffs pointed out that their aircraft were undertaking long navigational flights over the sea and dinghies should, therefore, be provided to give their crews a reasonable chance of rescue in the event of ditching. It was agreed that the heavy bombers (Harrow, Whitley, Heyford and Hampden) should be provided with a circular type of pneumatic dinghy ('H' type) adapted from earlier types, but which on ditching floated free, un-attached to the aircraft. It was possible to house the dinghy and accessories in a floating container, which could be thrown into the sea by one of the crew immediately the aircraft came to rest. The medium bomber types (Battle and Blenheim) were to be equipped with a small triangular dinghy ('C' type) in a similar container. A larger type for seven or eight persons ('J' type) was to be developed for the new heavy bombers under development, such as the Stirling. These dinghies were intended to keep the crew afloat until they could be rescued. No equipment was provided other than a topping-up pump, a drogue to act as a sea anchor, and three marine distress signals, which were of a poor design and seldom worked.

In 1938, the Navy experimented with a new smoke float, which emitted a large cloud of red smoke. They also called for an emergency ration for each member of the crew, together with a first aid kit. The RAF followed suit, but water – the most important item – remained a problem which could only be met by the standard service water bottle carried by each member of the crew. The provision of aids was based on the assumption that ditched airmen would not have to wait long before being rescued.

During the extensive Home Defence exercises carried out in the summer of 1938 and 1939, landplanes had to fly over the sea and special arrangements were made for air sea rescue. The RAF provided special safety boats and destroyers were made available by the Navy. In addition, coastguards were instructed to keep special watch for any distress signals. In September 1938, the facilities provided by the civil life-saving control officers at civil airfields were added to those that could be made available for rescue work. These officers could call upon civil aircraft equipped with radio and advise those flying over the area to search for missing aircrew.

In December 1938, the Air Officer Commanding-in-Chief Bomber Command (Air Chief Marshal Sir Edgar Ludlow-Hewitt) raised the question of the safety arrangements for his Command. He pointed out that the war plans then being developed required his bombers to fly over the North Sea. It was, therefore, essential that his crews should fly long-range training flights over the sea, but these had to be restricted because of the limited rescue facilities and the time taken to reach any of his crews forced to ditch in the sea. At this time there were just seven high speed launches in operation around the British coast, and a 400-mile stretch of the east coast without any cover at all. Although the crews had dinghies, these would be of little use if marine craft could not be dispatched quickly to their aid. There were also plans to increase the number of general reconnaissance squadrons and this would increase the need for more safety boats.

To consider these requirements a conference was held at the Air Ministry on 28 February 1939, presided over by the Assistant Chief of Air Staff (Air Vice-Marshal W. Sholto Douglas) and attended by representatives of Coastal, Bomber, Fighter and Training Commands. The chairman ruled that the conference should confine itself to peacetime requirements and not those that might be considered necessary in the event of mobilization. It was decided that the high speed launch organization should be controlled by Coastal Command and that an additional 13 launches would be necessary, to include two for the Middle East Command. Since it would take time to acquire the additional launches, those allocated to Penang and Ceylon were to be diverted to Grimsby and Great Yarmouth and a third was to be transferred from Glasgow to Blyth in order to meet the increased requirements for the North Sea area.

In July 1939 amended instructions were issued detailing the responsibilities of the Coastal Command Group Commanders for co-ordinating the aircraft and marine craft involved in rescue. Pending the provision of a chain of 19 high speed launches for rescue work based from Wick in the north of Scotland eastwards right round the coast to the Isle of Man, interim measures were taken to establish the available launches along the east coast and the English Channel.

On the outbreak of war the Assistant Chief of Air Staff ruled that no further launches were to be sent abroad until requirements at home had been met – the result of this decision was that the overseas Commands had only four launches at Singapore, Malta, Aden and Basra.

Chapter Two

Early Wartime Organization

T HE RESCUE ARRANGEMENTS for the early months of the war followed the general lines of the peacetime organization, but certain facilities were no longer available, such as the civil aerodromes and GPO W/T stations. In March 1940 new communications instructions were issued dealing with aircraft in distress over the sea. An aircraft in distress sent an SOS or Mayday (*M'aidez*) message and the RAF formation receiving the distress call passed a priority message to Fighter Command, whose movements liaison section then forwarded the message to appropriate naval authorities, RAF formations and the coastguards.

As the opening shots were fired in the Battle of Britain, there were still only 14 high speed launches in commission. The intensity of fighter operations over the Channel alerted the authorities to the increasing loss of airmen over the sea. During the last 21 days of July over 220 aircrew were killed or missing, the majority over the sea. As a result, at the end of July 1940 the Vice-Admiral, Dover (Vice-Admiral Sir Bertram Ramsey), and the Air Officer Commanding (AOC) No. 11 Group (Air Vice-Marshal Keith Park) organized a local rescue service with light naval craft, RAF launches and some Lysander aircraft borrowed from Army Co-operation Command. The value of the 'combined services' organization was soon apparent.

On 22 August 1940 the Deputy Chief of Air Staff (DCAS) (Air Vice-Marshal Arthur Harris) chaired a meeting that established the formation of a skeleton Sea Rescue Organization that provided the basis for all the developments that followed. All rescue craft came under the operational control of the local naval authorities, with the RAF remaining responsible for the air search and for informing the naval authorities. Approval was given to retain the Lysanders, which were placed under the operational control of Fighter Command where liaison officers were appointed to assist in handling the search organization. Thus, nearly 12 months after the outbreak of war, the first steps were taken towards the formation of an organization specifically allotted to the task of sea rescue.

The Sea Rescue Organization put into force in August 1940, valuable though it had proved in the Battle of Britain, was still found to be seriously wanting in many respects, and too narrow in scope to meet the increasing demands being made on it. It was becoming obvious that the co-ordination of the work of the rescue services under a central organization would be the only means of securing true efficiency.

In October 1940, aircrew losses were 260, the majority over the sea, which a more efficient rescue organization could have reduced. In December 1940, the Chief of the Air Staff (Air Chief Marshal Sir Cyril Newall) instructed that the Sea Rescue Organization must be drastically reorganized and expanded. At the subsequent meeting chaired by DCAS, it was agreed that the rescue of RAF personnel from the sea had become of such paramount importance that a Directorate should be formed, headed by an Air Commodore as Director of Sea Rescue Services and assisted by a Naval Deputy Director. It soon became apparent that the best location was Headquarters Coastal Command. The Secretary of State gave provisional approval for the formation of the Directorate on 24 January 1941 when Group Captain L.G. Le B. Croke was promoted and appointed the first Director of Sea Rescue, and the Admiralty appointed, as Deputy Director, Captain C.L. Howe RN. The title of the Directorate was soon changed to 'Air Sea Rescue Services', a title that would avoid confusion with the Naval Sea Rescue Services.

A set of regulations was drawn up for the new Directorate, which would be responsible directly to DCAS. Briefly, its responsibilities were:

1. the co-ordination of all sea rescue operations for aircraft and aircraft crews;
2. the provision of ancillary equipment to be dropped by aircraft at the scene of distress, to provide aircrews with a chance of survival until the arrival of the rescue craft;
3. the provision of adequate marine craft, moored buoys and similar aids to rescue.

The new Directorate took up its duties on 6 February 1941, and during the next six months the small staff established close relations with various organizations that had a role to play in sea rescues. In addition to dealing with actual rescue activities, the Directorate of Air Sea Rescue was responsible for the development of life saving equipment in conjunction with the Director of Operational Requirements. From its foundation it had four main problems to solve:

1. how to teach aircrews to ditch and abandon a landplane forced to land into the sea;
2. how to maintain life of the aircrew after they had abandoned their aircraft;
3. how to locate the aircrew;
4. how to bring them safely home.

These four key areas will be addressed individually in the chapters that follow.

For the purpose of sea search the British Isles was divided into four areas coinciding with the geographical boundaries of the four Coastal Command Groups (Nos 15, 16, 18 and 19) with sea rescue officers attached to each Group. Close-in search in a coastal area 20 miles in depth stretching from the Wash round the south coast to South Wales was the responsibility of Fighter Command's Lysander aircraft.

During the first four months of the new organization, successful rescues were raised from a bare 20 per cent to almost 35 per cent. Nevertheless, in June 1941 the DCAS (Air Vice-Marshal N.H. Bottomley) was concerned that the rescue services were not expanding in ratio to the increasing air offensive. His view was supported by the anxiety of the Commander-in-Chief of Bomber Command (Air Marshal Sir Richard Peirse), at the inability of the rescue services to meet the growing needs of his Command. The Admiralty also saw the need to review the administration of their light Coastal Forces, which included naval motor boats used for sea rescue. No naval officer had direct responsibility for this activity and it was felt that an officer who was fully alive to the importance of air sea rescue was needed to join the naval operations staff. The obvious choice was the Deputy Director of Air Sea Rescue, Captain C.L. Howe.

DCAS also saw that it would be an advantage if the Air Sea Rescue Services could be more closely knit with the allied work of Regional and Flying Control and he proposed the formation of a larger Directorate embracing all three organizations. It was felt that a senior officer of considerable standing should be chosen as the head and it was agreed that the appointment should be that of a Director General. The choice fell upon Marshal of the Royal Air Force Sir John Salmond. He accepted and took up his appointment on 23 September 1941.

The proposed organization he was asked to head consisted of the amalgamation of:

1. Directorate of Air Sea Rescue – concerned with the rescue of aircrews from the sea;
2. the Assistant Directorate of Regional Control – concerned with guiding aircraft to their bases;
3. the branch of the Directorate of Fighter Operations concerned with aerodrome lighting and navigational warnings.

The Air Sea Rescue Directorate was to be headed by Group Captain E.F.Waring, assisted by Commander G. Barnard RN. Three branches were established to deal with rescue policy, aircraft and ancillary equipment; the provision and allocation of marine craft and equipment; and liaison with Coastal Command.

In the meantime, a meeting that was to have a crucial impact on the longer-term development of the air sea rescue organization took place on 11 September, chaired by DCAS and attended by the

Assistant Chief of Naval Staff (Home) (Rear Admiral Power RN) and senior representatives from the major operational RAF Commands.

A review highlighted that successful rescues had increased since the formation of the Directorate of Air Sea Rescue (ASR), with 37 per cent of the 1,200 aircrew members who had crashed at sea rescued. The co-operation of the RAF generally, the Royal Navy, the Observer Corps, HM Coastguard, the RNLI and Trinity House was working well. Good progress had been made in providing airmen with dinghies and equipment to keep them alive and attract attention, and in instilling in aircrews a feeling of confidence in their safety equipment. The main difficulties encountered were the lack of rescue craft and the unsuitability of existing high speed launches for deep searches in rough water.

Improvements to the current organization and search responsibilities were discussed and it was agreed that operational executive control of the service should be vested in the Air Officer Commanding-in-Chief Coastal Command.

The meeting then discussed the use of the Lysander and Walruses of Fighter Command, the latter having just been introduced for sea rescues. It was felt that these aircraft could achieve better results if the search was extended from 20 miles to 40 miles from the coast. Operational aircraft undertook deep search. The serious losses of highly trained aircrew during the summer of 1941 indicated that speed in commencing the search was vital, and this was difficult to achieve with operational aircraft that had other more important demands. Furthermore, they could not take off until survival aids had been loaded, further increasing the delay. For a successful search close co-operation with surface craft was essential but was difficult to achieve with untrained crews. Little prospect of improvement in deep search could be hoped for unless aircraft could be specifically allotted to air sea rescue.

The need for deep search aircraft was agreed. It was decided that two squadrons of Hudsons, equipped with air-to-surface vessel radar (ASV) should be allocated for air sea rescue duties. Finally, the available types of sea rescue craft were fully investigated, and it was decided that high speed must be sacrificed for seaworthiness. Crews had to be kept alive in their dinghies until the arrival of slower but more seaworthy craft, which would stand a better chance of reaching them in a rough sea. The Admiralty representative reported that the Fairmile 'B' launch was being produced for the Navy and it was decided to approach them for 50 of this type to meet the RAF's requirement for 90 launches, against which 40 pinnaces were already in production.

The first nine months of the Air Sea Rescue Service had been an uphill struggle and the Director of ASR had faced some formidable problems. The losses in the sea of trained aircrew in 1941 averaged 200 each month, so it was no surprise that he secured a steadily mounting interest amongst the air staff in the rescue service. Major improvements to the organization, co-ordination and control of rescues had been made in order to achieve a higher success rate. The foundations had been laid for a rapid expansion of the service in anticipation of the dramatic increase in air operations mounted from airfields in the British Isles.

Chapter Three

Aircrew Training

FOLLOWING THE ESTABLISHMENT of the Directorate of Air Sea Rescue at the end of January 1941, one of the most pressing requirements the new organization had to address was the training of aircrews in ditching and dinghy procedures. Although it was 18 months since the opening of the war in Europe, most aircrews were uneducated in the use of the emergency dinghy and equipment and unfamiliar with the art of a successful ditching. All the assistance and safety and survival aids produced would be useless unless aircrews could be trained to carry out the correct ditching and escape procedures and, having done so, to use the aids they were provided with or might have dropped to them. The Directorate stressed to all Commands the urgent need to give aircrew opportunities to practise escape and dinghy drills.

When special lifesaving equipment was first introduced there were a few Group, Station and Squadron Commanders who were sufficiently keen to try and interest aircrews in their own safety. However, this was not typical across the RAF and little training was given regarding the correct distress procedure, handling of aircraft and dinghy drills. In 1940 No. 5 Bomber Group had some rescue enthusiasts who were led by the AOC (Air Vice-Marshal A.T. Harris) and they were sufficiently interested to conduct their own local rescue services and training.

Staff at the Directorate prepared lectures, instructional pamphlets and drawings, and the syllabuses at the Initial Training Wings, which all aircrew passed through before commencing flying training, were modified to include lectures on the duties of aircrew before, during

and after ditching. In April 1941 the first edition of a monthly
memorandum on flying training, *Tee Emm*, appeared in the crew rooms
of squadrons and flying units across the RAF. The introduction to the
first edition set the tone for the popular publication. Drawing on the
RAF's short history, but highlighting a tradition of the spirit of youth
and all that youth implies, the introduction suggested that *Tee Emm*
'should in a small way reflect this spirit by an occasional intrusion of
light heartedness into a serious subject'. Using the mythical and
accident-prone Pilot Officer Prune, it was an excellent medium for
passing on important information on airmanship and training. Articles
on survival and air sea rescue appeared at regular intervals until the
memorandum ceased publication in 1946. Three months after the first
edition of *Tee Emm*, special air diagrams were issued to illustrate the
ditching drills of the main aircraft. These showed colour step-by-step
pictures of the main features of the drill, and were issued in a most
attractive form in an effort to encourage the interest of aircrews.

In spite of this training drive it was apparent from rescue results and
reports of survivors that insufficient time and attention were being
paid to instruction in air sea rescue – aircrews generally refused to take
much interest on the grounds that it would 'never happen to me' –
and the Directorate had an uphill task in their drive to organize and
co-ordinate rescue training.

During one particular month five cases of loss occurred where
aircraft failed to return from flights over the sea and had not carried
out the correct distress procedure of sending a wireless telegraph
(W/T) message indicating that they were in trouble. This was only one
of the examples during early 1942 that made it clear that crews were
still very ignorant of the essentials necessary for a successful ditching
and subsequent rescue.

In March 1942, steps were taken to appoint an officer at every
station as the air sea rescue officer. He was responsible for all aspects
of air sea rescue equipment carried on the aircraft of his station, and
for the training of aircrews in dinghy drill and distress procedures.

An aircraft in distress was required to inform its base of its intended
ditching and the nature of the distress. Bomber and coastal aircraft
informed the control station appropriate to the area in which the

aircraft was flying giving course, height, speed, position and time, together with any other relevant details. The wireless operator continued to transmit until the aircraft was just about to ditch when, after giving the standard SOS distress signal, he clamped down the wireless key to allow the ground station to plot a bearing. Coastal Command aircraft also made a radio telephone (R/T) call if they were within range of a convoy. Fighter Command aircraft made their SOS using R/T on the sector fixer frequency.

Prior to landing in the sea the crew carried out the ditching drill. All lower escape hatches, bomb doors and internal access doors were closed to delay water entry, and inevitable sinking, after alighting on the sea. Upper exits were opened before crews took up the appointed crash position. The pilot, strapped in, endeavoured to land the aircraft into wind as slowly as possible, tail down, the other members of the crew bracing themselves against firm fixtures in the fuselage to break the shock of the impact. Having landed in the water each member of the crew carried out his previously appointed task, including assisting the others to embark in the emergency dinghy and taking out the necessary survival aids and equipment. Clearly, if this procedure and drill were not rehearsed frequently, personnel and equipment were likely to be lost. It was a difficult job for the station rescue officer to arouse interest and make lectures and demonstrations convincing. Some enterprising rescue officers invited those who had survived a ditching to visit their stations and brief the aircrews. There was no better way to convince doubting aircrew of the essential need to learn the appropriate drills than to hear the experiences of those who had survived terrifying ordeals.

The station air sea rescue officers had done their best to train aircrews in correct ditching and dinghy procedures, but the majority had insufficient knowledge themselves and had very little opportunity to undertake any training to gain this knowledge and experience. Their functions and duties had never been clearly defined because of a lack of facilities for their own training. In the eyes of many aircrew, these dedicated officers lacked credibility.

Towards the end of 1942 the increase in operations and the consequent number of forced landings at sea made it imperative that one officer on each station was fully trained in air sea rescue methods and procedures. In February 1943 a case was submitted to the Air Ministry for the formation of a special training course where practical exercises could be conducted using dinghies and rescue craft. In support of the case it was pointed out that, of the 1,761 aircrews that had come down in the sea in the last six months of 1942, 1,166 lives had been lost – 66 per cent of the crews involved in the incidents. An investigation highlighted the standard of training of aircrews and of the maintenance personnel responsible for rescue equipment as the main contributory causes to the high loss rate. To rectify the latter, a new trade of safety equipment worker was introduced.

On 26 February 1943, the Assistant Chief of Air Staff (Operations) gave authority for the formation of a School of Air Sea Rescue. He followed this up with a letter to all operational Commands urging a general improvement of standards of supervision and training.

The school was formed at Blackpool, where it could be accommodated on an established training station near the airfield at Squires Gate. The school was allocated three Anson aircraft and arrangements were made to use the marine craft at Fleetwood for exercises and dinghy sea training. The course was of two weeks' duration and could cater for 20 officers from the operational Commands and the USAAF. The school opened on 30 May 1943, and both theoretical and practical training was given on rescue procedures and familiarity with all types of rescue equipment. During its first seven months, the school trained 526 officers in rescue procedures and over 3,000 safety equipment assistants. This resulted in a greater awareness amongst aircrew of safety and survival measures, and an approved standard of maintenance of survival equipment.

The rescue of a Lancaster crew who had ditched near the Dutch coast provided a graphic example of the importance of having a fully trained officer and qualified airmen assistants at each squadron to make certain that all aircrews were familiar with ditching and dinghy drills.

The Lancaster was hit by flak when flying at 17,000 feet near the Dutch coast. The pilot jettisoned the bombs and started to return to base. The aircraft continued out to sea, losing height, and at 4,000 feet the pilot ordered the crew to prepare for ditching, which he should have initiated as soon as he left the coast. The wireless operator was not aware of this possibility until he heard the order, so valuable time, and height, was lost. When he transmitted an SOS the aircraft was too low for a fix to be obtained. He also failed to switch his Identification Friend or Foe (IFF) equipment to the distress position before commencing the distress procedure.

The pilot made a successful ditching and the dinghy was released satisfactorily. The crew took the emergency packs, pigeon containers (homing pigeons were regularly carried, as will be described in Chapter Five) and the radio transmitter into the dinghy before cutting the two cords which they assumed connected the dinghy to the aircraft. In fact, they cut adrift the main emergency pack containing the signals pistol, the loading coil for the radio and other emergency equipment, including water bottles. They found that one of the pigeons had been drowned because the lids of the containers had not been closed prior to ditching – this should have been the task of the mid-upper gunner. The other pigeon was wet, but they released it with a message attached. Unfortunately, it did not reach base, almost certainly because of its waterlogged condition.

After the crew had spent 24 hours in the dinghy, two RAF bombers flew close to the dinghy at low level, but the distressed crew were unable to attract the attention of the aircraft as they had no pyrotechnics. They tried to work the radio without success, unaware that the loading coil was missing. For the next four days they drifted in the direction of England, and the weather was so clear that they could see both the English and French coasts. They hoisted a shirt on the mast in the hope that they would be sighted, and early on the fifth day they were seen and picked up by a minesweeper when 8 miles off Dungeness. Their 130-hour ordeal in the dinghy might have been considerably reduced had they used the correct distress procedures, their knowledge of which had never been checked since they had arrived on their squadron.

The time to instil an awareness of distress procedures was at the Operational Training Units (OTU), where recently qualified aircrew came together to form crews to learn the operational skills before joining a squadron.

As the air sea rescue organization developed and the experiences of survivors were analysed, so the training programme for aircrew could be made more appropriate. With the rapid expansion of the air war – and with it the inevitable increase in losses, many at sea – survival techniques could be modified. The most important aspect was to disseminate this information to aircrew.

In addition to the regular articles in *Tee Emm* other articles appeared in the many publications available to aircrew. One to appear in the Coastal Command Review of July 1944 is worth recording, since it encapsulates all the advice for ditched aircrew and will provide a useful backdrop to much of what follows later in this book.

HOW TO SURVIVE IN A DINGHY

This is a difficult subject to discuss because the sea is so prolific of extraordinary occurrences. Just as we are beginning to think we know something of the conditions of survival, a crew is picked up alive when by all the known rules they should have died days before. Probably these unexpectedly long survivals are due to a great will to live, and to determination not to give up even if things appear hopeless. However, from the experiences of many people it is possible to work out a practicable routine and to outline what, from a medical point of view, ought to be done. Obviously every instruction must be preceded by 'if possible' because very often it will not be.

THE DITCHING

Assuming that the crew have properly adjusted their life-jackets and taken up ditching stations, the following points are most important.

Do not remove any clothing. Heavy clothing in the water does impede swimming and it does make it harder to climb out of the water into the dinghy, but it does not sink you. It becomes saturated with water and therefore about as heavy as water. Its buoyancy is about neutral, although it takes some time to expel all the air so that at first, heavy clothing actually buoys you up. In the dinghy the advantages of having all the clothing you can, even if it is wet, to serve as protection against the cold, are so great that you should wear as much as possible and discard none.

If you can, take into the dinghy one or more parachutes and any spare clothing. Since this is additional to all the rest of the emergency equipment, it will often be impossible, but they are very useful if available.

Do not go in the water from the aircraft unless you must. That may sound foolish, but before now people have dived in to rescue some quite unimportant piece of equipment. When the emergency arises you should instinctively avoid going in if it can be helped. It makes a tremendous difference if you can avoid getting wet through at the start. If you must go in, slide or jump in as gently as possible, hold your nose and close your mouth tight. Diving boldly into a rough sea with a Mae West on is unpleasant and makes your chances of swallowing sea water much greater. Sea water in the stomach increases seasickness very markedly.

If you are in the sea do not swim aimlessly. You may become exhausted very quickly in those conditions and then there will be no more swimming. Float long enough to make sure of an objective and then go for it. Wearing a Mae West in rough water you will get along best on your back.

If you have an injured man in the water, it is difficult to get him into the dinghy by pulling first his head, then his body and finally his legs aboard. As he comes in he tends to push you away from the buoyancy chamber against which you are kneeling, so that both you and the dinghy are unbalanced. Float him horizontally against the dinghy first and then roll him, first on to the top of the buoyancy chamber and then on board.

IN THE DINGHY

Having got away from the aircraft there are three things you should do at once. It is very important to have these fixed firmly in mind so that you do them instinctively. They may seem very difficult at the time and the immediate results will certainly not seem worthwhile, but the effect of neglecting them is very great later on. They are:

1. Bale the dinghy – probably the most important single means of preventing the effects of exposure.
2. Fix the weather apron.
3. Make arrangements to collect rainwater.

Quite often men are picked up after many hours in a water-logged dinghy, and they say they were 'all in' and could not bale it out. It is easy to understand how they felt and to sympathize, but if some instinctive urge to carry out a routine could have made them bale, they would have been in much better condition.

It is much the same with the weather apron. You are very cold, you fix it and probably do not seem much warmer. It is a nuisance and prevents moving around. It does not seem to help, but 12–18–24 hours later you will be in far better shape if you have used it.

Rain may fall in the first hour. You may be in the dinghy a long time therefore you cannot waste any rain. Arrange to be able to use the apron to collect it, so that it runs down into a depression. Have something ready to store it in and use the sponge to transfer it from the apron to the container. Wash the salt off the apron with the first few drops and collect the rest.

Next, sit on something if you can. If you sit on the dinghy floor only a layer of fabric intervenes between your nether regions and the cold Atlantic. This is very depressing. It is not safe to sit on the buoyancy chamber, so try to sit on an emergency container, a bit of crumpled up clothing, a parachute or part of it. It helps a lot.

Then assess your crew. You want to know who will be your right-hand man on whom you can rely in 6–10 days' time if you should still be there. All the evidence suggests that in survival at sea, mental make-up is much more important than physical strength. If two men are of equal character, the physically fitter would probably do better. On the other hand, a quiet determined individual, particularly if he is well educated, will generally survive well even if he is of poor physique. A very fit, strong man, noisy and demonstrative, and perhaps a bit empty-headed, will often succumb quite easily.

Then establish a routine, giving everyone some duties to do. Dinghy and lifeboat crews who lie in the bottom and do nothing rarely survive long exposure. Those who keep active and attentive do much better. If you have an injured man do not, out of kindness, excuse him all duties and leave him to lie idle. Try to find some job in the routine he can do and get him to do it. It is really kinder and helping him more.

If you are in good order, you should try to arrange some sleep rota. Often there is no room for this, but sometimes there is unfortunately not a full crew in the dinghy. Sleep in short watches of about two hours, and detail someone to watch over the sleeper so that he can relax without the fear of falling over the side. If you are really exhausted do not sleep, but try to stay awake. To help you, energy tablets are provided in the emergency flying rations and they have full directions printed on the box.

Now you can give some attention to the refinements of protecting yourself against exposure. If you have ditched at night, do not strip off your wet clothing in order to dry it until the day is a few hours old. You lose more heat by the exposure than you gain from the small amount of drying. When you do take things off to dry at high noon, do it in layers. If you have a relatively windproof garment, dry one layer from underneath it first, then replace it and dry another layer from underneath, retaining the wind-breaker meanwhile. Finally, when you have two (or more) layers of dryish clothing available to wear, remove and dry the wind-breaker.

Keep moving if possible. If you cannot move your limbs because of lack of space, tense and relax muscles without moving limbs.

Keep your flying boots on, provided they do not feel tight. They help to keep your feet warm. When the boots feel tight, however, it means that the feet are swelling and then boots hamper the circulation and do more harm than good. Remove them and never replace them. Wrap your feet up loosely and keep them as dry as you can. Parachute silk is good if you have any. If your feet are numb and swollen do not rub them.

Sunburn can be very troublesome. At sea you can get sunburnt under a white sky, apparently because the salt spray continuously washes away the sweat, which is a natural protective against sunburn. Improvised sun hats are good if they can be made, and a rolled up handkerchief or bit of parachute tied round the head and over the bridge of the nose in a roll keeps off some of the upward glare of the sea. The burn jelly in the first aid kit is being made into a dual-purpose job, which will protect also against sunburn.

WATER RATIONING

Without any water at all a man can survive four to six days. In exceptional cases you may last longer but this cannot be expected. The position seems to be that the body requires a minimum of 18 oz water per day to keep it in good order for long periods when resting. If about this amount cannot be obtained, it does not matter very much how much less is taken.

It is undoubtedly possible to ration water too strictly. There are many examples of men being picked up in very poor condition with considerable supplies of water available. They had instituted a very severe rationing scheme and might actually have died of thirst with water in hand. Again, the chances of rainwater within a few days are quite good in northern latitudes, and it is a mistaken policy to allow yourself to get into a very bad condition and then to obtain rainwater, only to find that you have gone too far to benefit much from it. Again, in air sea rescue the majority of contacts and rescues are made in the first five days. After that the rescue becomes more difficult, so that it is important that the dinghy crew should be as fit as possible during the time when rescue prospects are best and their co-operation is more fruitful.

A 'liberal' or a 'severe' rationing scheme shows similar results and decline after 10 days. However, if a severe regime is in place, there is a quick decline in capability within one or two days. On the other hand, a liberal rationing maintains a good performance for the first five days – when rescue is most likely – followed by a rapid decline over the next five days.

In a large dinghy there should be 56 oz of water per man. It is suggested that it should be rationed as follows:

1. First day   No water unless exhausted or wounded.
2. Second day   14 ozs per man.
3. Third day   14 ozs per man.
4. Fourth day   14 ozs per man.
5. Fifth day   2 ozs per man, and the same thereafter.

OTHER SOURCES OF WATER

Rain has already been mentioned but sea water is no use. The effects of drinking it are always bad and it should be avoided. It is known that in the laboratory small quantities of salt water can be added to fresh water and drunk without harm. But this careful adjustment cannot possibly be made in a dinghy, and the effects of a draught of sea water on a man short of water are always disastrous within a day.

Of course, when you have plenty of fresh water to drink you can take quite a lot of sea water as well (as we sometimes do when swimming), but the conditions are then quite different. It is also dangerous to wash out the mouth with sea water, because the risks of succumbing to the temptation to drink are too great.

In hot climates, provided that hostile fish are absent, bathing may be helpful as it cools the body and loosens the sweating.

Fish have been advocated as a source of water, but enthusiasm seems to have run ahead of fact. Twelve pounds of fish squeezed in a mechanical press will yield about one pint of fluid. Other methods of extraction, such as chewing and squeezing the cut up material in a handkerchief, are even less effective. The resulting fluid, though it has less salt than sea water, contains a lot of protein and this is a bad thing to take when short of water. Despite newspaper reports this is also true of sea birds, flesh and blood. Both fish and sea birds can be used as food if the water situation is good, but both are bad if water is scarce.

At sea, food is not nearly so important as water. Man can survive quite long periods without food. A tin of emergency flying rations contains about as much nourishment as a man normally eats in a day, so that the rations question is not very important. The emergency rations should be used in accordance with a strict routine so that they break up the day and help to keep your spirits up. The Horlicks tablets are sometimes criticized on the ground that they increase thirst. This may be true in normal circumstances, but when you are really short of water all dry foods tend to promote thirst and subtle differences disappear. The Horlicks tablets have an advantage (apart from their concentrated nourishment) in that they are not excessively palatable to most people and therefore they are fairly easy to ration.

DINGHY DISEASE

Certain ailments are liable to arise in dinghies and lifeboats. The chief of these, of course, is seasickness. It does not usually last more than 48 hours, though this is cold comfort to the sufferer. He should be laid as flat as possible, and should either close his eyes or look at a part of the dinghy which moves with him and not at the sea or sky. The seasickness remedy in the first aid kit should be tried. It is not 100 per cent successful, but it may help.

Dry mouths and cracked lips are a common problem for those who have to spend some days in the dinghy. Sucking metal objects like coins etc. may help at first. Any greasy substance except fuel oil can be smeared on the lips.

Sore eyes and eyelids can also be uncomfortable. Again apply any simple greasy material except fuel oil, and if they become very bad cover with a pad and bandage.

This article provided an excellent general guide to survival at sea and was based on the experiences of those who had been forced to confront a survival situation at sea and had succeeded. To assist aircrew to appreciate the fundamentals for survival, it was emphasized that the priorities were absolutely clear. Aircrew were encouraged (and still are) to commit to memory and virtually bury in their sub-conscious the phrase:

Protection, Location, Water, Food.

By doing so, if they found themselves in distress and there was ever a dilemma or confusion, they would automatically remember this phrase in order to get the essential priorities correct.

Simple published guidelines were not available during the early years of the war, but in line with all the other rapid developments in the air sea rescue arena, their need was soon appreciated. Once they became available, the responsibility fell on the training organization and the specialist staffs at the airfields and squadron operations headquarters to regularly brief the aircrews. Those aircrew that took the trouble to take note of this advice and practice survival training and dinghy drills – and, surprisingly, some did not – enormously increased their chances of surviving. The accounts that follow will illustrate just how successful some men were at putting the theory into practice when they found themselves in the hostile and alien environment at sea. In particular these accounts will emphasize that it was often the 'will to survive' that was the most significant influence.

Chapter Four

Survival Equipment

DINGHIES

The first type of inflatable dinghy, the 'A' type, of rough triangular shape and intended for a crew of three, was developed for use as a flying-boat tender in 1925. Over the next 10 years it was adapted for emergency rescue purposes. In 1935, a larger, circular pneumatic dinghy known as the Youngman dinghy was developed in three sizes, 'E', 'F' and 'G', which had an outer ring of two separate chambers forming the buoyancy compartment, filled in with a fabric floor. Housed on the top wing of the aircraft, it was released in the event of ditching and floated still attached to the aircraft, to allow the crew to embark and await rescue.

By 1940 the 'H' and 'J' type dinghies had been developed to provide greater carrying capacity and increased stability. The two-compartment buoyancy arrangement of the earlier multi-seat dinghies had been sacrificed, but a variety of leak stoppers were introduced. The floor was lowered, which allowed the crew to sit inside, thus making the dinghy less likely to overturn in a rough sea. The modified 'H' type (see plate 1) was used in the heavy bombers and was installed in a stowage compartment; when the aircraft came to rest on the water, the sea activated an immersion switch, which actuated the carbon-dioxide bottle that automatically inflated the dinghy. Scaled-down versions based on an improved 'H' and 'J' type were developed to accommodate three people: the 'M' type, and later a two-seat 'L' type. So, by the end of 1940, all multi-seat aircraft had been supplied with dinghies.

The fighter pilot, on the other hand, had to rely solely upon his flotation jacket (Mae West) to keep him afloat until help arrived. The possibility of providing a dinghy had been carefully considered, but the difficulties of stowing a dinghy in a small cockpit were such that the idea had to be abandoned. However, in the autumn of 1940, the availability of a German single-seat dinghy added new impetus to the idea. Pilots had been advised to bale out rather than try to ditch their fighters, so a dinghy was imperative. The 'K' single-seat dinghy was designed. This was a boat-shaped dinghy packed in a valise attached to either the parachute harness or the Mae West. At the beginning of 1941, 12,000 'K' dinghies were ordered and issued to all fighter pilots and Fleet Air Arm aircrew. Improvements on the original design were soon made with the inclusion of paddles, a telescopic mast, emergency rations and a flag to attract attention.

By August 1942, the issue of' 'K' dinghies to fighter aircraft had been completed, with three different types developed to fit the various seat parachute harnesses and seating arrangements. By this time most of the 'K' dinghies had been modified, with a protective apron and hood to shelter the occupant from the weather and the sea. The success of the 'K' dinghy prompted the authorities to issue them to crews in multi-seat aircraft who might be forced to bale out over the sea, and almost all aircraft except heavy bombers and trainers received them.

In the winter months, aircrew were picked up in their dinghies but had already died from exposure. The Deputy Director of ASR was convinced that not only would the introduction of a sail for the dinghies increase the chance of survival, but the psychological effect of making the effort to sail home would contribute to a survivor's resistance to exposure.

Only minor modifications were needed to convert a 'K' dinghy to sail. The telescopic mast and flag were replaced with a stronger mast with a simple rig and a red sail. With this modification and the protective hood and apron it was considered possible for an unskilled person to have a reasonable chance of sailing to friendly waters.

Experiments to find a suitable multi-seat sailing dinghy (later known as the 'Q' dinghy) were conducted in the autumn of 1942. At the end of September successful trials were completed and the air staff agreed that the new 'Q' dinghy should replace the 'H' model. The new dinghy was a boat-shaped yellow dinghy 16 feet long and with a 14-foot mast, rigged with mainsail and foresail coloured dark brown. It was also designed to carry a dinghy radio to operate with a kite aerial. Simple sailing charts printed on cotton fabric were prepared for inclusion in the dinghy to assist survivors to sail to friendly waters. Approval was given on 29 October for the immediate production of 50 'Q' sailing dinghies for issue to long-range maritime aircraft operating in the southwest coastal areas.

Further trials were conducted on the 'Q' dinghy and certain drawbacks were identified. These early models were found to be too difficult to assemble and sail by the average crew. Modifications were incorporated to improve stability and overall performance, and this hindered general production. Nevertheless, in May 1943 a rescue was achieved by means of a 'Q' sailing dinghy, which demonstrated that if a satisfactory type could be developed it would be a great assistance in the rescue of aircrew.

By the end of 1943, general production of the 'Q' sailing dinghy was progressing well and approval was given for their use in the heavy bombers as a replacement for the 'J' type. The sail arrangements of the 'Q' continued to be modified throughout the war.

EARLY DEVELOPMENT IN AIR SEA RESCUE EQUIPMENT

Before any attempt was made to organize and co-ordinate air sea rescue, a number of units developed their own survival aids to be dropped to their crews in distress to enable them to survive until passing ships could pick them up. These local improvisations included many and varied items in rescue aids thought fit by the individual units. Co-ordination occurred later, with the introduction of standardized emergency equipment packs made to accommodate only standard items of equipment, emergency rations and first aid.

Three RAF stations were prominent in developing their own supply-dropping survival equipment in 1940. The life-saving gear carried the name of the RAF station responsible for the design.

Thornaby Bag

The first of these was designed at RAF Thornaby, a Coastal Command station on the east coast of Yorkshire. It consisted of a strengthened fabric parachute bag using the kapok pads from a Mae West lifejacket for flotation. The advantage of these bags was that all the components were readily available on the station. Individual bags were made which contained watertight tins of food, drink, cigarettes and first aid equipment. The bag was never a great success since it was difficult to spot once it had landed in the sea and it was liable to burst on impact. Nevertheless, it was better than no aids at all and some successes were achieved.

Bircham Barrel

Another Coastal Command station, RAF Bircham Newton in north Norfolk, followed up the idea of the Thornaby Bag by experimenting with a type of supply-dropping container which could be carried on the bomb racks of the searching aircraft. It was made from the tail container of a 250 lb bomb with a reinforced inner frame and an inner canvas bag, all made watertight. Once again, all the components were readily available on the station. Further developments made the barrel more conspicuous once it was in the sea and also allowed the ditched crew to retrieve it more easily. By September 1941 clearance had been given for it to be carried on a wide range of aircraft.

Lindholme Gear

It was soon obvious that distressed aircrews needed something more than food containers to keep them alive until a ship arrived. Group Captain E.F. Waring, the station commander of the bomber base at RAF Lindholme, who was to play a major role in the air sea rescue arena throughout the war, invented and perfected a dinghy-dropping apparatus where an inflatable dinghy, food, clothing and first aid outfits could all be dropped in a series of five containers. The large container was from the tail unit of a 500 lb bomb and was where the dinghy was stored. In four smaller containers, as in the Bircham Barrel, were water, food and protective clothing. All the containers were strung together by floating ropes, which ditched aircrew could grasp and haul in. The advantage of this apparatus was the availability of a much larger dinghy of a more robust design for rough seas.

Following a successful rescue with the aid of a Thornaby Bag of a Whitley crew that had been in their dinghy for 72 hours, the Director ASR suggested that all Coastal Command stations should produce them for their own rescue attempts. The Lindholme Gear soon proved its value, and it was agreed that they should be commercially produced. In the meantime, RAF Lindholme produced 100 sets and these were distributed to Bomber and Coastal Command stations.

IMPROVEMENTS IN RESCUE EQUIPMENT

Considerable improvements had been made by the spring of 1942 in the individual items of equipment carried either in the aircraft or in the emergency packs attached to the dinghy. As with the 'K' dinghies, all multi-seat dinghies in production were supplied with rubber weather covers or aprons, attached to the buoyancy chambers and buttoned across the dinghy.

The normal marine distress signals stowed in the dinghy pack had never proved very satisfactory and frequently failed to operate. Aircrews were urged to take the aircraft's Verey pistol and cartridges. At the beginning of 1942 waterproofed red star Verey cartridges were included in the dinghy pack. From this idea a lightweight one-inch Verey pistol, capable of firing a red star cartridge, was developed during the spring of 1942. The cumbersome smoke floats were replaced with waterproof two-star distress signals, three of which could be carried in place of one smoke float.

Including tins of water in the dinghy's emergency rations solved the problem of stowing drinking liquid. Experiments continued to find the best type of food to be included in the emergency ration.

By the spring of 1942 an important piece of equipment had been added to the multi-seat dinghies – a floating knife. This replaced the jack knife, which had numerous disadvantages, not least that once dropped from cold hands it was likely to disappear for ever.

Thus, during 1942 aircrews were provided, either personally or in the dinghy and emergency packs, with the following aids to survival and rescue: a floating torch, whistle, first aid kit, fluorescene, paddles, baler, leak stoppers, floating knife, telescopic mast and flag, distress signal, Verey cartridges and dinghy cover. For sustenance, chocolate, emergency rations, Horlicks tablets and drinking water were included. By 1943, all these items contributed in small measure to the maintenance of life and successful rescue of many aircrews. Improvements continued to be made throughout the war and variations, depending on the theatre of war, were made to the basic items.

Chapter Five

Location Aids

O NCE DITCHED AIRCREW had successfully boarded a dinghy their chances of rescue were greatly enhanced, but the most difficult operation was to locate them. Distress signals received from aircraft enabled a DF (direction finding) fix to be obtained, but the accuracy and value were dependent on a number of factors such as distance, the weather and the quality of the bearings. Often there was a significant delay before a rescue craft could arrive at the scene, by which time the dinghy might have drifted a considerable distance from its original position. Sometimes the crew did not have time to transmit an SOS before ditching. It was essential, therefore, that survivors were provided with location aids to assist searching aircraft.

The most effective location aids were visual signals and radios. The RAF copied the German idea of providing Mae Wests and skull caps coloured yellow. Fluorescene bags, which on immersion stained the sea yellow, were included in the dinghies. The 'K' dinghy had a telescopic mast with a flag, and the Directorate of ASR encouraged the development of waterproof and more effective pyrotechnic signals. However, the most important development in the early days was the dinghy wireless set, which the rescue craft could home to. Another rescue aid used in the early days was the cage of homing pigeons that could be released, once the survivors were in the dinghy, with a message giving the position of ditching.

DINGHY WIRELESS TRANSMITTERS

Experiments to provide a suitable radio for ditched aircrew started in the middle of 1941 but progress was slow. After the capture of a German set, it was realized that it was superior to the British prototype, which was scrapped, and approval was given to produce 2,000 modified versions of the German set. Trials confirmed its suitability and a much bigger order was placed in January 1942 in order to provide one set for every dinghy. The transmitter (known as type T 1333) was designed to function on the international distress frequency of 500 kilocycles per second (kc/s). It was encased in a waterproof floating container and the aerial was a mast; experiments were also conducted using a kite. It was not possible to store the transmitter in the dinghy pack so it had to be stowed loose in the aircraft and taken out by hand at the time of the ditching. Unfortunately, a series of technical difficulties delayed introduction of the transmitter and none had been delivered by the following summer. In view of this grave situation an immediate demand for 1,000 American sets of a dinghy radio (an exact replica of the German set) was submitted.

By February 1943, 1,600 British sets had been delivered and the American sets were becoming available. In order that marine craft could home on to a dinghy transmitter, RAF high speed launches and the Royal Navy's rescue motor launches (RML) were fitted with the appropriate wireless receiver (R 1155) and the DF loop.

During the summer of 1943 large numbers of British and American dinghy radios were issued. By the end of the year it was recognized that the American set (SCR 578) was superior and it was agreed that the United State authorities would supply 12,000; production of the British set would be adjusted accordingly.

ASV OSCILLATORS

Locating a dinghy in the sea was an immense problem. It was recognized that what was needed, as an alternative to a dinghy wireless set, was an oscillator able to emit automatic distress signals capable of being detected on the searching aircraft's ASV radar. Since the dinghy radio could not be carried in a number of aircraft owing to the lack of storage space, there was an urgent need for some form of homing aid, but progress was painfully slow. It was not until the winter of 1943–4 that any significant progress was made. The radar oscillator, known as 'Walter', was carried by all aircraft flying over the sea. The aid had an endurance of 23 hours with a range of approximately 15 miles at 2,000 feet. Its great advantage was the indication it produced on a searching aircraft's radar screen, which could not be confused with any other.

THE PIGEON SERVICE

The Royal Air Force Pigeon Service, which had been established before the war, originally provided reconnaissance aircraft operating over the sea with a means of emergency communication in the form of carrier pigeons. Their use was later extended to bomber aircraft. Pigeons were rarely used when aircraft force-landed in the sea as they would not fly in bad visibility, at night or when wet. As the container in which they were carried in the aircraft was not waterproof, they were seldom in a fit state to undertake a flight after being taken into the dinghy.

Most of the pigeons were supplied from lofts run by National Pigeon Service volunteers. In October 1941 an Air Ministry initiative to create a more formal service met with little support from the operational Commands, although it did prompt the provision of a watertight floatable pigeon container, which replaced the basket in January 1942.

At the end of February a pigeon figured in a rescue, which aroused a good deal of attention in the press and emphasized that pigeons could be valuable in rescuing a ditched aircrew.

PIGEON TO THE RESCUE

During the spring of 1942, the Beaufort squadrons of Coastal Command were busy hunting the German capital ships. The

Scharnhorst and *Gneisenau* had recently made their audacious 'Channel Dash' and there were fears that one or both might try to join the battleship *Tirpitz* at Trondheim in Norway. Leading a detachment of six Beauforts at Sumburgh in the Shetlands was Squadron Leader Hedley Cliff (see plate 2), a veteran torpedo attack pilot who had recently returned from the Far East.

During the morning of 23 February 1942, Cliff was summoned to the operations room and briefed to take his six torpedo-armed Beauforts to patrol between Stavangar and Kristiansand in southern Norway. Cliff elected to take the most southerly patrol and he took off first at 2 pm in Beaufort L 9965 and headed for the Skagerrak. Nothing was seen so Cliff extended his search further to the south, but there was still nothing to report. At 4.30 pm he turned the Beaufort west and headed for Scotland at 500 feet. Without warning the port engine blew up and caught fire and the aircraft immediately started to descend. Cliff had little time to warn the crew but the wireless operator, Sergeant Venn, realized the acute danger and immediately sent an SOS and clamped his wireless key down. In less than 30 seconds, Cliff flew the Beaufort on to the sea.

The aircraft skidded for a short distance before the nose dug into the six-foot waves. The navigator and the gunner, Pilot Officers MacDonald and Tessier, scrambled clear and on to the port wing where they released the dinghy, which inflated in 15 seconds. Venn appeared holding the basket containing the two pigeons, which had been stowed near his position. On impact, Cliff was thrown heavily against the side of the cockpit and damaged his shoulder. He struggled to get free of his parachute but eventually emerged and was hauled into the dinghy. During this period one of the pigeons escaped and sat on the wing. The crew made frantic efforts to catch it, but it took off and was never seen again. A minute later the aircraft sank.

Once the crew had settled in the dinghy, Cliff took stock of the situation. It was rapidly getting dark, they were 150 miles east of the Firth of Forth, the temperature was only just above freezing and it was starting to snow. Apart from two bars of chocolate and a few Horlicks tablets they had no food, as all the food containers were stored in the aircraft and no one had had time to grab them. Cliff realized that exposure was their biggest problem and he instituted a roster for paddling, not with any expectation of making progress but in order to keep the blood circulation going. He absolutely forbade anyone from going to sleep.

They wrote their approximate position on a scrap of paper and rammed it into the special container fixed to the ring on the leg of 'Stinkie', the remaining pigeon, and released him. The bird was very reluctant to fly and the crew urged him to get airborne, almost overturning the dinghy in their efforts. Eventually the bird left, heading west. The crew settled to a freezing and acutely uncomfortable night huddled together in the bottom of the dinghy.

A faint SOS had been received at base, but it was indistinct and the fix was very unreliable. Once it became apparent that Cliff and his crew would not return, a Catalina was sent to fly along the Beaufort's planned return track from Kristiansand, but despite searching all night nothing was seen. At dawn a second aircraft was sent, but this also returned having seen nothing of the missing crew. Meanwhile at 8.30 am Mr James Ross, an ardent member of the National Pigeon Service, had checked his loft near St Andrews in Fife and found a very bedraggled, oil-stained bird which he eventually recognized as one of his. He immediately telephoned nearby RAF Leuchars and reported the arrival of the bird. The number on the bird's leg ring (40 NS 1) was checked and it was confirmed as one taken on board Cliff's aircraft. Unfortunately, there was no message in the container.

The experts gathered to work on the very slender evidence available in an attempt to narrow the search area. The oil on the bird caused much confusion: it was thought that it could have flown no more than 50 miles, so the search was concentrated in this area. An army post then reported that it had also received a weak SOS at the time Cliff was thought to have ditched. The naval staff reported that a tanker had been in the North Sea, and new calculations were made on the basis that the bird may have spent the night on the tanker – hence the oil – before flying again at dawn. Based on this theory, the search was extended further eastwards and six aircraft were sent to comb the new area.

At 11.15 am a Hudson of the Royal Netherlands Naval Air Service 320 Squadron found the dinghy. After dropping a smoke float, the aircraft dropped a Thornaby Bag, which the survivors soon recovered. The Dutch aircraft remained with the dinghy until Beaufighters, which had escorted a Royal Navy Walrus to the scene, relieved it. The amphibian alighted alongside the dinghy and Cliff was told that high speed launches were on their way and would arrive shortly – then, to everyone's surprise, it took off.

Very soon afterwards *HSL 118* from Blyth arrived and the survivors were picked up at 2.10 pm, landing at Blyth three hours later. When the crew arrived at Leuchars they related their experiences and discussed the role of the pigeon. Mr Ross had been invited to the discussion and he asked why they had not put a message in the container; he was surprised when Cliff confirmed that a message had been attached to the ring of 'Stinkie'. At this point Mr Ross exclaimed that the pigeon that had returned to the loft was 'Winkie'. So it was the escapee that had struggled back and not 'Stinkie' who, sadly, never returned to his loft.

Following this rescue, crews were reminded that pigeons are not good night flyers, and if darkness was likely to fall before the pigeon could reach its loft they should wait for dawn before releasing the bird. Although pigeons were carried in bomber and coastal aircraft throughout the first few years of the war, this was the only rescue in the European theatre that could be credited to the Pigeon Service.

Hedley Cliff returned to operations and finished the war as a wing commander, having been awarded the DSO. Tessier and Venn survived the war, but MacDonald was lost in a Liberator just before the war finished. 'Winkie' was awarded the Dicken Award (the animal VC) and lived for another 11 years. She was then stuffed and is now on view in a Dundee museum, just a few miles from her loft.

★

The use of pigeons never achieved great success apart from the efforts of 'Winkie', and there was a general lack of enthusiasm for the service. However, since the promised dinghy radio transmitter was so slow in arriving, it was agreed that the service should be continued but not expanded. To improve the service, RAF lofts were established to replace those run by the volunteer groups.

As the distances flown on operations increased during 1943, it became doubtful that pigeons could fly these distances over the sea. Bomber and Coastal Commands stated that they no longer required the service and in November 1943 it was withdrawn, although it was retained in some overseas commands where the supply of dinghy radios was still insufficient.

PART TWO

Northwest Europe

Chapter Six

Rescue Craft

HAVING LOCATED SURVIVORS following a successful ditching, the next problem involved the provision of aircraft and marine craft specifically allotted for their speedy rescue. Every vessel and aircraft in the area was a potential rescuer, whether they were Navy, Air Force, RNLI or any passing vessel. However, for an air sea rescue organization to be fully effective, it was necessary for specialist assets to be dedicated to the task.

RESCUE AIRCRAFT

From its inauguration, everyone concerned in air sea rescue was aware that the shortage of men and equipment made it impossible to allot aircraft specifically for the search and rescue task, and calls would have to be made on the operational commands for assistance. The difficulty in carrying out efficient rescues with such a handicap is illustrated by the struggles of the Directorate to obtain additional aircraft during its first year of operations.

In January 1941 the 12 Lysanders borrowed from Army Co-operation Command were the only aircraft employed specifically on search work. The searching they carried out was limited to a narrow coastal belt outside which the other Commands had to rely on their own rescue arrangements. In May these aircraft were transferred to Fighter Command with the addition of a further six, and they were allotted two each to nine fighter stations bordering the North Sea and the English Channel. Although an improvement, the numbers were woefully short of the requirements and, in September, Fighter

Command were successful in establishing four squadrons of Lysanders (see plate 3) Nos 275, 276, 277 and 278, which allowed the original area of search to be extended from the Humber to the Isle of Man.

The Lysanders proved to be a valuable stopgap until more capable aircraft became available. Although the aircraft was unable to carry the Lindholme Gear or other types of standard gear to drop to distressed aircrew, a special-to-type gear was produced for the aircraft in February 1941. The gear was made up of four small 'M' type dinghies, water, food and distress signals, all packed in a valise to fit in the small bomb containers, which could be dropped from the Lysander's stub wings.

The value of the Lysanders for ASR work is well illustrated in the rescue of two Hurricane pilots.

LYSANDERS LOCATE TWO HURRICANE PILOTS

Ten Hurricanes of 258 Squadron took off from Kenley during the morning of 16 June 1941 to provide escort to Blenheim bombers attacking Boulogne. Leading one of the sections of fighters was Flight Lieutenant A.M. Campbell. After dropping their bombs the Blenheims turned for home. Campbell saw one that had become separated from the rest of the formation and he went to the aid of the lone bomber. On the way back across the Channel four Messerschmitt 109 fighters repeatedly attacked him, one of which he shot down. He soon exhausted all his ammunition and dropped down to sea level in order to draw the fighters away from the bomber, which escaped. The attacks continued and soon there was a loud explosion as the Hurricane's fuel tank was hit.

Campbell remained with the aircraft until he saw flames and felt uncomfortably hot, when he pulled up to 1,500 feet and baled out. There was little wind, and as he hit the sea the parachute collapsed on top of him and he became entangled in the shroud lines, which restricted his movements. His 'K' dinghy remained attached to his lifejacket but it sank and he had great difficulty pulling it to the surface as the shroud lines tightened around his shoulders. Finally, he succeeded in getting the dinghy pack to the surface where he ripped off the cover, unfolded the dinghy and turned on the CO_2 bottle. The dinghy inflated in a very short time.

Campbell eventually managed to free himself from his parachute before clambering aboard the dinghy. He pulled in the drogue and started paddling with his hands towards the English coast, using the sun as a guide. The sea was calm but the effort of paddling kept the dinghy half full of water despite his regular attempts to bale it out.

After 30 minutes a bi-plane flying at sea level, escorted by six Messerschmitt 109 fighters, approached from the direction of France. He saw that the bi-plane was a German Heinkel 59 floatplane used by the Luftwaffe for air sea rescue. He got out of his dinghy and floated some 25 yards away until the fighters turned away, then clambered back on board only for the German formation to return 20 minutes later and pass a mile away. In the meantime, Campbell had spotted a Lysander on the horizon flying at low level; it appeared to have an escort of four Spitfires.

Suddenly, overhead, an air battle started and the four escorting Spitfires of 91 Squadron engaged the Me 109s, which had reappeared at about 3,000 feet. One of the German fighters was damaged but the Spitfire section leader, Pilot Officer D.H. Gage, was shot down and Campbell saw the aircraft dive into the sea – he saw no parachute. Providing top cover for 91 Squadron and the Lysander were Spitfires of 1 Squadron and they engaged the Me 109s, which had reformed after the skirmish with 91 Squadron. One of the German fighters and the He 59, which was not displaying the recognized International Red Cross markings, were shot down.

As the battle finished, Campbell found himself alone again and he once more started to paddle towards England. After two hours he could just make out the coastline when he saw a rescue launch patrolling, but his attempts to attract its attention failed. Another appeared in the area where the Spitfire had disappeared, and during the launch's search pattern it came close enough to notice Cameron's splashing and shouted attempts to attract attention. At 3.45 pm he was taken on board *HSL 123*, arriving at Dover four hours later none the worse for his adventure. Campbell soon returned to flying operations.

★

Five days later, on 21 June, Hurricanes of 1 Squadron were returning from escorting bombers to Desvres. Over Boulogne they ran into a large formation of Me 109s of JG 26. Pilot Officer V. Kopecky (Czech) flying Z 2909 attacked one and saw it spiral down towards the beach below. As he watched it spinning out of control, bullets smashed into his cockpit from two Me 109s approaching from the English coast. The throttles of his Hurricane were put out of action and the engine started to emit smoke.

Kopecky was just off the French coast at 12,000 feet and decided to try and make the English coast. He descended gradually to 2,000 feet when it became obvious that he could not reach land, so he called up his ground control and informed them that he would have to ditch in the sea. He lowered the aircraft's flaps and reduced speed to near stalling, opened the hood and the side door and then unfastened his Sutton harness. He lowered his goggles and braced himself for the tail-down impact. He was thrown forward, but the kapok in his Mae West helped him float free as the Hurricane sank almost immediately. Once clear he inflated his lifejacket and released the parachute harness. He then pulled the dinghy towards him with the lanyard, opened the press-studs, unfolded the dinghy, pulled out the pin and inflated the dinghy slowly with the aid of the CO_2 bottle; it inflated fully in 15 seconds.

He climbed into the dinghy 'in the correct manner as shown in the "K" dinghy diagram 2040', as he later narrated to the debriefing officer. The sea was calm but he found the swell made it difficult to paddle with his hands. (Soon after these two rescues, paddles were introduced into the 'K' dinghy pack.) He baled out the dinghy with his hands and soon saw a Lysander, escorted by four Spitfires. They saw him waving and the Lysander descended and circled him until *HSL 123* arrived. The launch had been called out to pick up Sergeant Aston of 92 Squadron and had just recovered him when it received a message from the circling Lysander and came over to Kopecky. Both pilots arrived in Dover at 7 pm.

Kopecky clearly knew his dinghy drill and carried it out exactly as briefed. Six months later, flying a 111 Squadron Spitfire, he crashed on take off and was seriously injured, losing a leg.

★

As early as 1940, recommendations had been made that a type of amphibious aircraft would be valuable to the rescue service. The Luftwaffe's extensive use of the Heinkel He 59 floatplane for ASR work had been noted. Appeals were made to the Royal Navy to provide Walrus aircraft but the Admiralty was unable to oblige. It was not until July 1941 that three of the amphibians were released from Coastal Command duties for use as rescue aircraft. Eventually, in August, the Royal Navy delivered six Walruses to Fighter Command to cover the coastal areas around Hawkinge, Coltishall and Portreath. They joined the Lysanders in the newly formed squadrons, so by late 1941, 36 Lysanders and 9 Walruses were allotted specifically for air searches and rescue.

In March 1942 a further squadron was formed for operations off the Scottish coast. By this time it was becoming clear that the Lysander, an old aircraft, was increasingly difficult to maintain, and spares were scarce. It was obvious that a replacement aircraft needed to be identified. Trials with another almost obsolete aircraft, the Defiant, were commenced in February. In April authority was given to form the first Defiant squadron, 281, at Ouston in Northumberland with a detachment at Turnhouse near Edinburgh. On completion of the trial, Fighter Command was given authority in May to replace all the Lysanders with Defiants, which were being steadily replaced in the night fighter role by twin-engine aircraft. By June a modified form of rescue equipment container had been designed for carriage on the underside of the aircraft's wings.

There were many daring rescues made by the men who flew the ugly but extremely effective Walrus. None better epitomize the gallantry of these often forgotten men than those involved in the rescue of Flight Sergeant Mike Cooper.

MINEFIELD RESCUE BY WALRUS

On 30 July 1942, 616 Squadron's Spitfires were returning from a close escort mission when Pilot Officer Bob Large and his close friend, Kenyan-born Flight Sergeant Mike Cooper (see plate 4), were shot down within minutes of each other as they returned across the Channel. Two high speed launches from Dover picked them up and they were soon returned to their squadron at Tangmere. Two months later, on 2 October, 616 Squadron was tasked for a similar operation escorting six USAAF Fortress bombers attacking an airfield just outside St Omer. Large was leading one section with Cooper once again flying as his wingman.

Over the target, they saw a section of Focke Wulf 190s climbing to attack the bombers. The two pilots dived to intercept the German fighters and Large soon shot one down. As they headed for home, a lone FW 190 followed them, and as Cooper turned hard to avoid it his Spitfire was hit by cannon fire. Cooper immediately headed for the Channel with his aircraft's engine damaged. Large confirmed that the crucial glycol engine coolant was streaming from the engine and, with the engine temperature rising and the aircraft likely to burst into flames at any moment, Cooper rolled the stricken fighter on to its back at 17,000 feet and baled out. He came down in the sea just 2 miles off Calais.

As he climbed into his dinghy, he saw the splashes of shells land close by. As the shelling stopped, four FW 190s set up a patrol over the top of him. In the meantime, Large had attacked Cooper's assailant until his ammunition ran out, when he headed immediately for Hawkinge, the nearest airfield, as he transmitted a Mayday call giving Cooper's position. After landing, his aircraft was immediately refuelled; meanwhile, he spoke to the air sea rescue office and discovered that they had misunderstood Cooper's position. Large immediately volunteered to take off again and orbit Cooper's position to allow a fix to be taken. His flight commander, Flight Lieutenant J.S. Fifield, accompanied him, and they soon found Cooper and transmitted another Mayday. Two Lysanders from B Flight, 277 Squadron, were scrambled from Hawkinge, with a Spitfire escort, and started a search but in the wrong area. Fifield spotted a second Lysander and led the pilot, Sergeant W.E. Uptigrove, to the dinghy, where Large had set up an orbit despite being attacked by the FW 190s. With the Spitfire escort keeping the German fighters occupied, Uptigrove took over the orbit.

In the meantime, Sergeant Tom Fletcher of 277 Squadron and his crew had been scrambled in their Walrus from Shoreham and flown to Hawkinge to be briefed. He was told that Cooper was sitting in the middle of a minefield, but its precise layout was not known. As a result, the Navy had decided not to attempt a rescue with their patrol boats or the RAF high speed launches (controlled by the RN at this time). Fletcher was given the options and he immediately decided to attempt a rescue.

As the Walrus headed across the Channel, more FW 190s appeared to see what the activity was about and Large attacked one of them, only to realize that his guns were empty – there had been insufficient time to re-arm them at Hawkinge. With two RCAF Spitfire squadrons escorting his Walrus, Fletcher was seen heading for the circling Lysander, so Large and Fifield decided it was time to leave. On arrival over Cooper's position, Fletcher dropped a smoke float to keep the dinghy in sight and to assess the wind. As he circled he could see several lines of mines and he managed to land between them. With a battle raging overhead, he quickly taxied towards the dinghy where Sergeant Len Healey threw Cooper a rope, which he was unable to hold. Fletcher had to taxi round again, avoiding the mines, and this time Healy managed to hook the dinghy and feed it down to the rear hatch where Flight Sergeant Roberts was waiting to grab Cooper and haul him on board. The shore batteries had opened up and the German gunners started to get an accurate range of the Walrus. With Cooper on board, and surrounded by mines and falling shells, Fletcher started his take off run and had just lifted off the sea when the Walrus flew directly over a floating mine. Spitfires closed around the slow-flying rescue aircraft and escorted it back to Hawkinge, where it landed as darkness fell.

Within a few days, it was announced that Large had been awarded an immediate DFC for his gallantry and selfless action in returning to the scene, knowing that his Spitfire was unarmed, to ensure that his friend was rescued. Fletcher and Healey were awarded the DFM and Roberts, on his first operation, was awarded a mention in dispatches.

The award of the DFM to Fletcher was particularly interesting. He had already completed five hazardous rescues when he deliberately landed in the minefield to rescue Cooper. His squadron commander commented that he had 'carried out [the rescue] with complete disregard of his personal safety and with great boldness and ability'. His AOC wrote that he thought the action, following the success of earlier daring rescues, was worthy of the award of the Victoria Cross. He referred to Fletcher's 'conspicuous gallantry' and that 'he ignored all dangers in order to pick up the pilot'. In the event, Fletcher was awarded an immediate DFM.

Mike Cooper returned to operations. On 16 August 1943 the engine of his Spitfire failed as he flew a sweep over France and he baled out for the third time. After landing in northern France, he was picked up by the Marie-Claire escape line, and after a hazardous winter crossing of the Pyrenees he arrived in Gibraltar on 20 December. He later flew the first Meteor jet fighters to enter service with the RAF. Bob Large became a 'moonlight pilot' flying Lysanders to France to deliver agents. The French government awarded him the Legion d'Honneur. Tom Fletcher became one of the most successful and colourful air sea rescue pilots and added a Bar to his DFM before being awarded a DFC.

★

An important step in improving the rescue services had been the decision in September 1941 by the air staff to form two squadrons in Coastal Command for deep search operations using ASV-equipped Hudson aircraft equipped with Lindholme Gear. Unfortunately, none could be spared, but Sir John Salmond pressed for their introduction. He pointed out that a high state of efficiency in air search could not be obtained without teamwork and adequate wireless communication between the search aircraft and sea rescue craft. This involved constant exercises, which could only be possible with specially trained aircrew for the rescue role. Adequate communication between aircraft and craft was impossible when operational aircraft, using various wireless frequencies, were used for searches. He maintained that Hudsons and rescue craft should both be fitted with VHF and HF.

The air staff accepted his claims and authorized the formation of two squadrons, Nos 279 and 280, to be equipped with Hudsons. However, there were too few available and by the end of 1941 the Air Sea Rescue Services were still served with just four squadrons of Lysander/Walrus in Fighter Command. Early in 1942 a few Hudsons were released to 279 Squadron at Bircham Newton, but the non-availability of more left Sir John Salmond with no option but to agree that 280 Squadron should be temporarily equipped with Anson aircraft, and they would also meet the shortfalls in 279 Squadron.

No. 279 became fully operational in March 1942, and soon proved the value of a deep search squadron if ditched crews carried out the correct distress procedures. Six crews (35 men) were rescued during May and June by rescue craft guided to the scene by the Hudsons. In June 280 Squadron became operational with Ansons and within days a crew had been rescued.

By the middle of 1942 operational commitments still prevented the release of the necessary number of Hudsons, and this not only hindered the work of the two existing squadrons but also precluded the formation of others. The latter had become necessary due to the increase in Bomber Command's operations, together with the arrival of the USAAF bomber squadrons in England. The Director of ASR suggested that a non-operational type should be introduced in order for the air sea rescue organization to develop. This resulted in the suggestion that the Warwick, a variant of the Wellington, should undergo trials to assess its suitability for search and rescue work, and in October VCAS gave his agreement for the trials to proceed.

By the end of October, it was clear that the Defiant was a poor substitute for the Lysander and Sir John Salmond highlighted the difficulties encountered by the ASR squadrons forced to use obsolescent aircraft. He pressed for more advanced aircraft, such as the Beaufighter, but none could be spared. However, it was agreed that certain increases and re-equipment should be made in existing Fighter

Command's rescue squadrons to give more adequate cover to areas that still had few rescue facilities. It was agreed that Spitfires should replace the Defiants and the remaining Lysanders for areas where enemy opposition might be encountered, and that Ansons should be used in areas beyond the reach of fighters. On 27 November new establishments for Fighter Command's five squadrons were authorized, representing an increase of 15 aircraft. These increases still left a large area of coastline from Montrose to Oban, an area where there had been 70 ditchings in the previous 12 months without cover. To cater for this deficiency, 282 Squadron was formed at Castletown with detachments at Peterhead and Scatsa in the Shetlands.

In March 1943, Air Commodore H.A. Haines, who had recently taken up the new post of Director of Air Safety following the retirement of Sir John Salmond, was informed that the air staff had approved the use of the Warwick with the formation of 4 squadrons for Coastal Command and one in Fighter Command, each with 20 aircraft. The plan also allowed for the Walruses to continue until replaced in 1944 by the new amphibian, the Sea Otter. The high-speed squadrons were to keep the Spitfire.

Delays in the production of the Warwick prevented the re-equipment of Coastal Command's deep search squadrons until the late summer. Five squadrons had been agreed but the delays, allied to the steady attrition of the Hudsons of 279 Squadron, prompted the Deputy Director of ASR to suggest that an incomplete version of the Warwick as an interim measure would be better than further delays. Accordingly, on 9 July, 280 Squadron was re-equipped with 20 Warwicks equipped to carry the new airborne lifeboat and Lindholme Gear. The re-equipment of 279 Squadron was expected to follow, but the build-up with Warwicks for both squadrons came forward very slowly during the summer and autumn of 1943. Coastal Command suggested that 279 Squadron should retain their Hudsons, which was agreed. In November, Fighter Command amalgamated 281 and 282 Squadrons with 10 Ansons and 7 Walrus, with 281 Squadron transferring to Coastal Command and re-equipping with the Warwick.

By the spring of 1943, the re-equipment of Fighter Command's rescue squadrons was also in full progress. Authority to use some

Spitfire Marks I and II to re-equip some of these squadrons brought about the requirement to provide rescue equipment capable of being carried and dropped from the aircraft. After trials, the Type 'E' rescue gear, which included an 'L' dinghy, emergency rations and 75 yards of floating rope to assist recovery by survivors, was developed. It could be carried internally in the Spitfire's emergency flare chutes. This allowed the fighters to retain their guns, giving the pilot the added confidence that he would still be able to engage the enemy should he be intercepted during his rescue operation. The Spitfire rescue squadrons remained in service until they were disbanded in February 1945.

In September, Fighter Command suggested the reorganization of the ASR squadrons. Up to this time Fighter Command were only responsible for rescue within 40 miles of the coast, with Coastal Command responsible outside this area. After discussions it was agreed in February 1944 that Fighter Command (now renamed Air Defence of Great Britain Command – ADGB) should be responsible for rescue in areas opposite enemy-held coasts, where fighter cover and escorts were often a necessary requirement for rescue operations. The area roughly enclosed a line from Southwold in Suffolk to the Hook of Holland, through the English Channel, and a line from Land's End to Ushant. Coastal Command was responsible for all other areas. The latter were to have three squadrons of Warwicks and one of Hudsons, each with 20 aircraft and operating from Bircham Newton, Thornaby, Tiree and Davidstow Moor. In addition, 269 (Met) Squadron based at Lagens in the Azores had been re-formed on 1 January 1944 to include an ASR Flight of six Hudsons and three Walrus. Until sufficient Warwicks were available to form Coastal Command's fourth squadron, it was agreed that Ansons should remain in the ASR squadrons of ADGB.

MARINE CRAFT

The high speed launch-building programme, agreed as war loomed, suffered from a number of difficulties in the early stages, and only 22 of the British Power Boat Company's launches had been produced by

February 1940. The original 64-foot model had been followed by a 63-foot type (known as the Whaleback because of its distinctively curved hulls and humped cabins), which had the advantages of a properly constructed sickbay, better seaworthiness and manoeuvrability. Both types, however, were difficult to maintain and suffered from a high degree of unserviceability. The heavy loss of fighter pilots in 1940 prompted a decision to increase the number of launches to 66, but it would be a further year before they were available. At the beginning of 1941 the Air Sea Rescue Service could only call on a limited number of rescue craft.

There were 14 of the RAF's 60-foot diesel-engine pinnaces at the main flying-boat bases. Although good sea boats for their size, they were very poor in rough weather. The 40-foot seaplane tenders were used as attendant craft for seaplanes and flying boats. They were of little value except for ditchings close inshore. The Admiralty provided a number of naval motor launches, manned by naval personnel, as rescue boats. These 110-foot launches had a reasonable speed (20 knots) and were good sea boats. An average of 20 were available along the Channel coast.

Although all these craft could be called on to aid a search, the majority could only operate in good weather. Other naval ships and launches could be called upon, but they had their own duties and were rarely available. The few dedicated rescue craft were needed to cover the North Sea and the eastern end of the English Channel, for which they were scarcely adequate. A valuable service for inshore work was available from the RNLI, and their crews made many rescues and were a valuable addition to the rescue effort.

The position regarding the type and supply of sea rescue craft in February 1941 was hardly satisfactory. To meet the necessary expansion of the rescue service there were two main requirements:

1. boats capable of cruising at low speeds in the area of air operations for a prolonged period, but with a speed of 25 knots available at short notice;
2. boats capable of high speed in rough sea for operations from selected harbours.

For the former, the naval motor launch, the Fairmile, was considered the most suitable. Although the Admiralty was willing to assist in air sea rescue whenever possible, naval operations had to take priority. For the search and rescue requirement, it was accepted that a new design was required that would be more robust and easier to maintain than existing types. The current types had been designed for high speed and thus their sea-keeping qualities suffered in consequence.

Obtaining these additional rescue launches to meet an immediate expansion of the Air Sea Rescue Service was another matter. No increase in production was possible, owing to both the heavy demands on the manufacturers and the interference that would be caused to the Admiralty programmes. In the meantime, the British Air Commission in Washington endeavoured to obtain suitable rescue craft from the Miami Ship Building Corporation, who were producing craft in fulfilment of an Admiralty order. Agreement was reached to divert two craft per month to meet RAF requirements.

In May the Director of ASR recommended to DCAS that the immediate requirements at home for the RAF should be 64 high speed launches and 50 pinnaces or seaplane tenders. This expansion scheme was approved, but VCAS sought to have the worldwide requirement identified. This resulted in an agreed estimate of 134 RAF craft with an addition of 44 for overseas commands and 110 naval craft.

Production delays throughout the second half of 1941 left the service well below the agreed establishment and short-term measures had to be introduced, but even these were beset with problems. However, in October the Admiralty agreed to allocate 50 Fairmile launches commencing in March 1942; such launches came to be known as rescue motor launches (RMLs). Attempts to accelerate the construction of 40 pinnaces to fill the gap before the RMLs became available were thwarted, and by the winter of 1941 only an inadequate rescue service could be maintained with the available craft, most of them unsuitable for winter operations and rough weather conditions.

During 1941 the enemy started to take offensive action when meeting rescue craft in the Channel, and in August two high speed launches were attacked and sunk by German aircraft. Whereas naval craft used for rescue work were well armed, RAF launches had little or no defence: just two Vickers .303-inch machine guns. Following this German aggression against life-saving operations, it was clear that rescue launches had to be better armed. On 12 August it was agreed that the 24 RAF launches operating at the eastern end of the Channel (irreverently called 'Hellfire Corner' by the air sea rescue crews) should be converted to take two Browning guns. Despite this clear need, no action was taken until the Under Secretary of State for Air visited Dover shortly after enemy fighters had attacked a naval rescue launch in April 1942, killing the captain. Very soon afterwards, steps were taken to mount two Vickers gas operated (VGO) guns on the launches operating in the dangerous areas of the English Channel.

By April 1942 only 7 of the 40 pinnaces ordered were in service, but the first naval RML was commissioned for service with the RAF Rescue Service. By 1 June there were 50 high speed launches in service at home, a modest increase of 18, against the establishment of 96. The dedication and determination of the crews of the high speed launches is a proud part of the RAF's history. The gallantry of Flight Lieutenant David Jones is typical of so many others that went unnoticed and unrecognized.

GALLANT LAUNCH MASTER

Flight Sergeant Eric Whitney and his crew took off from Lakenheath at midnight on 5 June 1942 in their Stirling (R 9314) of 149 Squadron. The aircraft was returning from Essen at 11,000 feet and was still 20 miles short of the Dutch coast at 2.45 am when it was struck by a Wellington diving out of control. The rear turret, tail trimming gear and part of the elevators were carried away, and with them the rear gunner, Sergeant K. Roderick. Almost simultaneously the aircraft was hit by two bursts of flak, one setting the bomb bay on fire and another bursting in the fuselage.

The aircraft became very hard to control, flying with the nose well up, the combined efforts of Whitney and his engineer, Sergeant R. Shields, being just sufficient to keep the bomber from stalling. All movable equipment was jettisoned. The front gunner, Sergeant W. Martin, extinguished the fire in the bomb bay and Sergeant B. Cheek, the wireless operator, set the IFF to distress and put out an SOS with a running commentary. To add to their troubles, the front gunner, who had gone aft to find out what had happened to the rear gunner, reported that a twin-engine fighter was closing in to attack. As three attacks developed, all flying controls were gradually shot away until the stick and rudder had no apparent effect on the behaviour of the aircraft, which went into a spiral dive to port. By this time, the aircraft was well out to sea.

At 1,000 feet the fighter had broken away and Whitney gave the order to prepare for ditching. The sea was calm with a slight swell from the northeast. The wind was light and visibility was good with no cloud and a good moon. Cheek clamped the wireless key down, the upper hatches were opened and the downward hatches closed, and the crew took up their positions. Whitney was struggling to regain some control. He opened the throttles on the port engines and throttled back those on the starboard. By 50 feet the nose was still high, and he had almost lifted the port wing when the bomber hit the sea at 80 mph. The wing broke off but the aircraft made a surprisingly gentle impact.

The fuselage remained afloat and the crew were able to clamber on to the wing, inflate the dinghy and climb aboard, none getting wet above the knees. They paddled away from the aircraft and the enemy coast, and three hours later the aircraft was still afloat.

Late in the morning an aircraft was heard and the crew used a fluorescene marker. The Verey flares failed to ignite, but after an hour a Beaufighter found them and dropped supplies. Three hours later they heard more engine noise, and shortly afterwards six Spitfires appeared escorting an RAF high speed launch.

HSL 127 from 27 ASRMCU had left Dover and sailed for the Belgian coast, with the experienced Flight Lieutenant David Jones (see plate 5) as master; he had already shown outstanding keenness and ability in carrying out many arduous and hazardous tasks. The dinghy was just 8 miles off the coast and in the middle of a minefield. The Spitfires provided protection from the air threat but Jones had to pick his way through the minefield. In broad daylight and just a few miles from enemy shore batteries, he picked up the crew, and by 6 pm they were safely ashore. The Commander-in-Chief, Dover, was impressed and sent a signal: 'I congratulate you on a well executed and highly successful long-distance rescue this afternoon.'

Six weeks after rescuing Whitney and his crew, Jones carried out another daring rescue 3 miles off Calais when he picked up Flight Sergeant C. Dennis and his 78 Squadron crew, whose Halifax had been severely damaged by a German night fighter and forced to ditch. He then played a prominent role during the Dieppe operation. After completing nine successful rescues, involving the rescue of 21 aircrew, Jones was awarded the DSC for 'his great courage in rescues of airmen close to the enemy occupied coast, particularly off Flushing and Calais'. Eric Whitney was commissioned and awarded the DFC.

★

With the progressive increase in air operations and the arrival of the USAAF, there was a clear need to increase the establishment of 96 launches. In August the home establishment was increased to 116, of which 70 to 80 would be pinnaces.

War production gained momentum slowly and the supply of the small fast craft increased. Thorneycroft, who had been concentrating on Admiralty requirements, also had more building capacity, and this allowed the building programme to be accelerated. From September, efforts were made to find a suitable replacement for the 63- and 64-foot designs, but to keep production going until a final type was agreed, more 63-foot launches were ordered.

The design of a new 68-foot launch was accepted when outright speed was sacrificed for better seagoing qualities. Operational experience had shown that it was more efficient for air sea rescue launches to be at sea on station or patrolling a specific area, and this became more important as the 1,000-bomber night raids increased and the US 8th Army Air Force mounted its daylight operations. A bigger launch meant more room all round, allowing a larger sickbay to be incorporated and a bigger bridge, which afforded much better visibility for the lookouts. Although not as fast as earlier launches, it was more comfortable at sea. All this added up to a more suitable craft, capable of staying at sea for a period of days if necessary.

Nicknamed the 'Hants and Dorset' the first 68-foot launch, *HSL 2677*, started sea trials on 28 August 1943. Ninety of these new launches entered service, all powered by three Napier Lion engines. This type of craft helped to increase rescue coverage around the coasts of Britain and the Mediterranean. They were used extensively during the invasion of Europe and after D-Day operated out of liberated ports.

In October 1943 the long-awaited twin Browning gun turrets began to be fitted to the high speed launches, two years after the requirement had been accepted.

In March 1944 a reorganization of Air Sea Rescue Marine Craft Units (ASRMCU) was undertaken in view of the changing operational environment. It was necessary to reinforce the south coast units, and for the most part this was achieved by disbanding units in areas which would be unaffected by invasion priorities. In May, the total marine craft available in the United Kingdom were:

Royal Air Force
High speed launches	130
Pinnaces	25
Seaplane tenders	27

Royal Navy
Rescue motor launches	50
Motor anti-submarine boats	14
Air rescue boats	14

ROYAL NAVY RESCUE MOTOR LAUNCHES

There has always been a tendency to think that the launches used for air sea rescue were the high speed launches of the RAF. The RMLs of the Royal Navy made a vital contribution alongside the RAF launches. They were based at ports around the United Kingdom and formed a branch of the Royal Navy's Coastal Forces. The RMLs were adapted from the Fairmile B-type motor launch, many of which were used for patrol duties and clandestine work. They were much larger (115 feet long), roomier and more powerful than the RAF launches, and although slower, they had excellent range and endurance and performed much better in rough seas.

THE AIRBORNE LIFEBOAT

All the rescue apparatus in use or proposed during the early years of the war was no more than a temporary means of sustaining life of aircrew in the sea. Unless the dropping of dinghies and food was not quickly followed up by the arrival of rescue craft, the aircrew's chance of survival was not very good. As the range of flying operations increased, some aircrew were forced to ditch or bale out in places too far from the coast to be rescued by marine craft.

Soon after the war started, a number of ideas were produced to provide a rescue vehicle. A glider-type boat was one suggestion, and a second idea was for a 32-foot motor dinghy to be dropped from a Hampden bomber. Neither was feasible, but the idea of carrying a boat by aircraft and dropping it to distressed aircrew had been born. Group Captain E.F. Waring, while still at Lindholme, had conceived the idea of carrying a motor-driven lifeboat under an aircraft and dropping it by parachute. The crew could then sail the boat to friendly waters where they could be rescued more easily.

When Waring moved to the Air Ministry in September 1941, he continued to work on his idea with the support of Lieutenant Robb RNVR, a boat-building expert, who showed great interest in the scheme. He made drawings of a type of boat he thought suitable. It was 20 feet long, was fitted with a sail, oar and motor, and could carry five to seven people. A boat descending under parachutes would drift downwind and probably out of reach of the crew in the water; therefore, it was fitted with a rocket-fired weighted drogue attached to the bows to form a sea anchor. The GQ Parachute Company devised a suitable parachute release gear. To prevent the boat capsizing, buoyancy chambers could be inflated by the action of the opening parachutes operating CO_2 bottles as the boat floated down. In a rough sea a crew might not be able to see the lifeboat, and if they did manage to reach it they could find it impossible to remain alongside. A rocket, installed at either beam, fired automatically upon impact with the sea, each rocket carrying 200 feet of buoyant line to be ejected, one either side. The distressed crew could then drift down on one of these buoyant lines and haul themselves to the lifeboat.

Waring's idea did not attract a great deal of interest initially, but Uffa Fox, the well-known builder of small sailing craft, heard of the idea and produced a similar scheme. He submitted the idea direct to the Minister of Aircraft Production (the Right Honourable J.T. Moore-Brabazon) at the end of December 1942. The Minister invited comment from the Director General of Air Safety, who gave him an assurance that a similar idea had already been submitted. Within a few weeks, the Minister had given approval to proceed with the development of the boat.

In January 1942 authority was given for Uffa Fox to construct an airborne rescue boat. He was asked to amend his design to meet the advanced ideas put forward by Waring and Robb, and the resulting design was virtually identical, in spite of the fact that it became known as the Uffa Fox Boat.

In February, approval was given for minor modifications to the Hudson aircraft, allowing it to carry the boat. Preliminary tests in August met with success, and on 19 September it was agreed to produce the successful version of the boat as the Airborne Lifeboat Mark I. At the beginning of October the decision to replace the Hudson with the Warwick meant modifying the lifeboat to fit the new aircraft. In view of the urgency to provide this rescue aid, it was agreed that the Hudsons of 279 Squadron would be equipped with this first version. Authorization was given for 24 Mark I boats to cover the period during which an improved boat was developed for the Warwick.

The first Mark I lifeboats started to enter service with 279 Squadron in January 1943. They were equipped with sufficient food, drink and comforts to cover seven days' requirements for a crew of seven. These included:

- for communication: a dinghy radio set, a Verey pistol and cartridges, a waterproof torch, smoke floats and an Aldis signalling lamp;
- for comfort and protection: waterproof outer suits with warm inner suits, first aid kit and massage oil;
- for food and drink: tinned water and drinking cup, condensed milk, tins of emergency rations, cigarettes and matches.

To aid the survivors on their voyage, a compass and charts were provided as well as materials and tools to effect repairs. All these were stowed in the boat's lockers, alongside petrol, oil, sails, masts and rigging, together with instructions to enable survivors with little sailing experience to operate the boat and navigate safely.

Teething troubles were encountered, but the majority had been resolved by May, when 279 Squadron was well equipped with airborne lifeboats. On 5 May the first operational drop proved the practical success of the new invention (see plate 6). The second successful drop of an airborne lifeboat under much more arduous conditions than the first proved beyond doubt the value of the lifeboat to the rescue services.

LIFEBOAT RESCUE FROM THE FRENCH COAST

As trainee bomber crews approached the end of the course at the Operational Training Unit (OTU), the majority were tasked to fly a short operation over enemy-occupied territory, usually northern France, to drop propaganda leaflets. These sorties, known as 'Nickel' flights, gave the novice crews an opportunity to experience the build-up to a bombing operation and then to fly over enemy territory where they might expect to meet opposition. The flights also served the useful secondary purpose of boosting the morale of those living in the occupied countries.

On the night of 13 July 1943, Wing Commander Norman Bray, a peacetime regular officer who had been awarded the DFC in 1938 for operations on the Northwest Frontier of India, took off in

Wellington 'F' (BJ 702) from Chipping Warden with his student crew from 12 OTU to drop leaflets in the Paris area. Shortly after crossing the French coast, the bomber was hit by flak, which damaged the port engine. Bray turned back but the Wellington steadily lost height; Flight Sergeant Bernard Fitchett, the wireless operator, sent an SOS and selected the IFF to emergency once the bomber had crossed the coast, where it received a hot reception from the German gunners. The aircraft's wing had also been damaged and Bray had difficulty controlling the bomber. He realized that he would not be able to complete the crossing of the English Channel and ordered the crew to take up their ditching positions before making a tail-down landing on the sea. The aircraft pitched forward and decelerated quickly, causing Bray to smash his face on the windscreen, but this did not prevent him from making a quick escape from the aircraft, which was rapidly filling up with water.

Standing on the wing, he saw three of the crew in the dinghy, which had released and inflated automatically. Sergeant Les Perkins, the front gunner, was trapped in the fuselage by his foot and Bray helped him to escape. All the crew managed to get to the dinghy before the Wellington sank, 15 minutes later. Bray's nose was broken and bleeding badly but he stemmed the flow after breaking open the first aid kit. All suffered from seasickness and cold, but once daylight came they were able to organize themselves and devise a plan for the rationing of water. At 9.10 am they sighted the French coast, and the navigator, Flying Officer G. Parkinson, fixed their position near Le Havre.

During the morning, a lone Spitfire sighted the dinghy, circled twice and waggled its wings before flying off. Throughout the day the crew took shifts to paddle away from the French coast before spending a fitful night. Early next morning a flight of Typhoons spotted the flares fired by the survivors and radioed a message to their unit. Within an hour, a Hudson of 279 Squadron took off from Bircham Newton carrying a lifeboat. As it flew over Tangmere, near Chichester, it picked up an escort of 12 Typhoons of 486 (RNZAF) Squadron before heading for the dinghy. At 10.45 am, 28 ASRU at Newhaven received a crash call, and *HSL 177* (see plate 7) and *HSL 190* left for a position 20 miles south of Brighton to await instructions.

The Hudson arrived in the search area and within 20 minutes the pilot, Flying Officer Lloyd Wilson from Melbourne, Australia, spotted the dinghy. The survivors fired a flare to allow Wilson to assess the wind. After a dummy run he dropped the lifeboat, which deployed perfectly under its three parachutes and landed close to the dinghy. The crew scrambled aboard and soon had the engine going; escorted by four Typhoons, they headed for the English coast 80 miles away.

Within minutes, a large formation of FW 190 fighters appeared and was immediately engaged by the New Zealanders, who shot down at least one of the enemy and damaged others. Four Spitfire squadrons were scrambled to relieve the Typhoons and take over the escort duties. At 4.15 pm, the two high speed launches were ordered to proceed a further 20 miles south to intercept the lifeboat. In the meantime, Bray and his crew were heading away steadily from the French coast, and after four hours they were 30 miles from the English coast when the two RAF rescue launches arrived. The launches had seen some of the Spitfires circling the dinghy, and Flight Lieutenant Alan MacDonald and his crew on HSL 177 reached the survivors shortly afterwards. The six Wellington survivors were soon fitted out with dry clothing and the launches headed for Newhaven with the Spitfires overhead. HSL 190 took the lifeboat in tow.

Bray and his crew were met by the naval medical authorities and were admitted to the RN sick quarters at Swanborough, where Bray received treatment for a badly broken nose and the others for cuts and bruises. Within a few days they returned to their unit.

Wing Commander Bray was loud in his praise for the conduct of his young and inexperienced crew. He also commented that all their lives had been saved because they adhered strictly to the training they had received at Chipping Warden. He concluded his report by saying: 'The whole show from beginning to end was a triumph of training and crew co-operation.'

This rescue from a position a few miles off the enemy coast was an excellent example of all elements of the rescue organization fulfilling their tasks perfectly. The pilot made a good ditching with the crew taking up the correct crash positions, allowing them to get clear of the aircraft quickly and board their dinghy. They took the correct precautions during the night and were ready to signal to the searching aircraft, which immediately alerted the rescue authorities.

The protection provided by the fighters was crucial and the speedy arrival of the Hudson, followed by a perfect drop of the lifeboat, allowed the survivors to board it quickly. They soon mastered the workings of the engine and had the lifeboat under way in a very short time. The high speed launches, with fighter escort, intercepted the lifeboat efficiently and soon had the survivors safely ashore, 40 hours after they had ditched.

★

Following the early success of the airborne lifeboat, further rescues soon followed. Shortly after the rescue of Wing Commander Bray and his crew, the Hudsons of 279 Squadron were in action again. The rescue of an RAF Mitchell bomber crew taking part in an air sea rescue operation, during which they were shot down, also provides an excellent example of the major contribution made by the Royal Navy's RMLs.

NORTH SEA RESCUE BY AIRBORNE LIFEBOAT AND ROYAL NAVY RESCUE MOTOR LAUNCH

At lunchtime on Friday 30 July 1943, Flying Officer Arthur Eyton-Jones and his fellow crew members (see plate 8) of 226 Squadron were preparing to go on leave when they were tasked to fly an air sea rescue operation to locate a USAAF bomber that had ditched in the North Sea. By 1.40 pm they were airborne from Swanton Morley in Norfolk in their twin-engine Mitchell bomber (FV 932). To provide an extra pair of eyes for the search, Sergeant J. Lecomber, a young air gunner flying on his first operation, was added to the four-man crew.

The Mitchell headed across the North Sea to a position north of the Dutch Frisian Islands. The weather was perfect as the aircraft climbed to 500 feet to commence the search, and the crew soon spotted an American dinghy with three people aboard. For the next two hours the Mitchell circled the dinghy, sending regular wireless messages back to base. Other search aircraft joined, and the increased activity must have alerted the German air defence system. Just before the Mitchell was due to be relieved, no fewer than eight Messerschmitt 210 fighters arrived on the scene and headed for the Mitchell. The pilot, Flying Officer Dick Christie, immediately turned west but escape was impossible. The air gunner, Sergeant E. Norburn, was killed as he engaged the enemy fighters and, almost immediately, the bomber's engines were set on fire.

With little time to warn the rest of the crew, Christie hastily ditched the aircraft. The Mitchell immediately started to sink and Eyton-Jones had great difficulty escaping from his navigator's compartment. He finally broke free; as he surfaced there was no sign of the aircraft, but an inflated dinghy with two men was nearby. The wireless operator, Flight Sergeant D. Bishop, and the young gunner, Lecomber, soon hauled him aboard. Christie was either killed or knocked unconscious on impact, as he made no attempt to escape.

The three men paddled around among the wreckage and picked up a first aid kit and three single-seat 'K' dinghies, which they inflated and tied to the main dinghy in order to be more conspicuous. The other search aircraft had scattered on the appearance of the German fighters, but one had seen the Mitchell ditch and transmitted its position. Eyton-Jones used the first aid kit to bandage a deep gash in his leg. Just as it was getting dark, a lone Beaufighter returning to England flew over the top of them and immediately climbed and started to circle. Before departing it signalled that it had sent a message and asked for help. After an evening meal of four Horlicks tablets, the survivors settled down for an uncomfortable night.

The three men were surprised that they did not see another search aircraft until the following afternoon when two Hudsons of 279 Squadron, escorted by four Beaufighters, appeared at 1.30 pm. One of the Hudsons was carrying one of the new airborne lifeboats. The pilot, Pilot Officer Watts, dropped a smoke float alongside the dinghy before making a number of dummy runs, finally releasing the lifeboat from 700 feet. Three large parachutes deployed and the lifeboat landed gently just 100 yards downwind, when the parachutes were jettisoned. It was a perfect drop. The three men paddled over. They were soon on board and were just slashing their dinghy to sink it when the air was rocked by cannon fire. It was the Beaufighters, sinking the remaining dinghies so that they would not be the cause of a false sighting in the future. Having seen the survivors board the lifeboat, the Hudsons left, but not before signalling the course to steer as 247 degrees.

Using the waterproof instructions in the lifeboat, the crew soon started the engines and set them at half throttle, but had difficulty fitting the rudder. The mast and sail were set and, with a wind from the southeast, the lifeboat headed for England. However, the crew had forgotten to watch the two engine hatches, and as the wind rose and the sea broke over the craft the engines stopped – both hatches were found to be full of water. They were pumped out but the engines could not be restarted. The mainsail was lowered and foresail set as the wind and seas continued to increase. Just as darkness fell, the tiller arm carried away at the rudder post and the craft immediately swung and lay across the seas, which poured aboard. This was the beginning of a wretched night.

The drogue was streamed, the foresail lowered and the mast was unstepped. The drogue failed to keep the boat from lying across the seas and, fearing that they might founder, the crew streamed both the mast and mainsail as a drogue. This improved things, but the heavy seas continued to cascade aboard. Eyton-Jones described the night as 'a period of pure nightmare'. At dawn on 1 August, the improvised drogue carried away and they were left helpless with no engines, mast, sails or rudder, and the seas constantly sweeping the boat.

With the craft lying across the seas, the starboard hatch filled with water and a dangerous list developed. Only by allowing an equal amount of water into the port hatch could the craft stabilize, although this caused it to lie low in the water. For the next six hours the crew pumped and baled until the water was clear. They then improvised a drogue using one of the survival wet suits, which proved effective.

During the afternoon the seas began to moderate and they were joined by a succession of aircraft until nightfall. They had time to explore other hatches, where they discovered more survival suits, and the relief of dry and warm clothing raised their spirits. They spent a more comfortable night, but the seas were still very choppy. They had established a routine of one tin of water, one of milk and nine Horlicks tablets each day between the three of them.

On 2 August the first aircraft arrived at 7.30 am, but the sea state made spotting the lifeboat difficult and the aircraft failed to see the craft. It was not until late in the afternoon that they were able to attract the attention of a Halifax, which then stayed with them for a number of hours. At 7 pm a Hudson arrived and stayed with them until dusk. As night fell and the other two slept, Eyton-Jones, who had not slept for the whole period, maintained watch but had a major scare when he dozed and almost fell overboard. He knew that in his weakened condition he would never have been able to regain the craft. At 8 am on 3 August, three Mitchells found them and these were relieved by others throughout the morning.

Overnight two Royal Navy launches of the 69th RML Flotilla had sailed from Grimsby to a waiting position near the Outer Dowsing shoal, where they spent an uncomfortable night in the heavy seas. During the early hours of the morning, the radio operator on *RML 547* received a message ordering the two launches to proceed immediately to a position 200 miles east of Newcastle to a 'powered dinghy'. Lieutenant Andy Andrews RNVR immediately set course with *RML 553* in company. Just after noon, *553* received a call on 500 kc/s, the international distress frequency, from a Hudson circling 16 miles ahead.

As the two launches drew near, a Mitchell swooped over *547* making the official 'follow me' signals, and shortly afterwards the rating manning the crow's nest spotted the lifeboat. Scrambling nets were lowered, and the three survivors were lifted gently on board and taken to the sickbay to be treated by the sick-berth attendant before being put to bed with a cup of hot, sweet tea as the lifeboat was taken in tow.

The rescue launches turned for home and the escorting aircraft disappeared. Late in the afternoon there was a major alarm when a German Junkers 88 flew between the two launches, but seeing the yellow decks (the international colour of the rescue services) the pilot waved and went on his way. The launches were diverted to look for other dinghies that had been reported, and it was not until late on the evening of 4 August that the survivors were finally landed at Grimsby, where they noticed that the ground would not keep still.

A huge effort was expended in rescuing Arthur Eyton-Jones and his two colleagues. Countless aircraft were involved and it was only the sixth time that the new airborne lifeboat had been dropped in anger. The crew displayed tremendous resourcefulness and determination under extreme difficulties, and the fact that a number of mistakes were made is fully understandable given the limited experience and the very adverse conditions. However, the airborne lifeboat had certainly proved its value. As Eyton-Jones commented, 'I am just glad that we spent that awful night in the lifeboat and not in our dinghy.'

Arthur Eyton-Jones returned to 226 Squadron and completed his tour of operations. He later completed a second tour on Mosquitos and was awarded the DFC. At the end of the war, Lieutenant Andy Andrews was mentioned in dispatches.

★

With the Mark I boat in service, trials were carried out to provide a lifeboat that could be carried by the Warwick. With air operations extending over greater distances, there was a requirement for a larger boat with an increased range. In April a specification for a new boat was drawn up (known as the Mark II) which was to be 30 feet long, capable of travelling 300 miles at a speed of 7 knots and with a capacity to carry 10 men. However, the development of this new Mark would take time, so a further 50 Mark I boats were ordered for modification and fitting to the Warwick for use until the Mark II was available. The modified type, known as the Mark IA, was available for trials in September. A boat was taken to the United States for use by a Fortress aircraft and a successful drop was achieved within a few weeks. On 7 January 1944 the first successful operation with a Mark IA lifeboat was achieved when a boat was dropped to the crew of a Mosquito in the Bay of Biscay.

SAILING A LIFEBOAT 120 MILES

In company with three other Mosquitos of 157 Squadron, Flying Officer Philip Huckin and his navigator Flight Sergeant Robert Graham took off at 2.50 pm on 7 January 1944 from Predannack in Cornwall. They were flying Mosquito HJ 660 and were heading for the Bay of Biscay on an offensive patrol and to provide fighter cover for the anti-submarine aircraft hunting for U-boats in the area.

The aircraft had been airborne for almost two hours when two Junkers 88 long-range fighters were seen. They were chased and Huckin closed rapidly with the rear aircraft, which he attacked, sending it crashing into the sea. During the combat, return fire from the German fighter hit both the engines of the Mosquito and it was immediately apparent that a ditching was inevitable. Huckin was 200 miles south of Land's End and too low to make a direct distress call to base, so he alerted the others to his situation and they transmitted an SOS call.

At 2,000 feet Huckin told Graham to take up his ditching position. The navigator placed one hand on the roof escape hatch and the other on the dinghy manual release handle, with his feet braced against the instrument panel. He was a bulky man and decided not to strap in as this hindered his movements. The pilot was strapped into his seat.

There was a long heavy swell and a choppy sea. The wind was moderate from the southwest. Huckin selected full flap and levelled out just above the sea at 110 knots. The first impact was slight, parallel with the swell, at which point Graham jettisoned the roof escape hatch and pulled the dinghy release handle. The second impact was firmer but the aircraft came to rest in a level attitude with the tail unit broken off. The navigator was out of the aircraft in less than a minute and the pilot, who took his 'K' dinghy with him, quickly followed. The two men inflated their Mae Wests, quickly boarded the aircraft's 'L' dinghy, which had inflated the right way up, and cut the painter attached to the aircraft. Three minutes after ditching, the Mosquito pitched forward and sank.

The two men baled out the dinghy without difficulty in spite of the adverse conditions of the choppy sea and long swell. They then checked their survival gear, which included emergency rations and water, dinghy apron and hood, paddles, mast and sails and six two-star red signals. Strict rationing was agreed, and since neither was hungry they decided to eat nothing at this stage.

Huckin decided, for comfort's sake, and out of consideration for his hefty navigator, to leave Graham in the 'L' dinghy and transfer to the single-seat 'K' when they tied the two together. With darkness falling, they streamed the drogue and spread the aprons for protection from the cold wind and sea spray. A strict watch was kept alternately and an effort was made to get some sleep, but the rain, cold and wet conditions made this impossible. Huckin took the kapok from his Mae West and made a cushion to sit on in an attempt to reduce the cold and damp.

At dawn they hove in the drogue, hoisted the sail for the 'K' dinghy and got under way, towing the 'L' type astern. They steered a northeasterly heading and estimated that they were making 1 knot. In the meantime, four Mosquitos from their own squadron took off at 7 am to search for them but sighted nothing. However, a second formation of four aircraft that had taken off two hours later sighted the dinghy at noon. Shortly afterwards five Beaufighters arrived, escorting a Warwick of 280 Squadron that was carrying a lifeboat. The captain of the Warwick, Flight Lieutenant George Chesher, made a perfect drop and the lifeboat landed 100 yards downwind of the dinghies.

Huckin cast off from the 'L' dinghy, paddled across to the lifeboat and was soon aboard. Graham joined him a few minutes later, having used the apron of his dinghy as a sail. They took the 'K' dinghy on board but jettisoned the larger 'L' type. In the boat the two men found a message: 'Steer 350 T. Good luck.' They quickly donned the survival suits.

The first attempt to start the motors failed. Huckin noted that the parachute had not jettisoned correctly and the rigging lines had fouled the propeller. He stripped off, took the floating knife, jumped into the sea and cut away the parachute. Once both propellers were clear, the starboard motor was started and a northerly heading was established. After running at 3 knots for an hour, the engine stopped because the drogue, which had not been properly stowed, had fouled the propeller. The port motor was started and they resumed their journey. The two men devised a rationing plan based on four weeks. They tidied up the boat and made good progress for the rest of the day without seeing any other ship or aircraft. Using a compass from the lifeboat's emergency pack, Graham took on the navigation responsibilities and maintained a plot and log throughout the incident.

At dawn on 9 January the port engine stopped because the fuel tank had not been refuelled before it ran dry – a necessary procedure. During the process of refuelling, the port propeller was fouled and all efforts to clear it failed. The mast was stepped and the sails were set. Although the two men had no sailing experience, they followed the instructions in the lifeboat instructions pamphlet and accomplished the task without difficulty. They made good progress in the strong southwesterly wind and estimated that they were 60 miles southwest of Ushant. Towards dusk, the wind increased; they stowed the sails and streamed the sea drogue, and rode out a gale for eight hours.

By dawn on the 10th the wind had abated, so the sail was set and good progress was made with an estimated speed of 3–4 knots. A Mosquito arrived in the afternoon and orbited before waggling its wings and departing due north. The men assumed this to be the direction to sail and course was altered. Later the visibility dropped to 100 yards and the cloud base was barely above the sea.

During the night a large aircraft was heard flying over the lifeboat and the men fired one of their two-star red signals, but it was not acknowledged. Unknown to the two survivors, the aircraft was a searching 224 Squadron Liberator from St Eval, Cornwall. It sighted a high speed launch, which was also out searching and in the event was only some 10 miles from the lifeboat. The Liberator tried to make wireless and radio contact with the launch, but this failed. It then made a number of runs over the launch, illuminating it twice with its Leigh Light searchlight before dropping flares and some cans of petrol. In the very poor visibility, the Liberator had mistaken the rescue launch for the lifeboat.

Throughout Tuesday 11 January the wind varied but was mainly from the west. Graham adjusted the course accordingly and the lifeboat continued to make progress northwards. Visibility remained very poor, and as the wind dropped off in the evening, the men decided to furl the sails and try to get some rest. Soon afterwards they thought they heard the sound of aircraft engines, but nothing materialized. Before long they heard the engine noise again and soon after two surface craft appeared, which, as they came nearer, they recognized as navy rescue launches. A two-star red was fired and they were seen. At midnight, the two survivors jumped on board *RML 534* where they were given a change of clothing and promptly put to bed. They were only 35 miles south of the Scilly Islands and 15 miles from the position estimated by Graham. *RML 526* towed the lifeboat into port.

The official report commented that Huckin and Graham had set a very high standard of initiative and skill coupled with great courage, fortitude and determination during their 103 hours afloat in the middle of winter. Neither man sustained injury throughout the incident, not even during the ditching. At no time did either feel that they would not succeed. This confidence stemmed from their sound knowledge of ditching and dinghy drills and survival at sea. Perhaps this was to be expected, since Huckin was the squadron's air sea rescue officer. No doubt his outstanding example alerted the rest of his squadron colleagues to the value of knowing the correct drills.

Two weeks after their ordeal it was announced that Huckin and Graham had been awarded an immediate DFC and DFM respectively. The citations were fulsome in praise of the two men for 'exceptional qualities of valour and determination, which never wavered and has set an example of the highest order'.

★

The airborne lifeboat proved to be a valuable addition to the air sea rescue organization. Of the 113 lifeboats dropped (15 by the USAAF), 61 were successfully boarded by at least one man. One successful rescue using an airborne lifeboat was by one of the RAF's most experienced Warwick ASR captains who had already made a number of successful drops, including the drop to the Mosquito crew whose experiences have just been related. Flight Lieutenant George Chesher and his crew had taken off to drop a lifeboat to survivors in the North Sea, not realizing that they too would soon be welcoming the sight of a lifeboat dropped to aid their own rescue.

RESCUERS RESCUED

Throughout the first week of October 1944, the Warwicks of 280 Squadron were constantly in action searching for ditched crews in the North Sea. It proved to be one of the busiest and most demanding periods of the squadron's activities. Amongst those they were searching for were a Beaufighter crew of 489 (RNZAF) Squadron who had been shot down on 1 October. Two Warwicks had located the two survivors early on 7 October before Flying Officer George Chesher and his crew were tasked to relieve them. They took off at 10.55 am from Langham in BV 368 and headed for the dinghy's last known position.

At 12.45 pm the crew sighted four dinghies tied together with two more nearby, and estimated that there were 10 survivors, almost certainly the crew of a USAAF Fortress that had sent out a distress signal. Chesher felt compelled to assist the 10 men; he dropped his lifeboat 20 yards away and saw the survivors scramble on board. As the Warwick circled, two Messerschmitt 410 fighters appeared from cloud and attacked it as the rescue aircraft's two gunners returned fire. One of the fighters was hit and left the scene with one engine trailing smoke. The other fighter carried out a series of attacks, wounding two of the Warwick crew and severely damaging the aircraft's hydraulic system. The aircraft's undercarriage fell down, both engines were hit and the tail was set on fire.

Chesher ditched the aircraft, which immediately broke into three parts and sank within 10 seconds. Fortunately, the dinghy inflated automatically and all the crew were able to scramble clear and get on board. The six men spent a miserable night, baling out water most of the time. The air gunner, Warrant Officer A. Donley, had been badly wounded during the attacks, Chesher had a shrapnel wound in his leg, and the navigator, Flight Sergeant B. Jones, dislocated his shoulder during the ditching. The crew managed to salvage the Lindholme container, and this provided welcome supplies. At 3.15 pm, two Mosquitos sighted the dinghy and radioed for help.

The dinghy was not sighted again before darkness fell, so four Warwicks were launched early the following morning to search for a number of missing aircraft, including Chesher's crew. Flying Officer L. Harvey found a dinghy with five men – the sixth was the badly wounded Donley, who was lying in the bottom of the dinghy. Harvey dropped his lifeboat at 12.20 pm but it hit the sea nose down and overturned. In the meantime, New Zealander Flying Officer E. Rhodes made radio contact with Harvey but was almost immediately attacked by German fighters. He quickly sought cover in the overcast cloud where he managed to evade the fighters. Harvey then alerted him that his lifeboat had capsized and was unusable so Rhodes headed for the area, where he soon spotted Harvey's circling Warwick.

Rhodes dropped his lifeboat accurately and the survivors quickly clambered on board before signalling to the two Warwicks: 'this is Chesher's crew – one man injured'. The survivors soon started both motors and steered a course of 255 at 6 knots for the next three hours to get clear of the enemy coast. German fighters were still very active, and one flew over the lifeboat and fired a star shell. A third Warwick, piloted by Canadian Pilot Officer L. Hagg, arrived on the scene and immediately set out to locate the standing patrol of rescue launches. His crew sighted them at 1.15 pm and started to direct them to the lifeboat, but the heavy German activity made this unsafe and the launches had to turn away when Hagg was also ordered to return to base. Attempts were made to contact the fourth Warwick, but it did not answer the radio calls and failed to return to base.

Two Beaufighters arrived to provide a fighter escort for the circling rescue aircraft, and one was soon attacking a Messerschmitt 410 and driving it away. At 2.45 pm Squadron Leader W. Harpur arrived to relieve the two Warwicks, but he soon had to seek cover in the nearby cloud as a German fighter closed to attack. An hour later he returned and remained with the lifeboat until darkness descended.

The lifeboat continued heading west through the night, first on one engine and then on the other. When the fuel ran out early the next morning they hoisted the sail to maintain their progress. Flying Officer F. Williamson had taken off at dawn in a Warwick and he soon found the lifeboat, which was now 80 miles clear of the enemy coast. Royal Navy *RML 27* had left Great Yarmouth, but Williamson was unable to contact it using the VHF radio. However, it was sighted some 7 miles away and he led it to the dinghy, which it reached at 9.08 am. The six survivors were soon transferred to the RML. *HSL 2697* (Flying Officer Postgate) arrived on the scene to take the lifeboat in tow, but after 51 miles it was damaged and not worth recovering, so it was sunk by the rescue launch's gunfire.

The rescue of this Warwick crew, who had themselves gone to the aid of survivors, took place under the nose of the Germans. Being experts in air sea rescue, Chesher and his crew were well placed to make best use of all the survival aids, not least the airborne lifeboat, which they sailed for 17 hours away from the enemy coast. Sadly, the rescue was completed at a cost: Flying Officer A. Mason and his crew were lost without trace. For his determined effort to drop his lifeboat and his subsequent conduct during the ditching and the rescue of his crew, George Chesher was awarded an immediate DFC.

Chapter Seven

The First Three Years

HAVING OUTLINED IN the previous chapters the development
and organization of the Air Sea Rescue Services in the United
Kingdom, in this chapter we will look at a variety of operations
and rescues in northwest Europe, with the aim of highlighting the
many different circumstances that faced both the aircrew in distress
and the rescue organizations.

Prior to the formation of the Directorate of Sea Rescue Services
towards the end of January 1941, the rescue of aircrew from the sea
depended very much on local arrangements. Much of the RAF's and
Royal Navy's small force of specialized air sea rescue craft were located
in the English Channel. With a large ground force established in
northern France, much of the capability was concentrated in the area
of the Straits of Dover. A few RAF high speed launches were available,
but no specialist craft were available for the Royal Navy, who had to
divert motor torpedo boats (MTBs) from their primary operational
role.

In 1940 the RAF's only specialized air sea rescue capability rested
with the high speed launches. Their first major contribution was not
the rescue of ditched airmen, but the evacuation of members of the
British Expeditionary Force (BEF) from the beaches near Dunkirk in
Operation 'Dynamo'.

OPERATION 'DYNAMO'

On 20 May 1940,Vice Admiral Bertram Ramsey, Flag Officer Dover, was ordered to make preparations in the event that the BEF had to be evacuated from northern France. Six days later he was ordered to implement the plan. By May 31, Ramsay had to call on his last reserves, the small craft, and this included the RAF's marine craft. Six launches were allocated to the rescue: *Pinnace 32*, four seaplane tenders (commanded by Pilot Officer Collins) and a Civilian Aviation Authority launch.

Pinnace 32 fouled its propeller on the outbound journey and had to return, taking no further part in the operation. The five seaplane tenders were towed across the Channel to conserve fuel. In the rough sea, the tow parted and the tenders made the last 12 miles under their own power. The launches transferred 500 men to the larger waiting vessels but *ST 254* grounded under the weight of the men trying to board, causing sufficient damage for it to be abandoned. A second fouled its propeller and was thrown on to the beach where it was holed. The other three continued their ferry work before returning to Dover in a poor state.

Two of the launches were made serviceable by 2 June and Pilot Officer Collins called for volunteers – everyone responded. *ST 243* and *ST 276* left for France at 2.30 pm, each with two Royal Navy berthing parties. As the launches approached the coast, both were bombed and machine-gunned by Junkers 87 'Stuka' dive-bombers. The gunners responded; a near miss severely damaged *ST 243*, but this did not deter Leading Aircraftman Lockwood, who continued firing his Lewis gun until the launch sank under him.

Corporal Les Flower, the coxswain of *ST 276*, took violent evasive action and, despite four more strafing attacks by the Stukas, Flower's skilful handling kept the launch afloat despite it receiving many hits. Flower moved to pick up the 17 survivors from *ST 243* from the sea, but the senior naval officer ordered him to proceed to Dunkirk and leave the men in the water. With great reluctance he obeyed the order and left to disembark the naval party at Dunkirk. Flower was then ordered to sink *ST 276*, but after a fierce argument with a naval officer who could not appreciate that RAF launches were not always commanded by officers, he took on board an RNVR junior officer, on the clear understanding that he remained in command of the launch. *ST 276* left the harbour at sunset and immediately headed for the position where *ST 243* had foundered. Despite the disabled state of their launch, Flower and his crew searched all night, reluctantly leaving the scene at dawn. With the exception of one man, Collins and his crew, together with the naval party, all perished.

Corporal Les Flower was awarded the Military Medal for his actions during Operation 'Dynamo', an unusual award for a member of the RAF who displayed his outstanding gallantry at sea.

★

In addition to the RAF and Royal Navy rescue services, other seagoing organizations gave valuable assistance in the rescue of aircrew down in the sea. During the early years of the war, when the RAF's air sea rescue organization was still in its infancy, the Royal National Lifeboat Institution (RNLI) made a major contribution.

ROYAL NATIONAL LIFEBOAT INSTITUTION

At the commencement of the Second World War, the RNLI had been saving life at sea for 115 years. Manned largely by volunteers, the men of the lifeboat service braved the worst of weathers to save life and were at the forefront of rescuing ditched aircrew who came down in coastal waters. With the lack of a formal air sea rescue organization in the first years of the war, the RNLI lifeboats provided one of the few chances of pilots being rescued during the period leading up to the Battle of Britain in the spring of 1940 and during the Battle itself.

One of the fighter pilots saved during this period was Squadron Leader John Peel (see plate 9), the commanding officer of 145 Squadron based at Tangmere in Sussex. On 11 July 1940 he was leading his squadron against a force of heavy bombers approaching the south coast when his Hurricane (P 3400) was hit by return fire.

Despite serious damage to his aircraft, he pursued an enemy bomber 25 miles off the coast and probably destroyed it. As he returned across the English Channel he was forced to ditch in the sea. At this time fighter pilots had not been issued with the 'K' dinghy and so had to rely on their Mae West life-saving jackets only, and hope that they would be picked up before succumbing to exposure.

At 6.25 pm the coastguards saw a fighter aircraft ditch southwest of Selsey Bill. Within minutes the Selsey lifeboat, *Canadian Pacific*, was launched and headed straight for the area. There was a strong breeze and a moderate swell, but within the hour the lifeboat crew spotted a pilot floating in the sea. Peel was pulled on board semi-conscious and in an exhausted state. He wrote later to his rescuers, 'When you arrived I had almost given up hope and I doubt I could have lasted more than a few minutes.' Wrapped in blankets, he was soon ashore safely and returned to his squadron later that night. The lifeboat had only been back at Selsey for a few minutes when it was re-launched to search for the crew of a German bomber that had been seen to crash offshore. After a two-hour search, all that was found was a patch of oil.

By July 1941, John Peel was a wing commander and leader of the Kenley Wing. On 9 July 1941 he led his Wing in support of a formation of Stirling bombers attacking Mazingarbe in northern France. On the return flight 20 Messerschmitt 109s were encountered and his Hurricane was shot down. He baled out over the English Channel and successfully boarded his 'K' dinghy. A Lysander, crewed by Sergeants Hurst and Glew, was scrambled from Hawkinge. They spotted the flag waved by Peel and called up a Royal Navy patrol boat, which picked up Peel shortly afterwards. He was back flying the following day.

Peel returned to operations and left the RAF in 1948 as a group captain having been awarded the DSO and the DFC.

A lifeboat rescue with a difference occurred on 8 August 1941 at 5.15 pm when the coastguards reported that an aircraft was down 10 miles south of Bembridge on the Isle of Wight. The Bembridge lifeboat, *Jesse Lumb*, was launched into a very rough sea and headed for the position noted by the coastguards. An aircraft circled over the lifeboat before heading off. After it had repeated the operation twice the lifeboat followed, but was unable to find a dinghy. She did, however, find the RAF's *HSL 116*, disabled and flying a distress signal. The high speed launch had been positioned in the English Channel during some of the day's fierce air battles and had been attacked by a German fighter. One of the crew had been killed and another seriously wounded. A rope had fouled the launch's propeller. The lifeboat managed to get a line aboard and took the RAF launch in tow. A wireless message to report the casualties was sent and the lifeboat delivered them directly to the hospital at Haslar, Portsmouth. The *Jesse Lumb* finally returned to her station 14 hours after answering the call.

During the morning of 3 September, the men of the Margate lifeboat saw a parachute descending out to sea. They immediately launched the lifeboat and headed for the area. The sea was calm and the wind light, but there was a mist, and after an hour of searching an RAF pilot was spotted floating motionless in the sea. He was very badly burnt and was lapsing into unconsciousness. He was gently lifted into the lifeboat, wrapped in blankets and made as comfortable as possible. A wireless call was made for an ambulance to be at the harbour, and when the lifeboat arrived the pilot was rushed to hospital. Then began a two-year ordeal for the pilot, Pilot Officer Richard Hillary.

Hillary had been on patrol with his fellow pilots of 603 Squadron when fighters of JG 26 engaged the formation. Hillary's Spitfire (X 4277) was hit and set on fire. After a great struggle, Hillary managed to bale out, but not before his hands and face had been severely burnt. He managed to open his parachute, but was virtually helpless once he was in the sea. An hour later the Margate lifeboat arrived.

During his time in hospital and convalescence Richard Hillary recorded his experiences and thoughts in his book The Last Enemy, *which is recognized as one of the classic books of the war. Although disabled, he returned to flying and was killed training to be a night fighter pilot on 7 January 1943. His ashes were scattered from the air over the sea where the Margate lifeboat had rescued him.*

Many bomber crews struggled across the North Sea only to ditch when almost in sight of land. Very often it was a lifeboat station that was able to offer the quickest response. During the early hours of 11 April 1942, the RAF airfield at Coltishall was alerted that a bomber had crashed in the sea 5 miles off the north coast of Norfolk. The Cromer lifeboat, *H.P. Bailey* (see plate 10), was launched at 3.58 am and soon found six airmen in a dinghy. It was the all-Polish crew of a 305 Squadron Wellington (W 5519) that had been badly shot up by a night fighter as it returned from a bombing operation over Essen. The injured pilot, Pilot Officer Czolowski, had ditched the aircraft and he and all his crew had managed to get aboard the dinghy.

A trawler had seen the aircraft ditch and arrived on the scene at the same time as the lifeboat. Between them they were able to recover the airmen, three of them wounded, and transfer them all to the lifeboat, which landed the six men at Cromer at 5.15 am.

The value and efforts of the Cromer lifeboat drew loud praise from Marshal of the RAF Sir John Salmond. He wrote to the general secretary of the RNLI on 5 May, 'The repeated launchings of this boat that so often result in rescue is most gratifying to me and the RAF squadrons. I wish to emphasize to you how grateful we are.'

Although not strictly speaking an air sea rescue, the actions of the Buckie lifeboat, *K.B.M.*, on the night of 15 September 1942 is worthy of inclusion in this section relating the important contribution made by the RNLI. At 8.53 pm the coastguards reported that the RAF's *HSL 170* was ashore on the rocks under the Buckie coastguard station. There was a strong WNW wind blowing, with a heavy sea, and the tide was one hour from low water. The lifeboat was launched at 9.30 pm and reached the rescue launch 10 minutes later. The lifeboatmen could see her by the light of the coastguard's Aldis lamp from the shore, with the seas breaking over her stern and the crew crowded into the bow.

The coastguards had managed to get a line to the RAF launch and rig the life-saving apparatus, so the lifeboat held off. The apparatus rescued one man by hauling him through the heavy seas and over sharp rocks, at great risk to the man. The rest of the crew then called for the lifeboat to help. The launch was high on the rocks and taking a pounding from the breaking waves. The coxswain of *K.B.M.*, Francis Mair, brought the lifeboat to the stern, but wind, sea and tide carried her away. Mair made a second attempt to go alongside, but, as he got closer to the launch, a heavy sea struck the lifeboat and lifted her towards the rocks. As the sea receded, the lifeboat crashed heavily on to the rocks and one of the crew was thrown overboard. The coxswain went full astern and was able to pick him up.

The next problem to beset Mair was the failure of the engine. One of the ropes from the life-saving apparatus had fouled the propeller. As the lifeboat wallowed dangerously, the rope snapped and the crew managed to restart the engine. Mair made another attempt to get alongside, but once again the lifeboat was struck against the rocks, forcing him to take it into deeper water. Eventually, the crew managed to get a grappling iron on to the launch and the lifeboat was able to close in. This brought it over the rocks again, and as each wave receded she crashed on them. Despite the risk of smashing up the lifeboat, Mair gradually worked her close to the launch, and the nine RAF men were able to jump aboard.

By skilful use of the engine, Francis Mair cleared the rocks, but by this stage he was standing in water since the bottom of the lifeboat was holed. He assessed that she was still seaworthy and he was able to get her back to harbour with the rescued men. On inspection, it was discovered that the bottom had been badly smashed; the whole boat was flooded, apart from the engine room, and had been kept afloat only by the air cases.

The rescue was carried out with great skill and courage, and Francis Mair was awarded the RNLI's 'Thanks on Vellum'. The crew was awarded an additional £1 to the standard scale of £1.50.

★

For those who came down further from the coast during the early days of the war, rescue was unlikely, but a small number of crews did survive. Luck often played an important part, but there were some remarkable feats of endurance as bomber crews struggled to cross the North Sea in their poor-performance bombers, often in the face of bad weather. The crew of a Whitley displayed an amazing willpower and determination to survive in midwinter.

PICKED UP BY TRAWLER

Twenty-six-year-old Squadron Leader Clive Forigny, the flight commander of 102 Squadron based at Topcliffe, took off with his crew on 1 March 1941 to attack Cologne in their Whitley bomber (T 4261). They found the target without difficulty and dropped the bombs from 12,500 feet before turning for home. Soon afterwards they discovered that the wireless was unserviceable.

On the return flight, the Whitley ran into thick cloud and the observer was unable to get any visual fixes to establish their position accurately. Forigny descended to 1,000 feet to get below the cloud, but they found themselves over the sea. The Whitley flew on but there was no sight of the English coast, and after nine hours in the air the fuel reserves were getting low. Florigny called Pilot Officer 'Revs' Rivaz, the rear gunner, forward to the cockpit and told him to prepare the crew for a landing on the sea. It was not possible to send an SOS because of the problems with the wireless.

Florigny dropped some flares to assess the wind and swell, and it was soon apparent that the sea was very rough and a gale was blowing. The crew took up their ditching positions and were uninjured when the bomber came to rest on the sea. The dinghy was thrown out and immediately inflated, but it started to drift away in the strong wind. The four men in the rear of the aircraft immediately jumped into the sea and three of them got on board. The fourth was a non-swimmer and was soon struggling. As Rivaz looked towards the aircraft he was horrified to see his captain standing on the floating fuselage while the distance from the dinghy widened rapidly. The men were helpless to assist as they found the dinghy impossible to control: it had inflated upside down.

The crew knew they could not reach their captain and that he would inevitably drown in the rough sea. It was an awful moment. All they could do was concentrate on hauling aboard the observer, who was still in the sea. As weakness overtook all of them and they feared they would be unable to save their observer, a wave washed him on top of them and into the dinghy. For some time they could only lie across each other, completely exhausted, but the immediate urgency of baling out the water made them start their efforts to prevent the dinghy becoming waterlogged. They could not risk entering the sea to try and right the dinghy so had to sit on the edge, with their feet in the middle forming a well. With the waves breaking over them continuously, they were soaked through but could not lessen their efforts to bale out the water using their service caps and helmets.

Since they had been unable to transmit an SOS they knew that it was unlikely that a search would start before dawn, which was still three hours away. They had to cling on to the dinghy as it rose and fell in the rough sea, and their ordeal was made worse by the biting winter wind. As dawn broke they saw an aircraft and managed to fire a distress flare. Almost at the same time they saw that the aircraft was German, and it continued on its way.

The men were appallingly cold and their legs and hands became numb, making baling very difficult. At about 9 am they saw a Hudson pass close by, but Rivaz's hands were so numb that he could not fire the Verey pistol until it had flown over. It was a depressing sight for the four men as it disappeared.

Two hours later they saw a Blenheim flying low as if it was searching. Rivaz again had to struggle with the Verey pistol, but he was incapable of holding it. The aircraft appeared to fly off, but it soon returned and started to circle the dinghy and the survivors could see the crew waving. Baling out operations were renewed with increasing vigour as the Blenheim stayed overhead. Soon a ship was sighted, and 30 minutes later a trawler came alongside. The four men were virtually helpless and had to be lifted on board. According to Rivaz, who later made a radio broadcast of his experience, the fishermen could not have been kinder. The crew were given dry clothing and hot drinks before being landed at Great Yarmouth five hours later.

The crew (see plate 11) were loud in their praise of the 34-year-old Rivaz and they later claimed that they all owed their lives to him.

For the eight hours in the most appalling winter conditions he had kept up their spirits during their ordeal.

The tragic loss of Squadron Leader Florigny was all the more poignant when it was discovered that his younger brother had also been on the same raid to Cologne, and he too failed to return and was posted as missing. The two brothers died on the same night and they are both commemorated on the Runnymede memorial.

'Revs' Rivaz returned to operations with 35 Squadron. On 18 December 1941 he was flying with his squadron commander, Wing Commander B.V. Robinson DFC, when their Halifax was hit by flak during a daylight attack against the Sharnhorst and Gneisenau at Brest. The bomber had to be ditched 60 miles off the south coast of England, but this time the SOS was picked up and a fix of their position obtained. A Lysander soon spotted them and it was not long before a rescue launch arrived. Rivaz was later awarded the DFC. On 13 October 1945, he was a passenger in a Liberator transport aircraft, which caught fire on take off and all on board were killed.

★

NINE DAYS IN THE NORTH SEA

The four-man crew of a 49 Squadron Hampden bomber (X 3134), captained by Sergeant Bryan Woolston, took off from Scampton just before midnight on the night of 30 June 1941 to bomb Dusseldorf. For Woolston and his wireless operator, Sergeant George Wood, it was their thirtieth and final operation before starting a rest tour.

The bomber had just crossed the Dutch coast at 17,000 feet when the port engine started to fail. The navigator, Sergeant P. Mackay, gave Woolston a course to steer and he turned for home. Within a few minutes, the engine failed completely amidst a shower of sparks and flames from the exhaust. The bombs were jettisoned over the sea, and despite the aircraft losing some height, Woolston remained confident that he could reach England. Six weeks earlier he had lost an engine during an attack against Hamburg and he had managed to creep back to make a successful crash landing on the Essex coast. However, his aircraft on this occasion was very difficult to control and it steadily lost height despite all the loose items being jettisoned. The gunner, Sergeant E.B. Chandler, also threw his guns and ammunition over the side. An SOS was sent (it later transpired that it was never received) and Woolston ordered the crew to take up their ditching stations.

The sea was very calm and there was good moonlight when Woolston throttled back the remaining engine until the aircraft was just above the surface, flying at slow speed with the tail down. The aircraft hit the sea hard, and George Wood thought they had landed on the beach. He immediately clambered on to the wing to find that they were on the sea and that the immersion switch had activated to inflate the dinghy, albeit upside down. Woolston quickly vacated the aircraft and dived into the sea to right the dinghy. During this operation he swallowed quantities of sea water and was violently sick for the next few hours. Before the crew could retrieve the Verey pistol, provisions and the two pigeons, the Hampden sank. The crew spent an uncomfortable night in the small dinghy.

When they took stock of their situation, they discovered that the two marine distress signals had been saved (they failed to work when they were activated a few days later), and their only food was a box containing 36 Horlicks tablets and some chocolate. They had a container with almost two pints of water and quickly realized that they would have to impose strict rationing, particularly the water. In the morning and evening they had half a Horlicks' tin-lid of water and three tablets each.

As the first day progressed the sun appeared, and for the rest of their ordeal the four men had to endure a heatwave. Woolston later commented that 'the hot spell undoubtedly saved us from dying of exposure'.

Towards the end of the second day they saw two Wellington bombers, but they flew on. To remain cool and avoid sweating, the crew immersed themselves in the water. On one occasion they spotted a mine close by and paddled away, now able to understand why there was no shipping around. By the third day they were all suffering from sunburn and they had to halve their meagre water ration; all the

1 *ABOVE: A crew with a 'H' dinghy. The CO_2 inflation bottle and various survival aids are visible (photograph courtesy of the Imperial War Museum, London CH 1264).*

2 *Squadron Leader Hedley Cliff, whose crew were saved by the pigeon 'Winkie' (photograph courtesy of the Imperial War Museum, London CH 5058).*

3 *A Lysander of 277 Squadron with life-saving gear loaded on the wing stub carriers (photograph courtesy of the Imperial War Museum, London CH 7571).*

4 *Mike Cooper and his groundcrew of 616 Squadron at 'readiness' (author's collection).*

5 *Flight Lieutenant David Jones, skipper of HSL 127, was awarded the DSC for his rescue under fire (Glynis James).*

6 *A Hudson drops an airborne lifeboat (TNA: PRO AIR 20/4710).*

7 *'Whaleback' HSL 177 picked up Bray and his crew a few miles off the French coast (photograph courtesy of the Imperial War Museum, London CH 12398).*

9 *Squadron Leader John Peel who was twice rescued from the sea (author's collection).*

8 *ABOVE: Arthur Eyton-Jones (centre) with his pilot, Dick Christie, who died in the ditching, and D. Bishop, the wireless operator, on the left (A. Eyton-Jones).*

10 *The Cromer lifeboat, H.P. Bailey, is launched (RNLI Cromer).*

11 'Revs' Rivaz (second right) and his three colleagues pictured after their rescue (YAM Archives).

12 Woolston and his crew after visiting HQ 5 Group Headquarters at Grantham. Left to right: 'Mac' Mackay, George Wood, Joe Woolston, Bas Chandler (G. Wood).

13 *Canadian fighter pilot Don Morrison DFM, shot down during the raid on Dieppe (Mrs D. Morrison).*

14 BELOW: *HSL 177 rescued Morrison after the Dieppe operation (Mrs D. Morrison).*

15 *ABOVE: The ASR badge worn by airmen members of the RAF marine craft crews (ACA Archives).*

16 *ABOVE: Wing Commander Ron Thomson DSO, DFC, captain of Fortress R/206 (photograph courtesy of the Imperial War Museum, London CH 14702).*

17 *LEFT: Squadron Leader Jack Holmes lets his Catalina drift towards the dinghy. Note the fuel jettisoned (Air Cdr J. Holmes).*

19 *Ron Foss pictured with his wife and son after receiving the CGM (ACA Archives).*

18 *Squadron Leader Jack Holmes DFC, who rescued the Thomson crew (Air Cdr J. Holmes).*

20 *The de la Paulle crew being picked up by Sunderland R/28 (J. Logan).*

Horlicks tablets had been eaten. They then ate the chocolate, eating a half piece each three times a day, but due to the lack of water they were unable to swallow all of it.

At the end of the third day three Blenheims flew by, but the two marine flares failed. The searching crews also failed to see the flashes from the signalling mirror. Nothing of note occurred over the next two days. The four men tried to paddle in a westerly direction, but they grew weaker and began to think that the end was near. On the sixth day their spirits rose when three launches came into view about 2 miles away, but they turned away without seeing the tiny dinghy. On the seventh day the water ran out after each had taken a mouthful. During the following day the crew felt very weak. At 9 pm a Hampden passed overhead, escorted by Hurricanes – once again the flashes from the signal mirror failed to attract their attention.

Throughout the ordeal, no one slept for more than 15 minutes at a time. At first the crew endeavoured to rest with their legs over each other's shoulders. This position worked until someone got cramp. Mackay, who was over 6 feet tall, suffered particularly. The scheme eventually evolved was for two to rest at a time as the others sat upright on the edge of the dinghy. Wood wryly commented, 'In another three days we should have had the system absolutely perfected!'

As the ninth morning dawned they all thought that they had 'bought it'. Woolston could no longer stand in the dinghy. Then at 8 am they saw a Hemswell-based Hampden and this time the aircraft spotted the flashing mirrors and turned towards them. Soon the aircraft was circling the dinghy, and after a few minutes the bomber signalled 'help coming' with the Aldis lamp. The aircraft continued circling for the next four hours; it dropped a dinghy, which the survivors recovered and immediately found some precious water. Wood thought the 'water tasted foul', no doubt due to the state of his mouth.

Two Blenheims with a Spitfire escort relieved the Hampden. At 12.30 pm *HSL 116* appeared and was soon alongside the dinghy. The crew were too weak to climb the scrambling net and had to be lifted on to the launch. None could stand, but they were soon resting on bunks with a tot of rum and a mug of tea. They were landed at Great

Yarmouth where they spent the next 10 days in the care of RAF doctors before returning to a wild celebration at Scampton.

The crew (see plate 12) had made a number of basic errors, but the training received by aircrews at this early stage of the war was still very rudimentary. The experiences of crews such as Woolston's did, of course, provide valuable lessons that could be incorporated into future training programmes. The pigeons should have been taken, and future drills identified a particular member of the crew to be responsible for taking the Verey pistol and flares. Throughout their ordeal, the crew had numerous opportunities to attract passing aircraft if the signals pistol had been available. In the event they were lucky to have such good weather, and the Hampden that sighted them was on a search for another crew from their own squadron. Nevertheless, they acted throughout in a very sensible manner, having determined a ration plan, which they strictly adhered to, and they kept as cool as possible in the hot conditions. Above all, they all possessed the most important quality for a survival situation: they kept their spirits high and their determination to survive never wavered.

After recovering in hospital Woolston and Wood were rested from operations and within a few weeks both had been awarded the DFM. They served in the Burma campaign and survived the war. Mackay returned to the squadron but was lost on operations. Chandler had a distinguished career as an air gunner, completing 98 bomber operations. He was awarded the DFM before joining 617 (Dam Busters) Squadron when he was awarded the DFC.

★

PADDLING FOR 58 HOURS

The commanding officer of 118 Squadron, Squadron Leader John Carver, was at the head of his Spitfire squadron when they took off at 5 pm on 13 March 1942 from Ibsley in the New Forest to escort bombers to the area of the Channel Islands. Nearing the Casquettes he saw a Junkers 88 fighter and immediately turned to engage it. Accurate return fire from the enemy rear gunner resulted in his Spitfire's radiator being hit. Shortly afterwards the cockpit filled with glycol fumes, the oil temperature rose and the engine started running rough, so he decided to set heading for home. To disperse the fumes he attempted to jettison the hood. The rear portion became detached, but the hood was held by the forward catch despite every effort to force it off.

He put out a distress call over the radio and tried to climb, but the state of the engine prevented him getting above 2,000 feet. One of his squadron climbed to 8,000 feet to allow the ground radar chain to get a fix of his position. Suddenly Carver's cockpit hood flew off and hit him in the face. On recovering from this shock he found he was at 1,300 feet and unable to maintain height. The speed was falling and he rolled the aircraft inverted, pushed on the control column and was thrown out of his Spitfire VB (W 3943).

On leaving the aircraft head first, his first pull of the rip-cord failed to open the parachute, but a second more positive pull opened it at about 500 feet. Partly stunned, he failed to inflate his Mae West during the descent and also lost one of his flying boots. On entering the water he struck the quick-release box of the parachute, but not hard enough to release the parachute, and it was still attached when he surfaced. Once he had released the harness he inflated his 'K' dinghy, which took about a minute. He thought he was clear of the parachute, but while boarding the dinghy he found he was entangled in its shrouds, eventually freeing himself with some difficulty. Once in the dinghy, he started to bale out the water and found there were no leaks. It being March, he had dressed appropriately and was wearing a thick vest and pants, a shirt, rolltop pullover and his tunic. He retained his one flying boot.

The wind was blowing at 15 mph from the south and was mild for the time of the year. There was a slight drizzle and the swell was about 4 feet. Having baled out the dinghy, Carver took stock of the situation. He covered himself with the dinghy apron and hood; despite the sea breaking over the dinghy the aprons were effective and kept it out. Although his clothing was wet, he was not unduly cold since the apron kept the wind off him. He opened the emergency pack and discovered two paddles, a baler and two leak stoppers. He was surprised to find no mast or flag, and there were no rations, although he had some in his escape pack. He decided not to open this until he was really hungry because he feared the contents would get wet – the tin was not waterproof.

By the time he was organized, darkness had almost arrived, and thinking that boats might be sent to his rescue, he kept awake and blew his whistle every 30 minutes. He did not know that he was too near the enemy coast for aircraft or marine craft to be sent to his aid and that Headquarters No. 16 Group had broadcast an international distress message.

The next morning he felt surprisingly fit and decided to paddle towards the south coast of England. By observing pieces of floating seaweed and by calculating the speed of the wind, which was still blowing from the south, he decided that he would have to cover 70 miles, and he allowed seven days for the voyage. He opened the food tin in his escape kit and rationed himself to one-seventh of the contents each day. This gave him two Horlicks tablets three times a day and a piece of chocolate.

Carver paddled all that day and occasionally lifted the apron to make a sail, and in this way he made better progress. During the morning he saw two Hudson aircraft but he had no means of attracting them. In the afternoon a convoy of ships passed him. These signs gave him encouragement and convinced him that he was making some progress.

He managed to sleep for some time during the second night, curling up in the dinghy and resting his head on the buoyancy chamber. He paddled all the next day and was able to catch some rainwater. Luckily, the wind remained in the south and the exertions kept him warm. Again he saw some ships, but was not unduly perturbed since he was convinced that he was making progress. On the third night he was dozing when he was awakened by the noise of ships' engines – he found himself in the middle of a convoy. He signalled SOS on his whistle and soon heard an acknowledgement shouted from the nearest ship, which was no more than 150 yards away.

After 10 minutes, the ship turned a searchlight on him and soon edged alongside the dinghy. Ladders were lowered along the side of the ship and he attempted to climb the nearest, but this was too much for him and he fell into the water, too weak to get a hold. At this point he inflated his Mae West – three days late! One of the ship's crew immediately jumped into the sea and got a lifebelt around him, and he was soon hauled aboard. The ship was HMS *Tynedale* and it was 1.30 am. He was just 7 miles south of Portland.

Carver felt weak for the first time during his ordeal. He was taken to the sickbay where he was dried and wrapped in blankets before having a brandy-laced coffee. His fortitude, resolve and determination kept him going, and he never thought of giving up. He had paddled 33 miles in 58 hours and his achievement remained one of the outstanding solo sea survival efforts of the war.

Based on Carver's experience a number of improvements were made to the 'K' dinghy, including the introduction of emergency rations and six two-star red signals, which could fire up to 150 feet.

Carver had already proved himself to be an excellent squadron commander before his experience in the English Channel. Shortly after his rescue he was awarded the DFC, and the citation made detailed reference to his conduct during his ordeal when his courage and determination 'were in the highest traditions of the service'.

Carver returned to lead his squadron after a short period of leave. On 6 June 1942, he led his squadron on a ground attack against targets in northern France. A large force of the Luftwaffe's latest fighter, Focke Wulf 190, attacked his squadron. Carver was shot down and killed near Cap Levy. He has no known grave and is commemorated on the Runnymede Memorial.

★

THE ONLY SURVIVOR

On the night of 8/9 April 1942 Pilot Officer M.A. Sproule was flying his first operation after joining 83 Squadron. It was a tradition that a new crew flew a 'Nickel' raid to drop leaflets as their first sortie before joining the main bomber offensive. The Station Intelligence Officer (Flying Officer R.J. Dyer) joined Sproule and his crew before they took off from Scampton in their twin-engine Manchester bomber (R 5837) to drop leaflets over Paris. Over Calais the aircraft was hit by flak and the starboard engine failed. The aircraft could not maintain height and Sproule turned for the English coast.

As the Manchester steadily lost height, the wireless operator transmitted a series of distress signals at 10.40 pm. This alerted the 11 Group controller, who was able to fix the aircraft 15 miles northwest of Gravelines. He immediately scrambled a Beaufighter of 29 Squadron to start a search. Other Beaufighters searched in relays and two RMLs sailed from Dover and searched all night without success.

Sproule managed to get the Manchester down on the rough sea and escape as it started to sink. He struck out for the dinghy, but there was no sign of the other seven men and it soon became apparent that he was the only survivor. Throughout the night there was a very heavy sea and visibility was bad. The search was restarted early the following morning once the visibility improved marginally. Spitfires of 91 Squadron took off at 7.15 am and Lysanders of 277 Squadron also joined the search. At 8 am Flight Lieutenant F.H. Silk spotted a succession of flares fired from a dinghy 20 miles northwest of Dunkirk, but the awful visibility prevented him from keeping it in sight. He noted the position and returned to Hawkinge to refuel.

Throughout the morning, the Spitfires and Lysanders managed occasional sightings in the continuous rain. The rescue controllers ordered *HSL 101* and *102* to sail from Dover with Hurricanes of 32 Squadron providing a close escort. Silk returned to the area, and after searching for some time he relocated the dinghy and set up an orbit under a very low cloud base. During the morning, successive relief aircraft were sent to orbit the dinghy and the high speed launches headed for the area. Swingate radar station, on the Kent coast, plotted the position of the orbiting Spitfires, and the control room at Dover kept the radar station updated on the position of the rescue launches, which they plotted on their own shipping radar. In appalling weather, relays of 32 Squadron Hurricanes were directed by Swingate and Foulness Control to provide a continuous escort for the launches.

The two radar stations provided invaluable assistance in directing successive patrols to the dinghy. Weather conditions were so bad that on several occasions pilots who had been orbiting the dinghy lost it, and more than once the patrol sent out was unable to find the dinghy at all. Without the direction of the radar sites, it is very doubtful that the searching aircraft would have succeeded. The Spitfire pilots were determined to stay with the dinghy, and Pilot Officer J.P. Maridor (French) of 91 Squadron stayed so long that when he landed at Manston his engine stopped before he had left the runway due to lack of fuel. He had been airborne for 2 hours 20 minutes in appalling conditions.

At 1 pm the two rescue launches spotted the orbiting Spitfire and headed for the position to recover Sproule, who had been in the dinghy for almost 15 hours. The Spitfires returned to base but the Hurricanes continued to provide escort as the two rescue launches headed for Dover. Very heavy seas prevented them reaching Dover until 6 pm.

This rescue highlights a number of interesting aspects. The perseverance of the Spitfire pilots is particularly praiseworthy, but the key to the success was the imaginative use of the two shore-based air defence radars and the co-ordination established with Dover and the launches. The Spitfires and Hurricanes flew 33 sorties in addition to 2 by Lysanders and 4 by Beaufighters. Sproule's squadron commander in his report commented 'the correct procedures by the wireless operator giving the correct position enabled the pilot to be found'. Sadly, it did not help him to save his own life.

The bodies of two of the crew were washed ashore, one in the Dutch Frisian Islands. The other five men, including Dyer the intelligence officer, have no known grave and are commemorated on the Runnymede Memorial.

★

FOURTEEN DAYS IN A DINGHY

Early on 4 June 1942 three Hampden aircraft of 415 (RCAF) Squadron were detailed to fly a 'Rover' sortie searching along the

Frisian Islands for shipping to attack. The torpedo-carrying aircraft took off from North Coates just after 1 am and headed out over the North Sea. The pilot of Hampden 'D' (AT 240) was Pilot Officer Holbrook Mahn, from Denver, Colorado, who had joined the RCAF at the outbreak of war. Also on board were his all-Canadian crew, the navigator, wireless operator and an air gunner. Two Hampdens returned to North Coates at 5 am, but Mahn and his crew failed to return.

One of the returning Hampdens reported seeing a red flash on the sea two hours after take off. With this report as the only clue to the fate of the missing Hampden, two Hampdens took off at 6.30 am to carry out a search. At the edge of the search area 100 miles east of the Lincolnshire coast, Squadron Leader W. Benn discovered a large oil streak. Five miles further on he found a pigeon container, some wreckage and a body floating just below the surface with a Mae West that appeared not to have been inflated. Two other aircraft were being held at readiness, but on receiving Benn's report the controller at Headquarters 16 Group decided that the aircraft must have been completely destroyed and there would be no survivors. He called off the search.

This was the end of the incident until 14 days later when, on the morning of 18 June, Group Headquarters were informed that *MGB 344* had picked up Mahn from a dinghy late the previous night. He was rushed to hospital in Great Yarmouth.

A detailed analysis was carried out in an effort to reconstruct Mahn's sortie. On the outbound route, flying at 200 feet, an engine failed and the aircraft crashed in the sea. The wireless operator, Sergeant Peebles, went down with the aircraft, but the other three managed to get into the dinghy, which had inflated on impact. The men had only two quarts of water, four packs of emergency rations and four chocolate rations. These apparently lasted for seven days. Sergeant Thomas, the air gunner, died on the ninth day and his body was committed to the sea. Flight Sergeant Stirling, the navigator, started to drink sea water and soon became delirious and unconscious. He died the following day and Mahn had to put the body over the side, leaving him alone in the dinghy on the tenth day. He managed to catch some rainwater in some canvas from the ration pack, and on the thirteenth day a gull landed on his dinghy; he was able to grab it and kill it, eating as much as he could.

As the Headquarters 16 Group report says, 'So far this report is built upon facts, the rest is based on the assumption that the aircraft ditched at the position of the red flash.' This connects with an incident late on 11 June when a Beaufighter of 235 Squadron, flown by Flight Lieutenant Birt, sighted a dinghy with two men, who waved. A Junkers 88 fighter engaged the Beaufighter and both registered hits on each other, with the Beaufighter sustaining damage to the wing. However, Birt remained in the area, but since he was unable to relocate the dinghy he returned to base. Based on the likely drift over the previous week, the discovery of this dinghy appeared to tie in with the position given of the earlier sighting of a dead body and wreckage.

Before a new search could be mounted, the intelligence staff at Headquarters Coastal Command intercepted a German signal giving the position of a German dinghy with two Luftwaffe aircrew aboard. This position was very close to the one reported by the Beaufighter. Bomber Command had very few losses on the night of 11/12 June, and those that occurred were reported to be in the target area. The operations staff assumed, therefore, that the dinghy was German, and no further action was taken.

A further twist happened during the late morning of the following day. A bomber of No. 3 Group was reported missing along a route that took it close to the reported dinghy. A Hudson, with Beaufighter support, took off to carry out a search. Intelligence staff reported that the Germans were also active in the area, which appeared to substantiate the belief that the dinghy sighted was indeed a German one. The search aircraft took off during the afternoon and headed for the area. Enemy air activity increased and the senior air staff officer recalled the searching aircraft. No further attempts were made to locate the dinghy.

Five days later, *MGB 344* left Great Yarmouth to patrol close to the Dutch coast. Just before darkness, a lookout saw the dinghy and the MGB investigated. The crew found Mahn lying alone in the bottom almost beyond help, beside him the remnant of the seagull. He was rushed back to hospital where it was discovered that he had gangrene in both feet due to the prolonged immersion in sea water.

Holbrook Mahn spent 18 months in hospital after his terrible ordeal and had to have both legs amputated below the knee. He returned to limited flying duties. In March 1946, he became ill and died in Addenbrooke's Hospital, Cambridge, and is buried in Cambridge City Cemetery, many miles from his native Colorado. His three Canadian colleagues are remembered on the Runnymede Memorial.

★

OPERATION 'JUBILEE'

The air sea rescue organization was heavily committed during Operation 'Jubilee', the landing and operations at Dieppe, which took place on 19 August 1942. The object of the combined operation was to capture and occupy the coastal town of Dieppe for a limited period and to draw the Luftwaffe into combat. Over 60 RAF squadrons were assigned to the operation: fighters to provide cover for close support, bombers and ground attack aircraft to hit land targets in the immediate area, and maritime and reconnaissance aircraft giving support. Most of the air operations were likely to take place over the sea, therefore the provision of search and rescue facilities was an essential part of the plan.

The Naval Force Commander was made responsible for rescue within 3 miles of Dieppe with the air sea rescue organization responsible within its normal boundaries. High speed launches from Dover, Ramsgate and Newhaven were tasked together with Fighter Command's rescue squadrons at Hawkinge, Shoreham and Martlesham.

The landings commenced at first light, with the RAF's 'Jim Crow' squadrons (low-level visual shipping reconnaissance patrols) on task. The rescue craft sailed for their allocated stations. Thirty-one craft took part, 14 RAF high speed launches and 17 Royal Navy RMLs, and coastal patrol boats of Dover Command. From dawn at 4.30 am onwards, 12 Defiants, 3 Lysanders and 5 Walrus were on continuous patrols over the Channel.

The withdrawal of the ground forces, which had suffered heavy losses ashore, began soon after midday, when the air operations intensified. The opposition proved much stronger than anticipated and more fighter squadrons had to be committed. Initially three fighter squadrons were assigned to provide cover over the town, but this was later increased to six and eventually nine. After the withdrawal was complete, fighter cover was maintained throughout the long return voyage, and by the end of the day, the greatest air battle fought by Fighter Command since the Battle of Britain was over.

The rescue launches operated under the umbrella of the fighters, but on occasions they had to speed to the rescue of a downed pilot, making them vulnerable to attack. Three RAF launches were sunk by air attack during the day, with the loss of 2 officers and 18 other ranks from the crews. Witnessing the bitter fighting and the loss of the launches was Canadian fighter pilot Pilot Officer Don Morrison DFM.

SHOT DOWN FIGHTER PILOT TURNS RESCUER

Amongst the squadrons supporting the many Canadian ground troops during Operation 'Jubilee' was 401 (RCAF) Squadron flying the latest Spitfire IXs.

Twelve Spitfires of 401 took off from Lympne in Kent at 1.25 pm led by the squadron commander, Squadron Leader K. Hodson. Their task was to patrol over Dieppe at 23,000 feet and engage enemy fighters harassing the withdrawal of the remnants of the ground forces. Flying in Yellow section was Toronto-born Don Morrison (see plate 13), one of the squadron's most successful pilots, who had shot down a number of enemy aircraft. The squadron had been over the town for 30 minutes when enemy fighters were seen. Morrison dived after a Focke Wulf 190 and shot it down. Large pieces fell off the German fighter and struck Morrison's Spitfire, damaging the engine. Losing height rapidly, he headed out over the French coast for the Channel, but the engine soon seized and burst into flames.

With the aircraft down to less than 1,000 feet, Morrison baled out of his Spitfire (BS 119) and his parachute developed fully just before he hit the sea – had he been over land he would almost certainly have been killed. In the meantime, his wingman had stayed with him and immediately transmitted a Mayday call. He continued to orbit over Morrison, who clambered into his dinghy, and within a short space of time saw him picked up by one of the RAF rescue launches that had been positioned just offshore.

Morrison was hauled on board *HSL 177* and given dry clothes, being told that the launch must stay on patrol. During the afternoon he watched a furious air and sea battle. Destroyers were laying a smoke screen to protect the withdrawing forces and the rescue launch patrolled looking for other downed pilots. At 5.20 pm cannon-firing FW 190s attacked two Dover-based rescue launches patrolling nearby. They were set on fire and the master of *HSL 177*, Flying Officer Frank Conway, raced to their rescue and immediately came under fire from other enemy fighters. Undeterred, the crew of *177* closed and started to lower the scrambling nets and pick up the RAF sailors. Fortunately, the fighters broke off and the rescue continued.

Morrison noticed a semi-conscious seaman drifting away. He immediately dived into the sea and burning oil to reach the badly injured man, bringing him alongside the launch where he was recovered on board. He was Leading Aircraftman Albert Dargue, the medical orderly of *HSL 122*, which had been attacked and set on fire by German fighters. Despite being badly hurt himself, Dargue tended the seriously wounded until *HSL 123* pulled alongside. Only four men were left alive and Dargue dragged the other three survivors on deck, but just as they were about to be transferred, *HSL 123* also came under attack and was severely damaged. As the launch caught fire, the master gave the order to abandon ship. Dargue inflated the Mae Wests of the three injured men then pushed them overboard before he jumped. Exhausted and weak from his wound, he could do little to help himself until Morrison rescued him.

Once *HSL 177* had picked up the 14 survivors the master headed for Newhaven at full speed (see plate 14), where the wounded were quickly evacuated to hospital. Morrison returned to his squadron and was soon back on duty. Following the Dieppe operation there were a number of gallantry awards for the men of the RAF's high speed launches, including an MBE for Conway and a BEM for the brave LAC Albert Dargue.

Morrison wrote a detailed report of his experiences but made no mention of his own courageous part. He was loud in his praise for the men who manned the RAF rescue launches and concluded his report: 'There can be no question as to the bravery of these men of the Air Sea Rescue Service who were often working within sight of the French coast. For myself, I would rather meet a FW 190 head-on in my Spitfire than meet one from a rescue launch.'

Morrison went on to achieve more successes in air combat, but on 8 November 1942 he was severely wounded in a dogfight over Calais whilst escorting USAAF bombers. He baled out and was captured. He was unconscious for 10 days and German doctors had to amputate his left leg. Eventually he was sent to Stalag Luft 3, where he learnt that he had been awarded the DFC, the citation drawing attention to his gallantry in rescuing the wounded medical orderly. He was repatriated with other wounded POWs in October 1943 and became a flying instructor in Canada before leaving the RCAF in June 1945.

★

In spite of the heavy attacks against the rescue launches 13 aircrew survivors were picked up during Operation 'Jubilee'. All were fighter pilots, most having baled out and taken to their 'K' dinghies. A Defiant dropped an 'M' dinghy to a survivor floating in his Mae West. He climbed aboard and was later picked up by a naval patrol boat.

There were many lessons to be learnt from the Dieppe raid, in particular the lack of armour plate protection for the gunners on rescue launches operating in a combat area. There was also a clear need for more capable armament, and the Admiralty agreed to supply 15 Oerlikon guns for the RAF's launches at Dover and Newhaven.

During October approval was given for 32 launches based at the east and south coast units to be provided with one 20-mm Oerlikon and four .303 Vickers guns on twin pedestal mountings. It was also agreed that armour plating should be provided for the more vulnerable areas of the launches.

ENTER THE UNITED STATES ARMY AIR FORCE

The arrival of the United States Army Air Forces (USAAF) in the United Kingdom in the spring and summer of 1942 had a major impact on the RAF's air sea rescue organization, which was itself only just beginning to get established. It was clear from the outset that the RAF would have to provide rescue facilities for the 8th Air Force once they began operations. The Chief of the Air Staff (Air Chief Marshal Sir Charles Portal) approached General Arnold, the Commanding General USAAF, suggesting that it would uneconomical to have two similar organizations operating side by side. It was agreed that United States aircraft would make a contribution to the RAF's rescue organization in due course. In the meantime, on 8 September 1942, the 8th Air Force were informed that all the resources and facilities of the United Kingdom's service were placed at their disposal. Within a month the crew of a Fortress was successfully rescued from the English Channel.

The Americans soon recognized that there were many conditions peculiar to air operations from England and that their crews must adapt. One significant factor, which had not received attention during training in the United States, was the inevitability of air operations against the enemy involving some flight over the sea. The aircraft were equipped with basic dinghies, but little thought had been given to ditching and sea survival procedures. A training syllabus, including briefings, was drawn up for crews arriving in the United Kingdom. Air sea rescue officers were appointed at each airfield and at Headquarters 8th Air Force Command. The latter also had liaison duties with his opposite number in the RAF organization. American airmen had been conditioned to parachuting from their aircraft when in distress, since most of their flying experience had been over the land. However, the US authorities were quick to appreciate the need to ditch aircraft and have appropriate survival aids, particularly with the onset of a European winter.

It took USAAF aircrew some time to appreciate the need to understand ditching procedures and the capability of the survival equipment, much of their own being unsuitable for operations over the seas around the United Kingdom. The loss of Brigadier General A.N. Duncan, the Chief of Staff, 8th Air Force, from a B-17 Fortress over the Bay of Biscay was a stark reminder of the problems. Other bombers in the flight saw the aircraft ditch and some of the crew escape wearing their Mae Wests, and at least one man got into a dinghy. A Fortress orbited the spot for six hours but had to return for lack of fuel. RAF Hudsons, with a Beaufighter escort, tried to locate the crash site and two destroyers were ordered to the area. The search continued for several days, but no trace of the crew was found.

It was clear that American crews had insufficient training in ditching drill and that there were deficiencies in their survival equipment. By the end of January 1943, RAF officers from the Directorate of ASR assisted the 8th Air Force in drawing up a memorandum of organization for search and rescue procedures and dinghy drills for United States aircraft. However, in spite of all the efforts to indoctrinate an understanding of air sea rescue into USAAF aircrew, losses continued. After a successful incident in October 1942, no further successes were reported until the following February, a month when nine crews were lost, involving 65 aircrew of whom only one was saved.

Based on this unfortunate start, the Assistant Chief of Air Staff (Operations) forwarded some comments and recommendations to the Commanding General 8th Air Force (Brigadier General Eaker) regarding aircraft modifications, better dinghy stowage, standardization of rescue equipment and other relevant issues. He also observed that, for all the efforts of the 8th Air Force staff, it was clear that aircrew were not practising ditching and dinghy drills and had taken little interest in rescue training. General Eaker recognized these weaknesses and confirmed that they were concentrating on the development of thorough air sea rescue indoctrination.

The few rescues recorded in the spring of 1943 were, for the most part, the result more of luck than of skill. One recorded on 4 March was an outstanding example of amazing luck compensating for a complete lack of training.

A Fortress returning from a bombing raid on Germany was attacked by enemy fighters and lost three engines in the ensuing fight. The aircraft lost height and at 5,000 feet the captain decided that a ditching was inevitable. No SOS was transmitted, as the wireless was out of order. The two pilots remained in their seats, but the eight remaining crew took up various positions in the radio compartment. On ditching the aircraft broke into several pieces, but all 10 men escaped. The dinghies floated out but the crew had great difficulty inflating them – they had not been stowed in their official stowage but had been wrapped in string and carried loose in the fuselage. It took 30 minutes to get the first one out of its bag and inflated, by which time three members of the crew had died in the cold sea.

One man saw an object floating nearby and grabbed it to give him some buoyancy. The seven men got into the first dinghy, and as they endeavoured to inflate the second they discovered that the floating object was the dinghy radio. Although they had not familiarized themselves with it during training, they managed to get the kite aerial launched and this triggered the automatic distress signal. Six hours later a search aircraft homed to the position and dropped a Lindholme Gear, which they retrieved. Within two hours a minesweeper picked them up.

The subsequent debriefing revealed that no dinghy drill had ever been carried out on their squadron, but they had seen a diagram of the dinghy. Unfortunately, none had studied it. The pilot's ditching procedure displayed a complete lack of knowledge of the appropriate technique, and he ditched into the swell instead of across the top and parallel. It was miraculous that none of the crew was drowned when the aircraft broke up as a result of the wrong ditching procedure. This whole incident served as an example of the serious consequences that follow a lack of training.

The rescue of the Fortress crew, due entirely to the automatic triggering of the radio transmitter, was the first successful incident attributed to its use, albeit through luck. The American radio was one of the most significant developments in the efforts to locate ditched aircrew. By the end of July, eight USAAF crews had been saved as a direct result of the dinghy radio. It had significant advantages over the British radio. It floated, was shaped to fit between the knees of the operator and had a signalling lamp for use at night. The RAF soon adopted it as a replacement for their own troublesome set.

American fighter pilots were not provided with dinghies and it was agreed that the RAF would supply some, together with RAF-type parachute harnesses, which were fitted with a quick-release mechanism. The American Mae West did not have a supporting collar behind the neck and an unconscious pilot soon drowned. A large number of Mae Wests were supplied to the 8th Air Force. By the summer of 1943 the RAF also supplied survival aids in an effort to standardize rescue equipment. During the summer a trailer was fitted with British and American survival and emergency equipment and it toured USAAF airfields to educate the aircrew.

As a result of the training drives and the work of the RAF and USAAF air sea rescue liaison officers, rescue figures began to improve in the summer of 1943. In June, 255 USAAF aircrews came down in the sea and 71 were saved, a 28 per cent success rate. In July, 139 out of 196 were rescued, and this included the rescue of 78 out of a total of 80 reported down in the sea on 25 July.

By the middle of July 1943 the increase in combined air operations, and the consequent higher rate of ditchings, was placing a considerable strain on the rescue organization. There was considerable goodwill and co-operation, and the 8th Air Force established a Command Air/Sea Rescue Officer while a USAAF officer joined the Air Ministry staff of the Directorate of ASR.

A major development occurred at the end of August when the 8th Air Force agreed to make available one aircraft from each Bomb Group for search operations when requested. As a result, the Lindholme Gear was cleared for dropping by the Fortress, Liberator and Mitchell bombers. The increasing efficiency of the rescue organization, and the USAAF's determination to educate their crews, is borne out by the rescue figures for the last six months of 1943, when 524 aircrew out of 1,364 were picked up, or nearly 40 per cent, as compared with the first half of 1942 when just 6 per cent were rescued.

During 1943 specimens of all British rescue equipment were forwarded to America for study, and for adoption or modification. In September the headquarters of the USAAF in Washington formed a new branch, known as the Emergency Rescue Branch, to deal with the supply and maintenance of all emergency equipment. In early 1944 this was followed by the establishment of an Air Sea Rescue Agency in Washington formed at the direction of the Joint Chiefs of Staff. To provide a direct liaison, Wing Commander R. Bicknell, who had experience of rescue equipment and procurement, joined the staff of the RAF Delegation in Washington.

Further evidence of the USAAF's determination to integrate into the RAF organization was the establishment of a Central Control Room at 65th Fighter Wing Headquarters at Saffron Walden. The American crews were more familiar with VHF radios, which they used for passing distress calls. If an aircraft advised that ditching was imminent, the controller at Saffron Walden passed the information to the appropriate RAF Fighter Group or Navy Sea Rescue Control Centre.

As formations of fighters began escorting the large bomber forces, spotter aircraft drawn from the fighter wings patrolled the bombers' return routes, reporting back to Saffron Walden the positions of aircraft forced down in the sea. Following the success of this system, in May 1944 the USAAF authorities authorized the provision of 25 P 47 Thunderbolt long-range fighters, based at Boxted, to be allotted specifically for rescue work. They were equipped to drop the RAF's 'M' dinghies and smoke floats (similar to the Lysander rescue equipment), which were supplied by the RAF. The RAF contribution to augment this service was an agreement to make available six Warwick aircraft, equipped with airborne lifeboats, prior to each 8th Air Force operation, in addition to two Walrus aircraft at Martlesham

Heath, all of which could be diverted to the scene of any USAAF incident at the request of Saffron Walden.

The new rescue squadron (later known as the 5th Emergency Rescue Squadron) commenced operations on 9 May, and within two weeks it achieved its first success in conjunction with a Warwick when a Fortress crew were recovered by airborne lifeboat.

The arrival of the USAAF in the United Kingdom and integrating them into the existing air sea rescue organization, together with the development and improvement of their own rescue service, is almost a copy of the RAF's experience. They had made many mistakes and it was an uphill battle to convince American aircrew to take rescue training seriously. However, USAAF leaders saw the need for air sea rescue and spared no efforts in preparing their aircrew. The dramatic improvements achieved during 1943 speak volumes for the combined efforts. A close relationship between the RAF, Royal Navy and USAAF had been established. In some cases American equipment was modified to follow RAF design, as were their dinghies and Mae Wests; in others, such as the dinghy radio, the Americans were able to eliminate the drawbacks of the British design. Thus, by the time of the greatest amphibious landing of all time in June 1944, the USAAF were completely integrated into the British air sea rescue organization and stood prepared for the major operations ahead.

★

Before concluding the chapter dealing with the first three years of the Air Sea Rescue Service, one noteworthy event should be recorded. For a few years the many people in the service had wished for some distinguishing badge to indicate the specialist nature of their work. In November 1942, His Majesty the King approved the issue of a badge to airmen members of the RAF marine craft crews engaged on ASR duties. The badge submitted for his approval consisted of a launch at speed, with the letters 'ASR' included in the design (see plate 15).

Chapter Eight

Battle of the Atlantic

The only thing that ever frightened me during the war was the U-boat peril.
(Winston Churchill)

There was no 'Phony War' for the men of Coastal Command who went to war on the first day of the Second World War, and continued in the front line until the final victory in Europe. The most momentous period of the war at sea became known as the Battle of the Atlantic, and it is generally agreed to have begun in June 1940 and continued until the German *Kreigsmarine* were denied the French Biscay ports following the Allied invasion of Normandy.

After the fall of France in 1940 when Britain stood alone, the trade routes across the Atlantic were the country's lifeline. Without the supplies of food, raw materials and manufactured goods (particularly armaments), the country would have starved and been forced into surrender. The new weapon at sea, the U-boat, had almost achieved this victory in the later stages of the First World War, and in 1939 Admiral Karl Doenitz, Flag Officer U-boats, recognized that a similar campaign against Allied shipping was of paramount importance if Germany was to be victorious. He spared no effort to sever Britain's crucial lifeline.

Coastal Command's war soon became an anti-submarine war. Ill equipped for the task at the outbreak of war, the Command obtained Catalina amphibious aircraft to supplement the few Sunderland flying-boat squadrons. Newly formed squadrons were equipped with obsolescent bombers such as the Whitley and the Wellington; both gave valuable service but they lacked the range and endurance necessary to prosecute the war deep into the Atlantic. The arrival of the very long range (VLR) Liberator in September 1941, albeit in small numbers, heralded a major increase in Coastal Command's capability. The introduction of more advanced ASV radars and the Leigh Light, a very powerful searchlight carried on the wing of the aircraft, added considerably to the effectiveness of the anti-submarine aircraft. The arrival later of the US Fortress and the transfer of two squadrons of Halifax bombers from Bomber Command further enhanced the Command's anti-submarine capability.

During 1942 successes against the U-boats increased and the plugging of the dreaded 'Atlantic Gap' by the VLR Liberators forced the U-boats to consider new tactics. However, the prelude to Operation 'Torch' in North Africa and the need to support convoys to and from Gibraltar added further strain to Coastal Command resources.

With the advent of the new technologies, VLR aircraft, HF/DF fixes, ASV radar, ASDIC, ULTRA decrypts and better depth charges (DCs) amongst others, further success was achieved. The great majority of U-boats were based in the Biscay ports of France where they had quick access to the Atlantic. However, they still needed to surface to charge their batteries and this, allied to Coastal Command's new capabilities, made them more vulnerable. It was quickly realized that sinking the U-boats as they transited the Bay of Biscay was likely to bring much greater reward than searching for them once they were loose in the great expanses of the Atlantic.

Intensive operations started in the Bay in February 1943, and for the next 12 months this area was to prove the most rewarding for the anti-submarine force. Admiral Doenitz ordered his crews to transit submerged during the night, to charge batteries during the day and to stay surfaced if attacked and 'fight it out'. This presented a wealth of U-boat sightings leading to attacks and sinkings. The dangers to the aircraft crews were immense as they could expect an onslaught of cannon and machine gun fire when the aircraft held a steady heading at very low level as it ran in to drop its depth charges.

To support the U-boats the Luftwaffe deployed a large force of long-range fighters of KG 40 at airfields bordering the Bay and they prowled the area looking for the anti-submarine aircraft. This drew a response from the RAF, who in turn deployed long-range Beaufighters and Mosquitos to counter them. The 'Battle of the Bay' saw some of the fiercest aerial fighting at sea.

With the loss of the French ports in the summer of 1944, U-boats transferred to Norwegian ports and continued to pose a major threat to Atlantic convoys and to those sailing to Murmansk and Archangel in Russia.

The maritime squadrons suffered some heavy losses at the hands of the submarines' gunners and the long-range fighters during the anti-U-boat campaign. Operating over the sea in harsh weather conditions, many of the aircraft, particularly the older twin-engine aircraft, had the added risk of mechanical and engine failure, which could force them down on the sea. Many crews disappeared without trace, but others survived in the most desperate circumstances and were brought home by the Air Sea Rescue Services.

NORTH ATLANTIC RESCUE BY CATALINA

Wing Commander Ron Thomson DSO (see plate 16), the squadron commander of 206 Squadron, based at Benbecula in the Outer Hebrides, decided during the afternoon of 10 June 1943 that he would fly the anti-submarine patrol between the Faeroe Islands and Iceland due to take off at dawn the following morning. He woke early and joined his crew for breakfast, where he sat with the station armament officer, Flight Lieutenant A. Barratt, a former bomber pilot who had been grounded following a serious crash. Barratt asked to join the crew 'for some coastal experience' and Thomson readily agreed.

After a detailed briefing by the operations specialists and the meteorologist, the eight men made their way to their Fortress aircraft R/206 (FA 704) where they donned their Mae West lifejackets before boarding. The big four-engine bomber, armed with seven depth charges, took off at 7.10 am and headed for the patrol area some 350 miles distant. Once in position, the crew commenced the search for enemy submarines. Using powerful binoculars to scan the seas, and protecting their eyes against the sun with special anti-dazzle glasses, they kept up a continuous search, hardly daring to lift their gaze from the desolate shimmering wastes below. By flying at 2,000 feet, Thomson was making as much use of the cloud cover as possible but, true to the forecast they had received, the clouds were small and provided little protection.

During his search, Thomson continued to monitor his engine instruments. He had just looked up from a routine check when he and his co-pilot, Flight Sergeant A. Chisnall, both sighted a surfaced U-boat dead ahead at 7 miles. The gunners immediately went to their positions and the wireless operator sent a sighting report as Thomson turned into the attack. The submarine started to take violent evasive action as the Fortress descended to wave-top height.

With his gunners firing at the conning tower, Thomson attacked, but he could feel his aircraft being repeatedly hit by return fire. The windscreen shattered in front of the co-pilot but Thomson pressed on and released six DCs as the submarine disappeared beneath the nose of his damaged aircraft. 'R for Robert' had been seriously damaged, but the controls responded and Thomson put the aircraft into a tight turn to see the results of his attack. The U-boat lay stationary and Thomson prepared for a second run. Suddenly the bow rose and the crew began jumping overboard. When the bow was vertical, the submarine started to sink and U-417 slid beneath the waves eight days after leaving Kristiansund on its first patrol.

Turning his attention away from the sinking submarine, Thomson realized that his aircraft could not remain airborne for long. Three engines had been hit, one was hanging uselessly from its mounting, and the airframe had been almost torn apart. Incredibly, Thomson and Chisnall had escaped injury and they prepared to ditch the Fortress. Flying Officer J. Humphreys, the wireless operator, sent an SOS as Thomson fought to keep the aircraft airborne long enough for the rest of his crew to take up their ditching positions. The nose of the aircraft struck a wave top and momentarily disappeared beneath a wall of green sea before rising to the surface.

The crew quickly escaped and Thomson climbed on to the port wing and unfolded the dinghy, which had started to inflate. The starboard dinghy must have been damaged as it failed to inflate and had to be abandoned. Just as the passenger surfaced and was hauled into the dinghy, the giant Fortress reared up and started to sink, almost taking the crew with it. They had had no time to collect the emergency rations and equipment.

Taking stock of the situation, it was apparent that the navigator, Flying Officer J. Clark, was suffering badly from a damaged back, but the rest of the crew were relatively unscathed despite few managing to get to their ditching positions and brace themselves in time. Using flying boots to bale out the water, they all felt tired, and the task required considerable willpower as successive waves broke into the dinghy. Within an hour almost everyone was seasick. At first each victim tried to twist round to vomit over the side, but this method upset the other occupants to such an extent that it had to be abandoned to prevent the dinghy from capsizing.

With the weather worsening and the waves increasing, the seven men made themselves as comfortable as the cramped space and miserable conditions allowed. At 5 pm the sound of aircraft engines could be heard and some of the men stood in the dinghy, almost capsizing it, and waved frantically. An aircraft appeared and started to lose height and turn towards them. As it flew over they saw the American markings and recognized it as a Catalina from Reykjavik in Iceland. The aircraft circled for the next hour, dropping smoke floats, and then, to their utter amazement, it made preparations to land despite the rough conditions.

Just as the aircraft was about to land it hit a big wave and crashed into the sea. The crew of nine quickly abandoned the doomed aircraft and Thomson and his colleagues saw them launch two dinghies and retrieve some survival aids. All nine got aboard and they remained in sight, only a short distance away, until darkness. The Fortress crew sat in gloomy silence with the dinghy hood over their heads, although this provided little protection from the breaking waves.

Early the next morning, they were visited by a Catalina and by a Fortress from their own squadron, both dropping supplies, but without paddles the survivors could not reach the containers. The Americans were still in sight but drifting further away.

During the night a gale blew with 50-foot waves and they doubted that they would survive until dawn, but by a combination of good fortune and the excellent design of the dinghy they were still afloat the next morning. However, their American helpers had disappeared. The crews were destined never to meet, for all perished from exhaustion or exposure.

The gale blew itself out and on the third day they were sighted by a Sunderland from 330 Norwegian Squadron. It attempted to land but had to abort after two attempts. By now, many aircraft were involved in the rescue attempt, and a Fortress flown by Flying Officer Hill arrived and dropped supplies. This time the drop was accurate, and the survivors recovered the two packs containing water and food, the first they had for 50 hours. A Catalina arrived and dropped more supplies and a radio and these were also recovered.

As darkness fell for their third night, they were once again alone, and most were suffering from cramp in addition to being soaking wet and very cold. Soon after dawn another Fortress arrived and was soon joined by two Hampdens, a second Fortress and a Hudson. With the sea relatively calm, Headquarters 18 Group decided to send a Catalina to make an attempt at a sea landing. A 190 Squadron Catalina, flown by the very experienced Squadron Leader Jack Holmes DFC, who had hastily gathered together a volunteer crew in the short time available, took off from the Shetlands and arrived on the scene at 11 am to join the other aircraft circling the dinghy. After dropping smoke floats to assess the wind, Holmes made a number of dummy runs to determine the best direction and conditions for landing. He then lowered the wing tip floats of his Catalina and started a long approach into wind. When about 200 feet high, the aircraft was caught by the slipstream of one of the circling Fortresses and Holmes only just managed to gain sufficient control to make a heavy landing before taxiing over to the dinghy, where he stopped the engines.

A line was thrown to the survivors and they were brought alongside the flying boat (see plate 17). Exhausted after spending three and a half days in a dinghy designed for four men, the eight men were taken on board and the weakest placed in the bunk as the others sat on the floor. Holmes realized that he was far too heavy for take off, so he jettisoned 140 gallons of fuel, leaving just enough to reach the Shetlands. He waited for a clear lane to open in the slight swell and then commenced his take off run, lifting the Catalina off the water at 1.34 pm. Six hours later, he landed at Sullom Voe where the crew were taken to sick quarters. They were found to be 'remarkably fit' considering their great ordeal.

The search for the American crew of the crashed Catalina continued but, sadly, no survivors were found.

Two months after their ordeal, it was announced that Wing Commander Thomson, Clark and Humphries had each been awarded the DFC. For his gallant rescue flight, Jack Holmes was awarded a Bar to his DFC. Thomson remained in the RAF and added the CB to his decorations before retiring as an air vice-marshal. Holmes also remained in the service, retiring as an air commodore in 1967 (see plate 18).

★

To supplement the overworked Coastal Command squadrons, No. 10 Bomber OTU was loaned to the Command and detached to St Eval in Cornwall. It took a large share of the patrols in the Bay of Biscay during the early phase of the anti-submarine campaign. The crews were near to completing their bomber training, and the patrols provided a useful experience before they joined their squadrons.

ENGINE FAILURE OVER THE BAY

Pilot Officer Paul Huigli RCAF, from Regina, Saskatchewan, and his crew were approaching the end of their bomber training at 10 OTU when they were sent to St Eval, near Newquay, to join the detachment tasked with flying patrols in the Bay of Biscay. At 11.46 am on 27 May 1943 they took off on their second anti-submarine patrol and headed south in their Whitley BD 282. They were proceeding on the outward journey at 150 feet under a very low cloud base when the starboard engine failed three hours into the flight.

The Whitley was immediately turned towards base and the wireless operator tried to send a distress call. The frequency was jammed by other transmissions but a brief SOS was heard by a patrolling Halifax, which immediately forwarded the message to Headquarters 19 Group operations room. Huigli warned the crew to take up their ditching positions, but in the very short time available not all of them got into position. As the aircraft approached the sea, Huigli had not had enough time to turn the aircraft along the swell and he had to land across, although he managed to land on the upside of the 12-foot swell.

The aircraft hit the water hard and started to fill with water rapidly. The bomb aimer fractured his ankle and the rear gunner his arm. As soon as Huigli recovered from the impact, he opened the upper exit and left, quickly followed by the second pilot and bomb aimer and they gathered on the port wing. In the meantime, the badly injured rear gunner had managed to remove the dinghy from its stowage and Huigli ran along the top of the fuselage and helped him to launch it. Before leaving the air-craft, the wireless operator threw the radio into the sea, and the navigator collected an emergency pack. The dinghy inflated correctly and the crew climbed aboard. The navigator used the floating knife to cut the painter but accidentally cut adrift No. 5 emergency pack. (Following this incident, the colour of dinghy painters was standardized to avoid this mistake.) The paddles were soon put to good use and the floating radio was recovered.

The dinghy, one of the new 'Q' type with sails, was soon baled out. Huigli decided to deploy the sea drogue and ride out the night close to the position passed with the SOS message. He also decided that they would not eat or drink for the first two days and then implement a strict rationing policy. The fluorescene marker was streamed.

Once the SOS was received, all aircraft already in the area were warned to search and two dedicated search aircraft were launched. However, the weather was so poor that the searching aircraft had to be recalled to base. Huigli and his crew saw a Whitley and tried to send a message with the radio. The distress flares had been lost when the No. 5 pack was accidentally ditched, and the aircraft flew on. The crew rigged the weather aprons and made themselves as comfortable as possible. The injured rear gunner was violently seasick and appeared to be suffering from shock, but the rest of the crew established a watchkeeping routine and most managed to doze at intervals.

During the night the cloud base lifted to 1,000 feet and by dawn there were signs that the weather was clearing, so the crew decided to ride on the anchor for a few hours to allow searching aircraft to investigate the position passed in the SOS. No aircraft was sighted so at 10 am they decided to hoist the sail and head for home. Huigli consulted the instructional diagram kept in the chart stowage and started to erect the sails.

The lower mast was inserted in the keel step with three sections collapsed; the centre section was attached with great difficulty to the lower section owing to poor fitting, and the side guys made fast. The topmast was then fully extended and the stays were passed round to each member of the crew in the bow, the stern and each side. Huigli stood up, held by the second pilot, and secured the topmast to the centre section. The two collapsed sections of the lower mast were then extended and all stays made fast. The navigator assembled the rudder and attached it. The mainsail was attached to the halyard and hoisted. The foresail was also set. Finally, the sea anchor was hauled aboard and at 11 am a course of 040 degrees was set for the Scilly Isles.

The dinghy aerial was hoisted and transmissions were made in the hope that the signal might be received. The survivors had been under way for about six hours when a Sunderland of 461 (RAAF) Squadron sighted the dinghy. One of the searching crew stated that the sighting of the dinghy was almost certainly due to the presence of the sails. The aircraft circled the dinghy and sought permission from headquarters to alight, which was granted at the captain's discretion.

Huigli and his crew furled the mainsail and dropped the sea anchor to await developments as the Sunderland attempted to alight along the swell. After a brief touchdown, the pilot opened the throttles and prepared to make a second attempt. The flying boat touched three or four times and the pilot appeared to make an attempt to get airborne, but the aircraft stalled and crashed into the swell. The nose and floats were carried away and the aircraft settled into the water with the wings just awash. On impact the 'J' dinghy inflated and the crew clambered on to the wings and all boarded the dinghy except the captain, Flight Lieutenant W. Dods, who was lost. In 16 minutes the Sunderland had sunk.

Huigli and his crew hoisted the sail and made their way to the Sunderland crew. They tied the two dinghies together, furled the sail, dropped the sea anchor and waited for assistance. Aircraft were sent out to search for the men and the French destroyer *La Combattante* sailed for the position given by the Sunderland before it alighted.

At dusk a second Sunderland saw the red Verey flares fired by the survivors, circled the two dinghies and dropped flame floats. Wellingtons of 172 Squadron maintained contact with the dinghy overnight. At 7 am a Sunderland of 461 Squadron captained by Flying Officer G. Singleton arrived on the scene. After surveying the scene he decided to land and signalled 'Destroyer coming – am alighting.' The Sunderland then alighted and taxied over to the dinghies and took the survivors aboard. At 10 am the destroyer arrived and the crews were transferred.

Singleton decided not to take off because he considered the sea too rough (although it had appeared to be calm from the air). The destroyer took the Sunderland in tow, but after three hours the tow rope snapped and Singleton decided to attempt a take off with a reduced crew. During the take off run in rough seas, almost 3 miles of buffeting, Singleton managed to get airborne with a gaping hole in the fuselage and with one of the floats ripped off. Unable to land on water, he made a safe crash landing beside the runway at Angle airfield near Pembroke Dock a few hours later.

A number of lessons emerged from this incident. It was the first use of the 'Q' sailing dinghy and it had proved a good test, confirming its value. Following the loss of the No. 5 emergency pack through cutting the wrong painter, changes were made to prevent a recurrence. This was the fourth occasion when a flying boat had alighted on the sea in an attempt to rescue a crew and crashed in seas which the captain had estimated as less rough than actually experienced. All had been Sunderland aircraft.

*Flying Officer Paul Huigli joined 424 (RCAF) Squadron. On the night of
24/25 April 1944 his Halifax was hit by flak over Karlsruhe and he was
killed. He was laid to rest in Rheinberg War Cemetery with four of his crew.*

★

To counter the U-boat threat against the convoys sailing to Gibraltar,
aircraft of Coastal Command were regularly detached to the airfield
on the Rock to provide anti-submarine cover. Returning from such
a detachment, Flying Officer G.H. Whahram ran into trouble as he
crossed the Bay of Biscay.

LIBERATOR IN AIR BATTLE

Flying Officer D. Johnstone was a radar specialist who had been
investigating signals emitted by German aircraft and submarines in the
Mediterranean. By the beginning of September 1943 he was at
Gibraltar waiting for a courier flight to return to the United Kingdom. He was due to fly home on the night of 1 September, but
hearing that a Coastal Command Liberator of 224 Squadron was due
to return the following morning, he approached the Canadian captain
of the aircraft, Flying Officer G.H. Whahram, and asked if he could
return with him and his crew. His main reason for the request was the
opportunity to see the ASV Mark 5 radar in operation.

Liberator P/224 (FL 959) was airborne from Gibraltar's runway at
10.30 am. Sitting beside Whahram was the second pilot, Flight
Sergeant Ron Foss. The anti-submarine patrol was uneventful until
they were 100 miles north of Cape Finisterre, where the murky
weather experienced off the Portuguese coast had cleared to leave a
thin layer of cloud at 5,000 feet. After investigating a small ship flying
the Irish flag, a fast-moving contact was detected on the aircraft's radar,
and moments later the gunners reported that four Junkers 88 fighters
were approaching. One pulled away to make a frontal attack.
Whahram turned to reduce the attack angle as he started to climb for
the cloud, but the fighter's first burst was accurate. There was an

explosion in the cockpit, and Whahram cried out and collapsed dead within seconds.

Foss immediately took control of the badly damaged aircraft and ordered Johnstone to drag the captain clear of his seat and take up his place to give assistance. After a struggle, Whahram's body was pulled clear, and the radar specialist was able to help Foss with the aircraft's controls and to give him instructions as the German fighters turned in for further beam and rear attacks. The first phase of the attack lasted about 20 minutes. Foss was able to thwart some attacks by using the sparse cloud, but the aircraft was hit repeatedly. The mid-upper turret soon became unserviceable but the rear gunner, Sergeant A. Maloney, claimed to have hit one of the fighters, which left the scene trailing smoke. A further burst of fire from the enemy fighters killed the gallant gunner.

With one engine feathered, another on fire and the other two misfiring badly, Foss decided that he had no choice but to ditch whilst he still had a small measure of control over the aircraft. All the crew had been wounded, with Foss hit in the hands and legs. The fighters held off as they saw Foss descend on fire towards the sea where, without the aid of flaps, he made a skilful landing under the dire circumstances. The aircraft broke in two and almost immediately sank, but the seven survivors managed to escape. Johnstone and Foss went down with the cockpit but managed to free themselves and reach the surface, where they saw three men in the dinghy and others swimming nearby.

The condition of those in the dinghy was:

Flying Officer J.C. Miller RCAF	back crushed, bullet wounds in back and feet.
Pilot Officer W. Collins	deep wound in the left leg.
Pilot Officer J. Wilcox	front of leg blown away.
Pilot Officer Johnstone	shrapnel wounds in hands and feet.
Flight Sergeant R. Foss	bullet wound in hand and shrapnel in knees.
Flight Sergeant N. Dilkes	bullet wound in left leg.

In the dinghy they found paddles, a pump, a signalling flag and a repair outfit. They also had two tins of water and five tins of emergency rations. There was no means of dressing the wounds except by covering them with handkerchiefs.

At 6 pm, an hour after they had ditched, a U-boat was seen. The survivors attracted its attention by flashing a mirror and it turned towards them. The decks were crowded with men. As the submarine passed, the survivors replied to a shout asking if they were allies by saying they were British – the U-boat sailed on to leave them to their fate. They spent a very difficult night cramped in the dinghy, which was designed to take five men only. (The second dinghy carried by the aircraft was not recovered.)

The dinghy drifted northwards for most of the following day. They tried to repair a single-seat 'K' dinghy they had salvaged in order to provide more comfort for Miller, who was in great pain. Unfortunately, their efforts failed. During the day they had a few Horlicks tablets and a small piece of chocolate. In the evening a Sunderland was seen 3 miles away but they failed to attract its attention and it flew on. The sea became rougher overnight and breakers broke into the dinghy, keeping the fitter men busy as they spent most of the night baling out the water. They continued to drift the following day, when their attempts to fish with a bent pin and chewing gum were unsuccessful. Another aircraft was sighted but it was too far away to see them.

On 5 September the weather was fine but the wounds of the most seriously injured started to develop gangrene. In the afternoon two more aircraft were sighted, but they passed on. It was then that the men had their first water, taking four tablespoons each before settling for another cold and cramped night.

During the evening of the 6th a Sunderland sighted them and dropped a sea marker. It made a second run and dropped cans of water, first aid material and some emergency rations, but no signalling aids. Another Sunderland took over the patrol and dropped a line of flame floats. As it got dark, a Catalina arrived and illuminated the area with its searchlight but was unable to spot them. A second Catalina also failed to locate them and the next morning they found themselves alone again.

The following day nothing came near them. Miller, the Canadian navigator, became delirious and sank into a coma. They gave him two injections from the first aid ampoules. Wilcox was also showing signs of collapse and they gave him more water, but during the night he became delirious, went over the side of the dinghy and sank out of sight. Miller died just after dark and they put him over the side after saying a few prayers.

During the morning of their sixth day in the dinghy, they were sighted by a Sunderland and a Catalina, the latter dropping more supplies. They were too weak to recover all the supplies, but amongst those they were able to haul aboard were 12 tins of water and some distress signals and flares. They spent the afternoon alone. Sergeant Bareham had become very weak and delirious and Collins was weakening. During the night a Catalina was heard and Foss and Johnstone let off some flares; the aircraft flew overhead and dropped a circle of flares around the dinghy. The sloop HMS *Wild Goose* of the 2nd Escort Group had been searching for the past few days and the Catalina called it to the area.

Two Sunderlands reached the survivors early the next morning and guided the sloop to the dinghy. At 9 am a whaler was lowered with Surgeon Lieutenant G. Stewart RNVR on board. The doctor found the airmen huddled close together, very wet, with their feet immersed in water, but surprisingly alert and fairly lively, except for Bareham. Only Foss was able to transfer to the whaler, which took the dinghy in tow to the sloop where the remainder were transferred individually. Bareham was described as 'comatose and unbelievably cold'.

They were taken to the sickbay where the doctor found them to be in very poor physical shape and displaying signs of marked dehydration. Except for their feet, they were wrapped in blankets and given sips of coffee. Bareham died a few hours after being rescued, but Collins appeared to respond well initially, although he had suffered badly in the dinghy and the gaping wound in his leg needed urgent treatment. He spent a fitful night and started hallucinating the following morning. At 1.30 pm he suddenly collapsed, and died a few hours later. It was a terrible blow to the three survivors that their two colleagues should succumb when they were finally safe, having survived such an ordeal for just over seven days.

The three survivors slowly improved, and when *Wild Goose* docked at Liverpool on 21 September they were admitted to hospital where they spent the next few weeks making a full recovery.

Within a few weeks, it was announced that Flying Officer Johnstone, the signals expert who 'hitched a lift', had been awarded the DSO. Dilkes, who had tended the emergency radio throughout the ordeal and helped his colleagues without complaint, was awarded the DFM. For Ron Foss, whose outstanding skill in ditching the crippled and blazing Liberator, and who did so much in the dinghy to help the others survive, there was the award of the Conspicuous Gallantry Medal (CGM), the most rare of all awards for gallantry in the air apart from the Victoria Cross. He was also commissioned and eventually retired from the RAF as a squadron leader (see plate 19).

★

FLYING BOAT CREW OF 12 RESCUED

Flight Lieutenant Jacques de la Paulle was born in New York to a French family. He was educated in France, and at the outbreak of the war he was studying medicine at the Sorbonne in Paris. He volunteered to be an ambulance driver, and for his gallantry after the German advance into France he was awarded the Croix de Guerre. After the fall of France he escaped back to the United States, crossed the border into Canada and joined the RCAF to train as a pilot in April 1941.

By the middle of 1943, de la Paulle had flown 10 anti-submarine patrols as the captain of a Sunderland flying boat of 422 (RCAF) Squadron. At 1 am on 3 September 1943 he and his 12-man crew took off from Castle Archdale in Northern Ireland in P/422 (DD 861) for an operational patrol on the western edge of the Bay of Biscay. The aircraft reached the patrol area five hours later.

Three hours into the patrol, and without warning, the starboard outer engine caught fire, exploded and dropped into the sea, taking with it the float and part of the wing. It also severed the fuel lines to the starboard inner engine, which started to fail. With the combined efforts of de la Paulle and his co-pilot, the American Flying Officer Romeo Freer RCAF, it was just possible to keep the big flying boat circling long enough for three SOS signals to be sent as hasty preparations were made to ditch the aircraft. The sea was rough and the starboard wing dug into the sea as the Sunderland alighted, allowing water to rush in through a large hole that appeared in the bows.

The flight engineer, Flight Sergeant Ken Middleton, had removed the astro dome, and together with the captain and the wireless operator he pulled the 'H' dinghy through the opening. As it fell off the wing, it pulled de la Paulle into the sea. The other two left the aircraft with the second pilot, who by this time was up to his neck in water and unable to grasp the emergency radio.

De la Paulle opened the dinghy (No. 1) as he floated in the water and it inflated immediately. Four of the crew climbed in as de la Paulle swam after the emergency pack, which had become detached and started to float away. The pack did not survive intact and the Verey pistol was lost. Almost immediately the dinghy deflated, probably because it had been torn by some of the wreckage.

The other seven members of the crew were on the lower deck of the Sunderland when it hit the water. Most had been able to brace for the impact and only minor injuries were sustained. There had been insufficient time to jettison the depth charges and the second navigator, Sergeant Joyce, had the presence of mind to tear the fusing wires away from them. One of the wireless operators released a pigeon, which flew away.

All seven men left by the rear of the aircraft and climbed into the second dinghy (No. 2), which operated correctly. They paddled away from the aircraft, now almost vertical, and were soon joined by the four men from No. 1 dinghy. The Sunderland sank 2 minutes later. In the meantime, the enterprising de la Paulle found the hole in the dinghy and dragged the waterlogged No. 1 dinghy across to the second. The leak stoppers were found, the hole was plugged and the dinghy was re-inflated with the bellows. The two dinghies were tied together, six men to each, with de la Paulle in charge of one and Freer taking responsibility for the other.

On the first day they tried to dry their clothes, and rations were apportioned on the basis that they could be at sea for at least 12 days. The mast was erected and used with the dinghy apron to sail in an easterly direction. All 12 Mae Wests were inflated and tied together to make a long tail to increase the chances of being sighted.

During the next three days they spotted a number of searching aircraft but were unable to attract their attention. Most of the crew were seasick on the first day, when none of them drank or ate. The next day they rationed themselves to a teaspoon of water and three Horlicks tablets each and some chewing gum. They made steady progress eastwards hoping to hit the Spanish coast, which the navigator, Pilot Officer A. Bolton, estimated was 150 miles away. The weather was warm during the day but each evening the wind rose and much of the night was spent baling water from the dinghy.

On the third day they were sighted by the tail gunner of a USAAF Liberator on an anti-submarine patrol, flown by Lieutenant Dudock, who immediately sent a sighting report and remained overhead to home a Sunderland of 228 Squadron to the scene. The Liberator flew over very low and dropped a bag. De la Paulle stripped off and swam to retrieve it. The bag contained a dozen oranges, three packets of cigarettes and a note saying, 'Don't go away. Help is coming.'

On arrival at 5.30 pm, Flight Lieutenant Howard Armstrong, the captain of the Sunderland R/228 (see plate 20), sought permission to alight and Headquarters 19 Group agreed for an attempt to be made at the captain's discretion. The survivors waved the flying boat away as they were aware of the heavy swell but, after jettisoning the depth charges and making two attempts, Armstrong managed to land safely under very difficult conditions.

The swell was such that the crew of R/228 frequently lost sight of the two dinghies as they taxied towards them. Eventually Armstrong managed to get close and the 12 men paddled to meet the aircraft, where they were dragged on board. The four engines were restarted and Armstrong started the take off run. The aircraft was virtually thrown into the air at 50 knots and it staggered just above the sea, slowly gaining speed. The survivors were given hot drinks and wrapped in blankets as the Sunderland made the long journey back to base.

The two pilots, plus the five Canadians and five Englishmen that made up de la Paulle's crew, arrived back at Pembroke Dock at 10.45 pm. As the Sunderland taxied on to its moorings, it ran out of fuel.

The survivors were loud in their praise of their captain, Jacques de la Paulle. One commented: 'The skipper was a model of leadership. The crew certainly had a great deal of respect for his abilities.'

The crew returned to complete a tour of operations. Jacques de la Paulle was awarded the DFC in April 1944, when the citation made particular mention of his leadership during the ditching episode. A few weeks after the rescue, Flight Lieutenant Armstrong was also awarded the DFC, but shortly afterwards he and six other members of his crew were killed when their Sunderland hit Blue Stack Mountain in County Donegal.

★

ELEVEN DAYS IN THE BAY OF BISCAY

Flying Officer Eric Hartley and his eight-man crew of 58 Squadron took off at 11.30 am on 27 September 1943 from Holmsley in the New Forest in their Halifax B/58 (HR 982) to patrol the Bay. It was his twenty-seventh operation, and flying with him as his co-pilot was Holmsley's station commander, Group Captain Roger Mead DFC, AFC. A pre-war regular officer, there was no need for him to fly operationally, but that was not Mead's style and he was keen to see for himself what his crews had to face. It was his first operation with a 58 Squadron crew.

Nearing the end of the patrol, at 5.18 pm a surfaced U-boat was sighted 8 miles away. Approaching at 50 feet, Hartley released eight DCs in a perfect straddle, but as the Halifax roared over the stricken submarine it was hit by return fire and the starboard wing was soon ablaze. The rear gunner, 19-year old Sergeant Bob Triggol, flying on his first operation, saw the U-boat rear almost vertically before it slipped beneath the waves, but he was immediately ordered to his ditching position. Hartley struggled with the controls of the Halifax and ditched just 3 miles beyond the attack position. The tail broke off the aircraft and Triggol went down with the aircraft. Sergeant M. Griffiths was dazed and, despite gallant efforts to rescue him, he floated away and was lost. The six remaining crew were able to scramble into the dinghy, which had inflated on impact. There was no sign of *U-221* or Kapitanleutant Hans Trojer and his crew. Trojer, the holder of the Knight's Cross, was one of the most experienced U-boat captains and on his fifth patrol as a captain. He and his crew of 50 perished.

Due to the speed of evacuation from the sinking aircraft, the emergency rations and survival aids could not be recovered. With few provisions, 700 miles from base and with the likelihood of their SOS going unheard due to the low altitude of the aircraft, the six survivors settled in for a long wait. Over the next two days they tried to make themselves as comfortable as possible in the overcrowded dinghy. They took stock of their situation and found that they had 5 pints of water and some emergency rations, which included Horlicks tablets, a few barley sugar sweets, chocolate and a tube of condensed milk.

On the second full day they were able to dry out some clothing and each had two Horlicks tablets at 6 pm and a mouthful of water, an event that became a nightly ritual. In order to conserve their meagre supplies they had decided not to eat or drink anything for the first 48 hours.

After two long and very cold nights, the swell increased significantly on 1 October with 35-foot waves, which constantly swamped the dinghy until eventually it was overturned. The crew were able to scramble on board but some kit was lost and they were exhausted by their efforts. Each man took it in turns to bale out, an all-night activity as the sea continually broke over the dinghy. The next day started with drizzle, and the men were able to catch some fresh water in their handkerchiefs, which they sucked dry. Over the next two days the weather improved and some clothing could be dried. They also made a makeshift sail from two shirts in an attempt to sail eastwards and nearer to the routine patrol areas.

On 4 October they reduced the ration of Horlicks tablets to three each day, but all their crude attempts to augment their supplies by catching fish proved fruitless. Roger Mead recorded in a rudimentary diary that spirits were high despite being in the sea for seven days, but over the next two days the sea became rough, accompanied by heavy rain, some of which they were able to catch.

On the ninth day another storm broke and the dinghy shipped water continuously; it required a great effort to prevent it becoming waterlogged. Each man tied himself to the dinghy and the fittest took it in turns to form a barrier by facing the incoming waves in an attempt to limit the water coming on board. This was exhausting work and two of the crew started to show signs of delirium, imposing a greater strain on the remaining four, one of whom had to remain alert to signal any passing aircraft or ship. Mead recorded the ninth night as 'an absolute nightmare, very rough and raining hard. Afraid of being tipped in the water at any moment.'

The crew had offered a prayer every night during their ordeal, but on this terrible night 'an additional prayer made for speedy deliverance, since we feel that although four of us could manage another three or four days, the position of the other two is becoming critical'. The dinghy continued to ship water for the next 24 hours but the four fittest managed to keep it reasonably dry and maintain a constant watch. Suddenly at 2.30 pm, Flight Sergeant Ken Ladds, who was on watch and who had played a prominent role throughout the ordeal, sighted the mast of a ship. Three Verey cartridges were fired and three Royal Navy destroyers turned towards them. Twenty minutes later the *Mahratta* was alongside the dinghy and the six survivors were carefully lifted on board (see plate 21), where they were cared for by the ship's doctor and crew at the end of their 11-day ordeal. Twenty-four hours later they were taken ashore by stretcher to the Royal Naval Hospital at Plymouth.

The crew could not have survived for much longer, but their determination was rewarded by what was a very lucky sighting. The destroyers were returning to England from Gibraltar and happened to pass close enough to the tiny dinghy for it to be spotted. The survivors took a few weeks to recover but all returned to duty.

Eric Hartley was awarded an immediate DFC for sinking the submarine and
for his leadership during the dinghy ordeal. Ken Ladds was awarded an
immediate DFM for his conduct. Roger Mead remained in the RAF after the
war and retired in 1958 as an air commodore, having added the CBE to his
other awards. A few weeks later HMS Mahratta *was sunk escorting a Russian*
convoy, and there were just three survivors of those who had been so caring to
the survivors of Halifax B/58.

★

ARCTIC RESCUE

By the middle of 1944 the war against the U-boats had turned very
much in favour of the hunters and the aircraft of British, American
and Canadian anti-submarine squadrons had gained the initiative.
With the loss of the French Biscay ports, many U-boats were
transferred to Norwegian ports.

Just after 2 pm on 18 July 1944, Squadron Leader Reg Nelms and
his Australian second pilot, 'Slim' Sommerville, took off their heavily
laden 86 Squadron Liberator (FL 907) from the runway at Tain in
Ross-shire. The nine-man crew (see plate 22) had been tasked to carry
out an anti-U-boat patrol well inside the Arctic Circle as part of a
screen protecting a large Royal Navy force withdrawing from the
area following an attack against the German battleship *Tirpitz* moored
in Kaa Fjord in north Norway. Eight hours later, Inverness radio
picked up an SOS message from the aircraft – nothing else was heard.

The Liberator had been flying at 1,000 feet at 8 pm when a
surfaced U-boat was seen 8 miles away. As the aircraft turned to attack,
the submarine dived. Nelms dropped a sea marker to fix the position
and commenced a square search of the area. The crew were rewarded
two hours later when the Canadian rear gunner, Flight Sergeant Cliff
Contant, made a second sighting astern the aircraft. Using cloud cover,
the aircraft attacked and the U-boat opened fire at 3,000 yards with
30 mm cannon as the submarine's captain turned hard to port. This
sudden turn threw the straddle of six DCs to starboard of the
submarine, so Nelms decided to carry out a second attack. Another

stick of DCs was dropped just as the Liberator was hit in the starboard inner engine and wing. The aircraft was soon blazing and Nelms realized that the aircraft was doomed: he had no choice but to ditch the bomber. In the few moments remaining, the wireless operator, Sergeant Robert Gregory, sent an SOS as he looked out of his cabin window to see flames streaming from the starboard wing. Oberleutnant zur See Otto Westphalen and his *U-968* escaped.

The flaps were badly damaged during the attack, causing the Liberator to hit the sea at a higher speed than ideal for ditching. The speed on impact was so excessive that the aircraft broke in two, and the heavier front part of the aircraft ploughed on through the waves for another second or two before finally sinking. The second navigator, Flight Sergeant Graham Richardson RNZAF, was killed when the aircraft broke up, but the other six survivors from the front of the aircraft managed to scramble clear, and whilst swimming in the wreckage were lucky enough to find three one-man 'K' dinghies. The larger dinghy and other survival aids went down with the aircraft. Flight Sergeant W. Daly and Sergeant D. Cossey were in the rear half of the aircraft, which was some 200–300 yards away; despite much effort they could not be reached and they were never seen again.

The six survivors paired off and squeezed themselves into the one-man dinghies, the smaller man sitting on the lap of the larger under conditions so cramped that very little movement was possible. They tied the three dinghies together and sat huddled up, with their uniforms soaked with icy water, waiting to be rescued. The pairings were Reg Nelms and Robert Gregory, Slim Sommerville and the flight engineer Sergeant Jock Toner, and Flight Lieutenant Ken Gray the navigator and Cliff Contant, who was badly injured. They were 200 miles inside the Arctic Circle northeast of Iceland, and 700 miles away from base. They had no drinking water, and between them had only two pocket-sized emergency ration packs containing Horlicks tablets. Although they helped save his life, Gregory commented later that the combined smell of urine, rubber fabric from the dinghy and Horlicks tablets put him off the energy tablets for life.

Fortunately Gregory's SOS had been picked up and a rescue operation was quickly put into operation. Initially it was expected that the large naval force, which included three aircraft carriers and the battleship *Duke of York*, would help with the rescue of the crew, so an air search was delayed. In the event, the Royal Navy decided it could not risk the safety of its force by detaching a destroyer. After this delay, a 210 Squadron Catalina took off on the long and time-consuming transit to the area where the aircraft had ditched, but the aircraft was unable to locate the survivors. The senior air staff officer at Headquarters 18 Group immediately ordered a maximum effort for the following day.

The six men suffered great discomfort, spending all of the time sitting in each other's laps unable to move for fear of capsizing the tiny dinghies, which in their weakened state would have been the end. Nelms and Gregory passed the time by recalling as many Latin phrases as they could. By night they tried, with little success, to keep each other warm and they suffered acutely from thirst. After 48 hours it started to drizzle, and Robert Gregory remembers putting his handkerchief on the side of the dinghy to soak up the fresh water before screwing it up into a ball and sucking on it.

The dinghies drifted from the point where the Liberator had crashed, and this hampered the search. Twice the men saw aircraft, which failed to spot them, but after 36 hours a Liberator from their own squadron, en route to its patrol area, sighted them. Flown by Flight Lieutenant Ross, the aircraft circled as the position of the survivors was signalled to the maritime headquarters. Food and an emergency radio were dropped but the food packet broke up on impact.

At 8 am the next day, 60 hours after they had ditched, they saw a Catalina heading straight for them. They fired the last of their distress signals and were thrilled and relieved when they saw the flying boat make a dummy approach before landing close by.

Twenty-five-year old Squadron Leader Frank French, who had recently been awarded the DFC for sinking a U-boat, captained the Catalina of 210 Squadron. He had taken off from Sullum Voe in the Shetlands six hours earlier and flown through the night. Brilliant navigation by Flight Lieutenant A. Jackson RCAF from Hamilton,

Ontario, had brought the rescue aircraft to the exact position of the survivors. The dinghies were sighted 3 miles away, just before the flares confirmed that the survivors had seen the Catalina.

French flew round the dinghy and dropped a series of smoke floats to assess the wind and the swell. After a dummy approach he prepared to land. Waiting for the big 'seventh wave' he judged his landing perfectly before taxiing to the dinghies. One of his crew climbed on to the wing and threw a rope to the survivors and hauled them alongside. The exhausted men managed to scramble aboard before the wounded Cliff Contant was lifted into the aircraft. French remained at the controls as the Catalina was rocked by the fresh swell.

Once on board, the men were stripped of their wet clothing and put into warm kapok sleeping suits, made as comfortable as possible and given warm beef tea. With the added weight for take off French had to jettison some fuel. After being on the water for 45 minutes he started the engines and took off to begin the long flight back to base. A signal was sent to HQ 18 Group confirming the safe rescue, which elicited a brief reply 'Well done' from the Air Officer Commanding.

Just after 2 pm French brought the Catalina on to the water at Sullum Voe, where the survivors were quickly transferred to the sick quarters. The modest French commented, 'We were lucky. Conditions were as good as one can ever expect in these northern waters.'

Although this rescue occurred in the summer months, it is nevertheless a remarkable story of fortitude and determination to survive in such northern latitudes with minimal survival aids. The rescue was made at very long range from base, 700 miles north of the Shetland Islands, and is almost certainly the most northerly successful rescue. The crew of the Catalina also deserve special praise, particularly the navigator for his precise navigation and the pilot who exercised great skill during the landing and the time spent on the sea in a difficult and potentially dangerous swell.

Squadron Leader Reg Nelms was awarded the DFC and 'Slim' Sommerville and Robert Gregory were both mentioned in dispatches. At the end of the war, when the full details of the events were available, Sommerville was appointed MBE. For his outstanding air and seamanship during the hazardous rescue,

Frank French was awarded the AFC. Otto Westphalen was awarded the Knight's Cross and survived the war. In 1966 he made contact with some of the Liberator crew.

★

After D–Day and the resulting loss of most of the French ports to the German U-boat force, the anti-submarine activities in the Southwest Approaches and the Bay of Biscay reduced dramatically. However, the port of Bordeaux remained available and anti-submarine patrols continued. Some U-boats had sailed weeks earlier and were returning short of fuel; they had no choice other than to head for Bordeaux.

One of the last actions against a U-boat in the Bay of Biscay resulted in an act of supreme gallantry by a RCAF navigator. Although this episode has appeared in other publications, it would be remiss not to include it in a book that is devoted to air sea rescue.

SUPREME GALLANTRY

At 5.30 pm on 27 August 1944, Englishman Flying Officer G.E. Whiteley and his crew took off from Limavady in their 172 Squadron Wellington XIV (NB 798) for a patrol in the Bay of Biscay. Just after midnight, a very weak distress call with a position was intercepted from the aircraft, which failed to return to base. Other Coastal Command aircraft were alerted and a search for the missing crew commenced.

Whiteley and his crew had located *U-534* on the surface off the mouth of the Gironde at Bordeaux. They commenced an attack with the aircraft's powerful Leigh Light searchlight, and as it illuminated, the Wellington met a withering burst of gunfire which set the port engine on fire as Whiteley dropped his depth charges astern of the U-boat. The aircraft was crippled and immediately force-landed on the sea. Four of the crew survived the ditching.

Warrant Officer Gordon Bulley RCAF, one of the wireless operators, found himself underwater but he managed to escape from the aircraft and reach the surface. Flashing his torch and shouting, he spotted Whiteley and one of the air gunners, non-swimmer Sergeant John Ford, both badly injured. The navigator, Flying Officer Rod Gray RCAF (see plate 23), had joined Bulley with a single-seat 'K' dinghy, which he was struggling to inflate. He too was badly injured but he assisted Ford into the dinghy and insisted that Whiteley join him in the hopelessly inadequate dinghy, whilst he and Bulley tied themselves together and clung to the side.

Throughout the rest of the night and into the early morning, Gray maintained the morale of the others although suffering from very severe leg wounds – it was thought that the lower part had been severed, but he never spoke of the extent of his injuries. He refused to exchange places with either of the men in the dinghy. During the morning, after many hours in the water clinging to the dinghy, he succumbed to his injuries and his comrades reluctantly cut his body free.

In the meantime, a search had started for the missing Wellington and at 2.19 pm on 28 August, a 10 (RAAF) Squadron Sunderland, captained by Flight Lieutenant W.B. Tilley DFC, RAAF, found the single-seat dinghy with three men. Shortly afterwards, he was joined by another 10 (RAAF) Squadron Sunderland; on board was Group Captain R. Mead DFC, AFC, the station commander of RAF St Eval, who had himself spent 11 days in a dinghy in the Bay of Biscay (see earlier in this chapter).

Tilley circled the dinghy with the other Sunderland and a 172 Squadron Wellington, which had also appeared on the scene. After circling for almost an hour, he decided that the plight of the survivors was clearly very acute and he could not wait for a surface craft to arrive. He jettisoned the depth charges and alighted on the calm sea. A desperate scene met him and his Australian crew, with the injured men draped over each other in the tiny dinghy and Bulley clinging to the side (see plate 24), where he had been throughout the whole 15-hour ordeal. The men were gently assisted into the Sunderland and Tilley took off. In view of the state of the three survivors, he abandoned his patrol and immediately headed for Mountbatten, near Plymouth, where the three could receive hospital treatment.

When the full story of the ordeal of the survivors came to light, Flying Officer G. Whiteley was awarded the DSO, the DFC went to

Warrant Officer Gordon Bulley and Sergeant J.W.C. Ford received the
DFM.To Flying Officer Roderick Borden Gray, the gallant Canadian
from Marie, Ontario, went the posthumous George Cross, the
supreme gallantry award for courage not in the face of the enemy, for
his magnificent courage and unselfish devotion to the welfare of his
colleagues despite his own appalling injuries.

★

Although the U-boat war had moved to the North Atlantic, the flights
into the Atlantic south of the British Isles made by the men of the
meteorological reconnaissance squadrons continued. Their job in
support of flying operations over Europe had become increasingly
important as the war progressed. Their work is rarely mentioned, yet
the crews flew long-range sorties over the sea areas surrounding the
British Isles and out into the Atlantic, to observe the weather that was
heading for Western Europe and would inevitably influence the
following day's operational plans, particularly the strategic bomber
offensive. Even when bad weather grounded operational squadrons,
the crews of the met squadrons still took off to gather the essential
weather data.

RESCUE BY PORTUGUESE TRAWLER

At 1.30 am on 24 November 1944, a 520 Squadron Halifax (LK 966)
took off from Gibraltar for a weather reconnaissance sortie (code-
named 'Nocturnal') to the west of Portugal and out towards the
Azores. At the controls was Flying Officer C. Crawford RCAF, and
his all-British crew included two specialist meteorological observers.
Once at the start of the patrol the aircraft descended to 200 feet to
take the first of a series of sea-level pressure readings. The Halifax
continued at this height for the next two hours, gathering more
weather data before commencing a climb to the 500-millibar level
(approx 18,300 feet) taking temperature and pressure readings every
50 millibars. As soon as the last reading had been taken, the aircraft
descended to 10,000 feet to conserve oxygen.

Just after 6 am the constant speed unit of the starboard outer engine developed trouble and the engine had to be feathered. The wireless operator immediately informed base and Crawford ordered the crew to jettison all loose equipment so that the aircraft could maintain height. Forty minutes later the port outer engine cut without warning and the port inner started to vibrate. The Halifax started to lose height and a distress call was transmitted. It soon became apparent that the aircraft would not be able to reach Gibraltar and Crawford headed towards the Portuguese coast.

At 5,000 feet the aircraft entered solid cloud, and with the aircraft approaching the coast, Crawford turned on to a northwesterly heading to avoid the risk of hitting the mountains just inland. A further SOS was sent, and when the Halifax broke cloud at 1,500 feet the navigator identified the marine beacon at Cap Espichel and an updated position was passed to base. In the event, this message was not received, probably because the aircraft was by then too low, but it was intercepted on the international distress frequency by a Spanish merchant vessel.

The vibration in the port inner engine worsened, so Crawford decided to ditch before it failed completely. He ordered the crew to their ditching positions and the wireless operator clamped down his transmission key. Dawn was breaking and Crawford could see just sufficient to assess the swell. He kept up a running commentary over the aircraft's intercom as he descended to the sea. At 7.50 am he ditched the Halifax perfectly and none of the crew was thrown from their position. There was an initial inrush of water and the aircraft settled with 4 feet of water inside the fuselage.

The crew salvaged six 'K' dinghies, two parachutes and the dinghy radio, along with two large ration containers and a camera. On impact, a fuel line broke and filled the fuselage space with fumes and one of the wireless operators, who had gone back to salvage more equipment, was overcome and had to be rescued. The aircraft's 'Q' dinghy inflated and the crew paddled clear of the floating Halifax in case of fire.

The crew could see two lights in the distance, and as daylight increased they were identified as two ships. The survivors fired a red

Verey flare and kept this up at 10-minute intervals. There was a heavy swell and a number of the survivors were seasick for a short time. In the meantime, the six 'K' dinghies were inflated and secured to the 'Q' dinghy, and some of the crew transferred, together with some of the equipment. Water was breaking into the dinghy and it needed constant baling, one man using his flying boot. One of the wireless operators had salvaged the aircraft's K.20 camera and he took some photographs of the floating Halifax.

The two ships converged on the dinghy, and after two hours a large Portuguese trawler, the *Barca de Pesca*, reached the men and took them on board 20 miles southwest of Lisbon. All the salvaged equipment was dumped overboard, except the dinghies and camera. The wireless operator with the camera was first to board the trawler and he took a series of photographs as the other survivors were helped on board. The crew of the trawler attempted to tow the aircraft into Lisbon, but it eventually sank after floating for almost three hours.

The nine men were landed at Lisbon and met by the Air Attaché, who took the exposed film. After four days enjoying the peaceful life of the Portuguese capital, the crew were flown back to Gibraltar.

Chapter Nine

The Bomber Offensive

PRIOR TO THE GERMAN *Blitzkrieg* on 10 May 1940, RAF bombers had been restricted to the bombing of shipping and harbours, and to dropping propaganda leaflets. Following the German bombing of Dutch and French towns, Bomber Command was authorized to attack targets on mainland Germany. The Command could muster some 200 bombers only, with just a proportion available each night. They attacked targets independently, approaching from different directions and at a time of the individual crews' choice. The bombers available were all twin-engine aircraft of a pre-war design.

The night offensive began in earnest in 1941, but the lack of navigation and bombing aids limited the Command's effectiveness. The first of the new four-engine heavy bombers, the Stirling, entered service in 1941. Although a significant advance with its increased bomb-carrying capability and better defensive armament, it also lacked the appropriate aids for accurate target-finding and bombing. A critical report by a civil servant, Mr R. Butt, highlighted the poor effectiveness of the bombing campaign, and his findings generated a major review of RAF strategic bombing policy.

The appointment of Air Marshal Arthur Harris in February 1942 heralded some dramatic changes. A report assessed that 4,000 bombers would be needed, and a new directive issued by the Air Ministry stated that instead of attacking individual targets in a city, the whole city was to be attacked. The era of 'area bombing' had arrived. Harris adopted the philosophy of concentration of effort to saturate the enemy air defences by getting the maximum number of aircraft over the target in the minimum time. The bomber stream was born.

Harris put his theories to the test in spectacular fashion on the night of 30/31 May 1942 when he launched his first 1,000-bomber raid with Cologne as the target. To achieve this number he had to send almost 400 obsolete bombers relegated to the training role with the OTUs and crewed by instructors and students near to completing their bomber conversion course. The raid lasted 90 minutes; later in the war, when tactics were refined, 1,000 bombers would be over the target in 20 minutes. The arrival of the four-engine Halifax and Lancaster bombers, with their much increased bomb loads, gave the Command a much greater hitting power, and these two powerful aircraft became the mainstay of the Command for the rest of the war.

The introduction of the new navigation aids was a major step forward and this was followed by electronic counter-measures, such as 'Window'. By early 1943, Bomber Command had been trans- formed with the new aircraft and capabilities. In addition, the' Mosquito was arriving in service and a new bomber group – No. 6 Canadian – was building up with the Halifax and later the Lancaster. A major development in the spring of 1943 was the introduction of the target marking aid 'Oboe', which, together with the increased bomb-carrying capacity, allowed Bomber Command to devastate areas. The so-called 'Battle of the Ruhr' started in March 1943, and in July it was the turn of Hamburg, where the new navigation and bombing aid, H2S, proved its worth.

The development of the Pathfinder Force, which had been formed in the second half of 1942, paved the way for more concentrated and accurate bombing by the Main Force. The third of Harris''battles', the opening phase of the Battle of Berlin, commenced in August 1943, but with the lengthening nights it reached its climax during the first three months of 1944.

Throughout this rapid escalation of the bomber offensive, conducted on a huge scale compared to the early days of the war, it inevitably drew a major response by the Luftwaffe. The development of the German night defence system, under the astute and brilliant leadership of General Kammhuber, posed enormous dangers for the bombing force. A series of 'belts', made up of early warning radars, fighter zones, searchlights and massive anti-aircraft defences, created a formidable obstacle for the bomber crews. However, it needed over a million men and enormous industrial effort to provide the machinery, all of which could have been dedicated to offensive operations had the Allied bombing campaign not been on such a significant scale.

In the spring of 1944, the bulk of the bomber forces were directed to support the forthcoming invasion of Europe and targets in France became the priority. These operations involved less time over enemy-occupied territory and the defences were not so formidable. However, some, such as the attack on Mailly-le-Comp on the night of 3/4 May 1944, resulted in very heavy losses.

The main offensive against Germany resumed after D-Day, but as the Allied armies advanced, the bombers were able to route over an increasing amount of territory in Allied control, thus helping to reduce losses. Also, emergency landing grounds became available on the continent and some severely damaged bombers did not have to cross the North Sea, thus lessening their chances of having to ditch.

The introduction into the strategic bombing campaign of 'The Mighty Eighth' of the USAAF, flying from airfields predominantly in East Anglia, created a new dimension for the Air Sea Rescue Services. Created for the specific purpose of conducting unescorted daylight high-level precision bombing operations, the force was to suffer many problems before the advent of the long-range escort fighter, and losses were heavy. By D-Day, the 8th Air Force had become the largest strategic bombing force ever committed to battle.

From the latter part of 1942, the round-the-clock bombing operations of the RAF and the USAAF created huge demands on the Air Sea Rescue Service. During 1943, aircraft lost or believed lost at sea, the great majority being bombers, numbered 1,188, involving 5,466 aircrew. The rescue service was responsible for saving 1,684 lives. This amounted to almost double the 1942 figure, reflecting the increased effectiveness of the air sea rescue force and the much greater scale of the bomber offensive.

The rescue of Sergeant George Honey and his crew graphically illustrates the efforts and courage that the men of the Air Sea Rescue Service were prepared to make to snatch men from under the noses of the enemy. It also highlights again the combined nature of so many successful rescues.

RESCUED OFF THE DUTCH COAST

The seven-man all-sergeant crew captained by Sergeant George Honey took off from Pocklington in East Yorkshire at midnight on 22 June 1943 to bomb Krefeld in their Halifax 'T' (JD 206). Just after crossing the Dutch coast the aircraft was badly damaged by a burst of flak over the aptly named town of Oberflakke. Three engines soon failed and Honey turned west for the North Sea as he ordered the bombs to be jettisioned. A ditching was inevitable and Honey got the aircraft down successfully, despite the bomb doors remaining stuck in the open position, but it had not been possible to transmit an SOS call. The crew scrambled clear of the sinking bomber and boarded the dinghy, which had inflated automatically.

The aircraft had come down just a few miles off the Dutch coast, and the crew deployed the drogue to limit the easterly drift that would inevitably have led to their eventual capture. At 6.30 am a passing Mustang spotted them and noted their position. The next sighting was not until 3.30 pm that afternoon, when two Typhoons saw them and transmitted their position to the emergency services. A comparison of the two positions indicated that the dinghy had not drifted nearer to the coast, so it was decided to make a rescue attempt under the noses of the Germans. There was always the possibility, of course, that the Germans had intentionally left them alone as bait in anticipation that an attempt would be made. Nevertheless, the decision to go ahead was made.

At 4.40 pm a message to prepare two aircraft for an operation was received at the headquarters of 277 Squadron's Walrus Flight at Martlesham Heath on the Essex coast (see plate 25). With the dinghy perilously close to the Dutch coast, it was apparent to the senior pilot of the detachment, Flight Lieutenant Jack Brown DFC, that his slow, lightly armed Walrus aircraft would need a fighter escort. The plan devised required two Typhoons to provide escort to the dinghy, where four Spitfires would take over the responsibility. For the return flight, more Typhoons were to relieve the Spitfires. The plan was approved and Squadron Leader Manak of Czechoslovakia, the commanding officer of 198 Squadron, also based at Martlesham with their Typhoons, joined Brown to finalize the plan.

Two Walruses, piloted by Warrant Officers Bill Greenfield and Tom Ormiston, were airborne at 6.37 pm and headed east. Halfway across the North Sea, Manak's two Typhoons arrived to provide close escort. Just after 7 pm Honey and his crew saw the two rescue aircraft 2 miles to the south and they fired their Verey pistol. The two Walruses saw the red flare and immediately turned towards the dinghy. The sea had become much rougher and Greenfield dropped a smoke float before landing, soon followed by Ormiston.

Greenfield picked up Honey, the flight engineer and one of the air gunners and Ormiston picked up the four remaining crew members. The sea state, together with the heavy load, prevented the Walruses from taking off, and they started to taxi westwards in the hope of finding calmer conditions. Four Spitfires, led by New Zealander Flight Lieutenant Roy Hesselyn DFM and Bar, a Malta veteran, arrived to provide cover. After 30 minutes of slow taxiing, Greenfield, who had the lighter load, decided to attempt a take off, and with the help of his crewman, Norman Leighton, he managed to drag the Walrus off the sea as it was about to be struck by a large wave. Shortly afterwards, two unidentified fighters flew past just 50 yards away and Leighton waved. It was only after landing that he discovered they were German Focke Wulf 190s.

Greenfield headed for the Suffolk coast with two of the Spitfires escorting him and at 9.10 pm he landed back at Martlesham, where his three passengers were taken to sick quarters. Meanwhile, Ormiston was struggling with worsening conditions and his aircraft became difficult to control. The rescue just 15 miles off the Dutch coast had attracted the attention of the Germans, and Hesselyn and his number two, Warrant Officer Boddy, continued to provide an escort. Hesselyn saw two fighters appear from the sun and immediately ordered

Ormiston to take evasive action as he and Boddy turned to intercept two FW 190s. Hesselyn saw his bullets strike the engine and cockpit of one of the aircraft, but he did not see it go down. Ormiston, however, saw a tremendous splash on the water at the same time and it was assumed that Hesselyn had shot the enemy fighter down.

With Ormiston struggling to control his Walrus, Jack Brown decided to take off from Martlesham in another Walrus, with two more Spitfires as escort, to render assistance. However, when he intercepted the waterborne Walrus, it was clear that the 10-foot waves made it impossible to land, so he remained in the area to give directions to a Royal Navy MTB (D 16) that had sailed to assist. Once the MTB was in company with Ormiston, Brown left the scene to return to base short of fuel, landing back at Martlesham just after midnight.

Ormiston's struggle continued as he made slow progress westwards with waves breaking over the cockpit and he needed all the assistance he could get from his crewman, Flight Sergeant Errington, in order to maintain control of the pitching aircraft. Eventually, at 2 am the following day, after taxiing in rough seas for just over six hours, the fuel ran out. The waves by this time were 10–15 feet high and it took the MTB 20 minutes to get a tow rope attached to the aircraft.

The Walrus was towed for one hour, during which time the sea was so rough that the MTB became invisible every time the Walrus dipped into a trough in the waves. The aircraft was taking terrific punishment and Ormiston felt that it was liable to break up, so he asked the MTB to take off his four passengers and the crew. This was accomplished with great difficulty before the Walrus was cut free and abandoned. The MTB arrived at Felixstowe at 6.30 am and the six exhausted men were given all the care they needed.

At 4.50 am news reached 277 Squadron that the Walrus had beached itself on a shoal and Brown decided to take a group of engineers to try and salvage the aircraft. They boarded a high speed launch in the hope that they could refuel the Walrus and taxi it back to a safe berth. They had not been at sea long when they saw the destroyer HMS *Mackay* with the aircraft in tow. The launch hailed the destroyer and eventually Brown boarded the Walrus, where he found an officer and two naval ratings standing waist deep in water operating the bilge pumps amidst bouts of seasickness. Brown assisted and made some necessary changes to the towing arrangements, which reduced the amount of water being shipped on board.

Eventually the Walrus arrived at Harwich and was towed across to the RAF's flying-boat base at Felixstowe. The aircraft, caked in salt and the oil dropped by the destroyer to help settle the sea, was in a very sorry state and had sustained considerable damage. However, after a lengthy overhaul, Walrus (X 9563) returned to active service and survived the war.

For his outstanding efforts, Tom Ormiston was awarded the DFC. Shortly afterwards, together with Greenfield and Leighton, he was decorated by the USA for rescuing USAAF bomber crews. George Honey was commissioned and completed a tour of bomber operations on the Halifax with 35 Squadron and was awarded the DFC on completion of his tour.

★

AFTER THE BATTLE OF HAMBURG

Towards the end of July 1943, the city of Hamburg was virtually destroyed by a series of heavy raids mounted by the RAF at night and the USAAF by day. Bomber losses were high, with many coming down in the sea, and the last few days of July 1943 provide a clear picture of the way in which the Air Sea Rescue Service had developed and the scale of effort needed during the days of the main bomber offensive.

Rescue work had carried on throughout the day of 25 July following the RAF's devastating attack on Hamburg the night before and the follow up daylight raid by the USAAF. At 5.30 pm an SOS was received from a Fortress returning across the North Sea. For the next 50 hours, distress signals, reports from returning aircraft, sightings by search aircraft, automatic transmissions on 500 kc/s from dinghy radios, reports from the Royal Observer Corps and coastguards all came in thick and fast. Air sea rescue aircraft, supplemented by those of Bomber Command and the USAAF, were called upon to help in what became the largest air sea rescue operation since the Battle of Britain. There were as many as 70 rescue aircraft in the air at one time, covering large areas of the North Sea.

Amongst the 78 rescued on 25 July was the crew of the 'Happy Daze' a Fortress of the 94th Bomb Group operating out of Bassingbourn near Royston. Lieutenant John Keelan and his crew were homeward bound from Kiel when three Focke Wulf 190s attacked the bomber as it crossed the Danish coast. It lost 25,000 feet in a few minutes and Keelan was forced to ditch the crippled bomber 75 miles north of the island of Borkum. The aircraft broke in two and sank in less than a minute. The two dinghies inflated automatically and nine of the crew scrambled on board and tied the two together. Sergeant Thomas Brown was missing.

The crew had taken the radio, a flare pistol and some rations. For 19 hours the dinghies drifted with the southeast wind, and throughout the night SOS signals were sent every 30 minutes. They paddled westwards and at midday they sighted two Halifax bombers, which they attracted by firing flares. One circled the dinghy and dropped a Lindholme Gear, which the crew recovered, and they quickly donned the waterproof suits and tied the three dinghies together.

During the evening two Hudsons of 279 Squadron appeared, followed shortly after by a third carrying a lifeboat. Flight Lieutenant Fitchew had been on patrol searching for another Fortress crew when he was called to the crew of 'Happy Daze'. He dropped a smoke float and carried out a dummy run before dropping the lifeboat just 75 yards from the dinghy. The lifeboat drop worked perfectly and two of the survivors paddled over, boarded it and rowed over to the others after hauling in the drogue. As soon as all the equipment had been transferred and the survivors were safely aboard, the Hudsons destroyed the dinghies with gunfire, signalling a course of 270 degrees as they departed.

After 15 minutes the ditched crew had both engines started and had set course at half throttle (see plate 26). They made good progress through the night and the navigator, Lieutenant William Greulich, using the charts in the lifeboat, maintained the westerly course. Early next morning, a Danish fishing boat, the *Betty*, came alongside, when the crew received a friendly welcome and the Danes agreed to head for England. The lifeboat was hauled aboard and soon after, *HSLs 184* and *2551* appeared and escorted the ship to Great Yarmouth, which was reached at 10.45 pm.

This was the fourth successful lifeboat rescue and was a perfect example of how effective the method could be when all elements worked correctly. It also clearly demonstrated the progress made by the USAAF air sea rescue officers and their training efforts, which had obviously registered with Keelan and his crew.

In the meantime, the crew of a Hudson on patrol, and carrying an airborne lifeboat, saw another Fortress ditch. Seeing the crew experience difficulty boarding their dinghies, the airborne lifeboat was dropped to them. Within a few minutes of ditching, the crew were on board and soon sailing towards the English coast. They were eventually met by rescue launches, taken off and landed at Great Yarmouth.

The Cromer lifeboat reported that it had picked up the crew of a Wellington and shortly afterwards it radioed that it had picked up another 10 men, this time the crew of a Fortress. This was followed by reports from aircraft that they were orbiting dinghies in five different positions, as much as 200 miles apart. Positions were signalled to high speed launches and to RMLs, which were loitering at rendezvous points ready for action, and they were soon on their way. Then came the news that a fishing vessel from Sheringham had picked up a USAAF bomber crew. HQ Fighter Command reported that, following the sightings of two dinghies 12 miles off the Norfolk coast, two Walrus aircraft had landed and picked up a further 10 Americans. However, they were unable to take off with their additional load, so the survivors were transferred to a rescue launch.

While this was taking place, another Hudson was dropping a similar lifeboat to an American crew down to the northwest of Heligoland. The nine men soon boarded the dinghy and started the second stage of their journey back from Hamburg. After they had covered 65 miles, a report was received from a search aircraft that had been shadowing them, saying that the crew and lifeboat had been taken on board a Danish trawler which had been fishing off the Dogger Bank and which had started heading towards Denmark. High speed launches were sent to intercept the trawler and recover the men at all costs. Area headquarters had signalled the escorting aircraft to persuade (the method was left to the discretion of the captain) the trawler to steer due west. This was done, and at 8 pm on 27 July the trawler was intercepted by two launches. One of them took the survivors on board and the other offered to escort the Danes to England. They agreed, and the two craft continued their journey in company. When almost in sight of land, one of the launches broke down, and was towed into Great Yarmouth by the Danish trawler.

Reports of sightings continued to be received by flying control at the Area Combined Headquarters, who were organizing the searches. High speed launches raced to a fresh position and picked up another Fortress crew. Then came a message from an aircraft that another Danish trawler had picked up 10 more Americans from their dinghies. RMLs on patrol in that area were sent to the scene and homed to the position by the searching aircraft. The trawler was found and the crew taken off.

As dusk approached on 27 July, two Spitfire pilots were reported in their dinghies near the French coast. Two Walrus set off with fighter cover and both fighter pilots were rescued. Thus, in a little over 48 hours since the first SOS was received, over 100 airmen had been rescued.

From first light on 28 July, the great work continued. Two dinghies were sighted 200 miles east of Newcastle and off went two Hudsons with airborne lifeboats. The dinghies were soon located and another successful drop completed. This crew were soon under way, but after covering 40 miles they were seen to stop. Another Hudson was called and was soon airborne with a fresh supply of petrol and oil. Tins of petrol were dropped in Thornaby Bags – for the first time an airborne lifeboat was refuelled from the air. The survivors recovered the fuel and were soon under way again. At 6.15 pm on the 29th, still under its own power, the lifeboat was met by rescue launches, and the entire party docked at Great Yarmouth late that night.

At noon on the 29th a message was received from North Foreland radio that it had picked up an automatic SOS on 500 kc/s almost due

north of them. This coincided with another report from the 4th
Bombardment Wing control of a Fortress in distress 73 miles northeast
of Middlesborough. Further bearings were received from other radio
stations. By 2.20 pm, two dinghies containing 10 men were located
by a search aircraft. A high speed launch homed towards it, and by 10
pm the 10 airmen had been landed at Blyth.

Fresh sightings and positions continued to be received, together
with reports of successful rescues. By dusk on the 29th, a further
135 aircraft had been searching in the North Sea alone. At dawn
the following day, six searches were airborne. An attempt to drop a
lifeboat 50 miles off the Danish coast had to be abandoned when
enemy aircraft appeared and one of the search aircraft was shot down.
By the end of the day, a further 39 survivors had been picked up.

The hectic efforts over this period indicate the enormous progress
made in just over two years by the Air Sea Rescue Service.

★

Few men could survive the ordeal of a ditching in the North Sea at
the height of winter, when exposure could take a life within hours.
For a complete bomber crew to survive such an ordeal required all
the aspects of a ditching and subsequent survival techniques and rescue
to work perfectly. It also needed excellent co-ordination, correct
drills and procedures and, above all, courage and determination. All
are in evidence in abundance in the rescue of a Lancaster crew in
January 1944.

A MODEL RESCUE IN SEVERE CONDITIONS

Just before midnight on 5 January 1944, a 626 Squadron Lancaster
(ME 577) took off from Wickenby, near Lincoln, to attack Stettin, a
target at very long range even for the best of the RAF's four-engine
bombers. Captain of the Lancaster was Australian Flight Lieutenant
Noel Belford. The outbound journey was uneventful and the 4,000
lb bomb and incendiaries were dropped over the target four hours
after take off.

Four hours into the return journey, the wireless operator, Sergeant T.S. Trinder, requested a MF/DF fix, which placed the bomber off the Danish coast. Over the next hour a series of bearings and fixes was passed to the aircraft as it crossed the North Sea. At 9 am Belford descended to 8,000 feet, and his crew started to jettison all loose items as it became clear that the aircraft was running out of fuel and would have difficulty reaching the English coast. Ten minutes later, Trinder passed an SOS with the aircraft's position and the possibility that the aircraft would have to ditch. The navigator, Flight Sergeant Arthur Lee, passed a continuous stream of positions to Trinder who continued to transmit them, allowing the Group Headquarters to keep a constant plot of the aircraft's progress.

At 9.30 am Trinder passed a further message that the aircraft had fuel for another 25 minutes. The captain then asked all the crew to repeat the ditching drill before they took up their positions. At 9.43 am 'SOS, Aircraft Ditching 53.31N 01.29E' was transmitted, after which Trinder screwed down his transmission key. The ground station obtained a fix 30 miles to the east of the aircraft's estimated position, and 3 minutes later, the plot ceased.

It being daylight, Belford was able to assess the sea conditions, which could best be described as bad. There was a very strong wind (30–40 mph), a heavy swell and a rough sea. He decided to ditch into wind although this was across the swell. He made a powered approach and endeavoured to land tail down. However, the swell was so deep that the nose still ploughed into the crest of the swell and the fuselage split just ahead of the bomb doors. The crew were all in their ditching positions, having discarded their parachute harnesses, and the four in the rear of the aircraft scrambled clear. The two gunners suffered minor injuries and the pilot smashed his face against the control column, but they were able to escape from the aircraft and all seven men inflated their Mae Wests.

The dinghy inflated inverted and started to drift away. It was grabbed and the crew turned it over and boarded it, but the sea was so rough that some of the emergency kit was lost during the transfer. One emergency pack was retrieved and the bomb aimer, Sergeant John Lee, took a parachute. The dinghy floated away quickly and 45 minutes later, the Lancaster was no longer visible. The crew used their flying helmets to bale out the dinghy and the parachute was used as a very effective weather apron.

Two hours after ditching, a 279 Squadron Hudson piloted by Flying Officer Gaze, and his all-Australian crew, arrived on the scene. The Lancaster navigator, Flight Sergeant Arthur Lee, fired a Verey cartridge and the Hudson turned to fly overhead the dinghy. Three USAAF Liberators were diverted to the scene and also circled the survivors. An airborne lifeboat was dropped but one of the retarding rockets failed to fire; it quickly drifted away in the rough sea, and despite furious paddling by the survivors, they could not recover it. Gaze remained overhead for three hours before a relief arrived, which dropped a Lindholme dinghy within 50 yards, but again, the crew, paddling furiously in the rough sea, could make no headway and it too was blown away.

The shadowing aircraft remained until dusk. At 11 pm a 280 Squadron Hudson arrived overhead and the survivors fired a distress flare. The aircraft orbited and dropped a flare just outside the range of the dinghy. Two more signals were fired from the dinghy and another flare was dropped, this time almost on top of the dinghy. At the same time, gunfire was heard and star shells seen. RML 498 had arrived on the scene.

The regular W/T messages sent by the aircraft's wireless operator allowed the rescue services to be alerted, and within 10 minutes of the ditching message Headquarters 16 Group had launched the Hudson. The sea state was too bad for the RAF's rescue launches to venture out, but during the afternoon the Commander-in-Chief, The Nore, decided that RML 498 should sail with instructions that she was to return if the commanding officer considered the risk to his ship too great. The RML sailed from Great Yarmouth at 4.36 pm. The weather was deteriorating, with a wind of Force 7. Allowing for winds and tide, a course was set for the anticipated position of the dinghy for 10.30 pm, but once she was out to sea the increasingly heavy seas made steering extremely difficult and it was estimated that it would take at least an additional hour to reach the dinghy. RML 498 arrived at the estimated position just after midnight but could see no sign of aircraft or flares. Appreciating that the speed made good on the voyage out had been reduced by the impossibility of steering closer than 30 degrees either side of the course, it was decided to head further north.

After 30 minutes the RML was told that ASR aircraft had made contact with the dinghy 100 miles east of Withernsea. The launch then saw the flares dropped by the circling aircraft and the answering red Vereys from the survivors, and immediately headed in the direction. Red Vereys were fired at one-minute intervals and this was a great assistance to the crew of the rescue launch, who were finally able to illuminate the dinghy with the searchlight. The launch moved slowly towards the dinghy in the very rough conditions. Considerable difficulty was experienced trying to get the Lancaster crew on board, as they were too exhausted to help themselves. Eventually all were safely recovered and rushed below deck, dried, wrapped in blankets, filled with hot soup and rum and bundled off to bed. *RML 498* set course for Great Yarmouth at 1.25 am at a speed of 5 knots. The sea remained very rough and winds increased to gale force; it took the rescue launch 10 hours to reach Great Yarmouth.

At midday, *RML 498* sailed up the estuary at Great Yarmouth and called to other moored boats with the loud hailer, 'We've got seven, we've got seven.' The moored boats replied with continuous blasts from their sirens and their crews waved and shouted a welcome, which the Lancaster crew returned enthusiastically. After a farewell with the crew of the naval launch the seven airmen were taken to a naval hospital for observation. The reporting officer of the rescue commented, 'The launch crew attended to the survivors very efficiently and the three "tea [sic] total" survivors recovered extremely quickly from the effects of exposure, having partaken of Navy Rum!'

This was a remarkably efficient rescue, which started with the prompt action of the aircraft captain Belford and his wireless operator, Trinder (see plate 27). The Group operations staff quickly generated the rescue services and the RAF, USAAF and Royal Navy played a major role in the successful rescue. The rescue needed to be efficient since the life expectancy of men who had been immersed in the sea and exposed in an open dinghy in a January gale could be measured in hours. The foresight to take a parachute into the dinghy played an immense part in the crew's survival.

Many people come out of this rescue with great credit. The RAF report commended the Lancaster's pilot, ' for his excellent captaincy and airmanship during the ditching and rescue when his conduct was exemplary'. The 626 Squadron signals leader commented, 'I consider this crew owe their safety to the wireless operator carrying out the ditching procedure correctly.'

The final word is left to the C-in-C, The Nore, who said: 'This success was due to the high courage and fine seamanship of the Commanding Officer of *RML 498* and his crew, together with the excellent co-operation of aircraft from 16 Group ASR squadrons. It is an example of the good work carried out by the Air Sea Rescue Service.'

★

The crew of a Halifax were not so lucky and were in their dinghy for three days during the coldest part of the year. For there to be any survivors was almost a miracle, but it is astonishing what reserves of human willpower can be drawn on, even in the most dire situation.

WINTER ORDEAL IN THE NORTH SEA

By January 1944 the so-called Battle of Berlin mounted by the heavy bombers of Bomber Command was at its height. A Halifax (JD 165) of 102 Squadron flown by Flight Sergeant D. Pugh and his crew attacked Berlin on the night of 28/29 January 1944. As they pulled off the target, the Halifax was hit by flak, which damaged the rudder controls and holed two of the fuel tanks in the starboard wing.

The rear gunner, Sergeant A.A. Burgess, was badly buffeted in his turret by a very close burst of flak and suffered concussion, so the captain told him to change places with the mid upper. The aircraft flew normally as the flight engineer, Sergeant R.F. Purkiss, repaired the rudder controls. However, fuel was being lost, and as the Halifax left the Danish coast it was clear that the aircraft would have to ditch. Pugh managed to keep the bomber flying, but as the aircraft descended to 2,000 feet he ordered the crew to their ditching positions. The time was 8.45 am and the crew estimated that they were some 90 miles east of Dundee.

The wireless operator, Sergeant A. Cohen, had put the IFF to distress at 15,000 feet before he transmitted an SOS with the aircraft's position. This was acknowledged and a fix was passed. In the meantime, the remainder of the crew took up their appropriate ditching station, except Purkiss, who stayed to assist Pugh.

The bomb aimer positioned himself on the starboard rest position with his feet on the aircraft's front spar. The navigator was on the port rest position and remained plugged into the inter-communication socket. The rear gunner was still in a dazed condition and the mid upper gunner, Sergeant C. Williams, took care of him and placed him with his back to the rear spar. He then collected the axe and an emergency pack with paddles and a dinghy cover before taking up his position on the port side with his back to the rear spar.

At 500 feet, Cohen clamped the transmission key and took up his position in the centre of the rest position. He first collected the dinghy radio and gave the kite aerial container to the bomb aimer. Purkiss remained with the pilot until the last minute and had no time to reach his ditching position so leaned against the wireless operator and braced his feet. He had collected the Verey pistol and some signal flares. All the hatches were opened and each member had collected flying rations and some torches. The crew had taken all the appropriate ditching actions.

The sea was very rough, with waves 15–20 feet high, and there was a medium swell with a westerly wind of 30 knots. It was daylight and the weather was good. At 200 feet the port inner engine cut, presumably through lack of fuel. Pugh put down some flap and reduced speed to 110 knots as he held the bomber's tail down. The tail touched first as the aircraft ditched – the final alighting was compared to the heavy braking of a car. Water rushed through the nose of the aircraft and into the open hatches in the fuselage. The rear crew were immediately immersed in the icy water.

Williams was first to leave the aircraft and Purkiss quickly followed him. The dinghy had inflated automatically and the crew escaped successfully, taking all the survival equipment as they clambered on to the wing, where they inflated their Mae Wests. The aircraft floated on an even keel and the crew cut the painter and floated away. The aircraft was still visible an hour later, no doubt its empty fuel tanks keeping it afloat. The crew had carried out all the correct drills and had a good supply of survival aids. The one thing against them was the winter weather and freezing temperatures.

Within one and a half hours most of the crew were seasick and unable to do much for themselves. The wireless operator was badly affected; he still tried to rig the wireless mast but his hands were too numb. All the crew sat on the floor of the dinghy with their feet to the centre. After a desperate night a heavy wave crashed into the dinghy, and the weight and speed of the water was such that it capsized the dinghy and all the crew were thrown into the sea. The navigator was trapped underneath but eventually freed himself. Sergeant E. Campbell, the bomb aimer, helped Pugh to right the dinghy. Pugh managed to get back into the dinghy after a considerable effort, and was then able to pull in the navigator, Flight Sergeant J.C. Graham, followed by Williams and Cohen. The other three remained in the sea, clinging to the ropes.

Those already in the dinghy were exhausted but Pugh struggled to get the rear gunner on board. He managed to get him half in but the gunner could not help himself and, with waterlogged flying boots and sodden flying clothing, his weight was too much for Pugh. The mid upper tried to assist, but with hands completely numb the two men could not save Burgess, who became exhausted with his efforts, let go of the rope and wished his two colleagues 'good luck'. In the meantime, the hands of Campbell and Purkiss became numb and they had to let go of the rope. They drifted off, neither shouting for help. There were now four survivors in the dinghy.

The four men suffered a great deal over the next two days. They had lost almost all the survival aids when the dinghy capsized, and the intense wet and cold made handling of the ration containers impossible. Exhausted and suffering from hypothermia, they were unable to take any exercise and their plight could hardly have been worse.

On the second day, a Warwick sighted them and dropped two Lindholme dinghies, which landed close by in the rough sea. However, the paddles had been lost and the crew were in such a bad condition that they were unable to recover the life-saving aids. An air sea rescue launch could be heard, but owing to the poor visibility, steep waves and the crew's inability to fire any signals, the dinghy could not be found.

Incredibly, the four men survived through the next 24 hours. Another Warwick arrived and dropped a Lindholme, but the crew could not retrieve it. The sea was slightly calmer; Pugh noticed that the drogue was fraying the dinghy fabric and he was able to cut it free with the floating knife. Eventually, at dusk, with the Warwick still in attendance, some parachute flares were dropped and *HSL 131* (Flight Lieutenant Cook) from 11 ASRMCU at Montrose was homed to the dinghy. The crew were helpless and they had to be lifted into the launch where they were immediately wrapped in dry blankets as the launch headed at full speed towards Montrose. Sadly, it was too late for the navigator, Graham, who died before the launch reached base.

The three survivors were admitted to Stracathro Hospital near Brechin, having been in the sea at the height of winter for three days and two nights. Three weeks later they were still bedridden and Cohen and Williams had not managed to walk.

Before joining 102 Squadron the crew had carried out a number of dinghy drills and the wireless operator had been tested on the distress signals procedures. Their ditching drill was perfect and, until the dinghy capsized, they had carried out all the correct actions. With their physical condition deteriorating, they made a number of mistakes during their ordeal; notably, they should have pulled in the dinghy drogue when the Lindholmes were dropped, allowing them to drift on to the crucial supplies. However, the conditions could hardly have been worse and it is testimony to their fitness that three were able to survive in conditions where most men would have died within a few hours. The squadron air sea rescue officer, who debriefed them in hospital, commented, 'All things considered I think you will agree that they put up a pretty good show, especially when one considers their physical condition after the overturning of the dinghy.'

COMBINED RESCUE OPERATION

A rescue on 29 June 1944 illustrates the level of co-operation achieved between the RAF, the Royal Navy and the USAAF rescue organizations. At 11.35 am the crew of a Fortress of the 390th Bomb Group called up Saffron Walden and gave the position of their imminent ditching. This was the only call received from the aircraft, but further signals came from accompanying fighters stating that 10 aircrew were in 2 dinghies 20 miles off the Dutch coast. The Naval Headquarters at Great Yarmouth and Headquarters 16 Group were notified immediately and *HSL 2551*, whose master was the veteran 43-year-old Flight Lieutenant George Lindsay, was already on patrol supporting the return of the American bomber force and was ordered to the scene. One of the escorting P 38 fighters was instructed to intercept the launch and guide it to the dinghies. Three hours later, Lindsay entered a minefield in order to pick up the survivors. He accomplished this quickly, and not wishing to linger so close to the enemy coast he set course for England at top speed.

A Junkers 88 bomber had been shadowing the rescue operation, and once the survivors were on board the high speed launch it took advantage of the low cloud to attack it 110 miles east of Great Yarmouth. Bombs ripped the rescue launch apart and it was soon ablaze. P 47s had been scrambled to act as escort for the launch, but on arrival at 6.45 pm they found it burning and abandoned with more than 20 men in the water. Lindsay saw one of his crew was badly injured and he swam to assist him to a barely floating dinghy. He then struck out to help another of his crew, but when he was seen again he was floating in his Mae West having died of exposure.

HSL 158 (Flying Officer Sutch) and *184* (Flying Officer Clark) raced to the rescue and picked up eight of the Fortress crew, rescued for the second time, and 13 of the crew of *2551*. In addition to Lindsay, three of his crew and two American airmen also died. As some of the survivors needed instant medical attention a 278 Squadron

Walrus, flown by Sub Lieutenant J. Robinson and Flying Officer R. Green, took off from Martlesham at 8.20 pm carrying two USAAF doctors to the scene, where they were needed to give the necessary attention to the wounded. The Walrus landed on the choppy sea and the doctors were transferred to *HSL 158* to tend the wounded. In the meantime, *HSL 2679* (Flight Lieutenant Herrick) had put to sea from Gorleston with a naval surgeon on board who was later transferred to *HSL 184*. The Walrus was unable to take off and was escorted back by one of the RAF rescue launches. Eventually, the party arrived at Great Yarmouth at midnight.

Flight Lieutenant George Lindsay, who had recently been mentioned in dispatches, was buried at sea on 4 July. Four Royal Navy and RAF rescue launches, carrying senior Royal Navy, RAF and USAAF officers, escorted the launch carrying Lindsay to a spot in the North Sea he had known so well. As his body was committed to the sea, three USAAF Fortresses flew overhead and dipped a wing in salute, followed by three Warwicks representing the RAF's ASR squadron.

★

Bomber Command had been heavily engaged in the build-up to the Allied landings in Normandy in June 1944. Much of the Command's effort had been directed against the road and rail network and the V1 flying bomb sites in France. By September Sir Arthur Harris was released from his commitments to assist the Allied advance and the all-out bombing campaign against Germany was resumed.

ROYAL NAVY RESCUE A CANADIAN BOMBER CREW

On the night of 15 September 1944, Flight Lieutenant Vic Motherwell and his crew of 420 (Snowy Owl) Squadron RCAF were the standby crew and expecting to have the night off. Due to illness amongst one of the crews planned for the night's operation against Kiel, Motherwell's crew were added to the battle orders. It was to be his fourteenth operation, but for the rest of his fellow Canadians it was to be their thirteenth.

Halifax NA 629 was airborne from Tholthorpe in Yorkshire just before 10 pm. The aircraft was new and had recently been delivered to the squadron. It had the dubious distinction of being a non-starter on two previous operations due to malfunctions. Shortly after leaving the English coast near Flamborough, all the navigation aids failed and navigator Flying Officer Ian McGown had to resort to dead reckoning. Approaching the Danish coast, searchlights and flak were seen to starboard indicating that the aircraft was on track north of Flensburg and a turn towards Kiel was made.

Just after the bombs were dropped there was a loud bang and the hydraulic pressure dropped to zero. The bomb doors remained open and the wing flaps started to droop. The undercarriage partially lowered, and all this additional drag required an increase in power to enable the bomber to maintain height in the bomber stream. As soon as the enemy coast was cleared, Motherwell started a slow descent in an attempt to conserve fuel. It soon became apparent that the bomber would not be able to make England and the crew considered the various options open to them. They decided to press on rather than head for Holland and bale out over enemy territory. McGown gave Motherwell a course to steer for Cromer in the hope that they could bale out over the English coast.

At 3,000 feet the fuel tanks were reading empty and the bomber was still 50 miles off the coast. With the undercarriage down and bomb doors open Motherwell knew that he must make a powered approach, so he decided to ditch before the engines cut and he ordered the crew to take up their ditching positions. McGown kept the wireless operator, Flight Sergeant L. Engemoen, updated with the aircraft's position, and Engemoen continued transmitting until it was time to clamp the key down and take up his position.

There was a heavy swell and 20-foot waves as Motherwell landed the Halifax into the strong westerly wind. He got the speed down to 90 knots holding the nose high under power, and the tail hit the crest of a wave and the aircraft rapidly decelerated. He completed a masterful job landing the aircraft on the sea in the most difficult circumstances and all the crew were able to get clear as the fuselage filled with water. The rogue Halifax had just 13 hours' flying time when it finally slipped below the waves.

The dinghy inflated and the crew scrambled aboard. It was an eerie scene, pitch-dark, the wings awash and the red-hot engines cracking with steam rising as the water engulfed them. Motherwell escaped from the top hatch above his cockpit and walked along the top of the fuselage; he was virtually dry when he stepped into the dinghy, which had floated to the tail. The crew cut the line and drifted clear of the aircraft. They were kept busy during the night baling out the dinghy as waves constantly broke over it. By first light, all the crew, except the Saskatchewan 'landlubber' Engemoen, had been seasick and conversation was limited

Back at Tholthorpe, two Halifaxes were made available for search duties and they took off during the morning. By late afternoon Motherwell and his crew had decided to hoist the sail and accepted that they might drift towards Holland, but shortly afterwards Flight Lieutenant E.S. Heimpal RCAF, pilot of one of the searching Halifaxes, sighted the dinghy and dropped a series of flares. Within a short time other aircraft appeared overhead, including a Hudson that dropped a Lindholme Gear. The crew were able to retrieve the dinghy and supplies, which included dry suits. A Halifax climbed to transmit a position report, and just as it was getting dark a Walrus appeared on the horizon.

Flying the 278 Squadron Walrus was Lieutenant Noel Langdon RNVR (see plate 28) with his crewman Leading Airman R. Atkins. After circling the dinghies, Langdon landed on the rough sea and immediately disappeared from the view of the survivors as the Walrus sank into a deep trough. Slowly Langdon taxied to the dinghies where the eight men were taken on board, Motherwell as the captain being last to leave the dinghy in true naval tradition.

With 10 men crammed into the Walrus, it was impossible for Langdon to take off and he started to taxi slowly towards England. After one hour, Lieutenant Don Mackintosh RNVR brought his *RML 512* alongside and all the survivors were transferred to the launch, given dry clothes and the obligatory tot of rum. Last to embark were Langdon and his crewman. The Walrus was taken in tow and the combination headed for Great Yarmouth. However, one of the circling aircraft detected a German E-boat and it was decided to cut the Walrus loose and increase speed towards England. During the early hours of 17 September *512* arrived at Great Yarmouth, where the survivors were checked by a Navy doctor and put to bed.

The following day, the Navy retrieved the Walrus, which had survived the night, and it was towed to Great Yarmouth and beached on a sandbank. Ground crew examined the aircraft and pronounced it fit to fly, a tribute to the strength of that sturdy, unglamorous aircraft. Langdon was taken out to the aircraft by boat and he taxied out to sea, took off and returned to his airfield at Martlesham. The aircraft was soon back in service.

Vic Motherwell and his crew (see plate 29) returned to Tholthorpe, and after a brief survivor's leave most returned to complete their tours with No. 420. Motherwell became the flight commander on promotion to squadron leader. For his outstanding airmanship and leadership he was awarded the DFC. For remaining at his position transmitting SOS messages until the last possible moment, and for his conduct in the dinghy when most of the crew were suffering badly from seasickness, Lyle Engemoen was awarded the DFM.

All the crew survived the war. Noel Langdon was awarded the AFC at the end of the war having completed 65 ASR sorties during which he was responsible for rescuing 19 personnel. Vic Motherwell flew with Air Canada for 30 years and in 1999 he and four other members of his crew flew to England for a reunion with Noel Langdon and Don Mackintosh.

★

Not every bomber crew that ditched at night needed the services of the air sea rescue organization. The crew of a Manchester bomber struggled to get their damaged aircraft back to England, but were forced to ditch before reaching the coast. The dinghy inflated and the crew climbed aboard. They carried out all the appropriate drills and waited for dawn, when they hoped that rescue would soon arrive.

The bomber remained afloat close by and they paddled clear to avoid being dragged down when it eventually sank. As it grew light they noticed that it was still afloat. Soon they saw the tower of 'The Stump', Boston's church. They had spent the night in 3 feet of water and were able to walk ashore!

Chapter Ten

Return to Europe

T HE ORGANIZATIONAL CHANGES made to the Air Sea Rescue Service during late 1943 and early 1944 were geared entirely to the invasion plans for the liberation of Europe. On 29 March 1944 a meeting was convened by the Air Officer Commanding-in-Chief, Coastal Command (Air Chief Marshal Sir Sholto Douglas), and attended by senior representatives from other Commands and the Directorate of ASR, to determine how soon these changes could be implemented. By this time the three Warwick squadrons of Coastal Command were fully equipped and operational and aircraft were available for the Warwick Flights of Air Defence of Great Britain Command (ADGB).

As a result of this meeting, the alteration to the areas of responsibility of Coastal Command and ADGB came into force on 15 April. Rescue work in the assault area was ADGB's responsibility, and this required the reinforcement of the south coast, resulting in the redeployment of rescue squadrons and air sea rescue marine craft units.

Following the redeployment of Nos 276 and 278 Squadrons, small Flights of rescue aircraft were established at 7 south coast airfields with a total of 80 aircraft. Outside the assault area, the USAAF rescue squadron of Thunderbolts and the four Coastal Command squadrons provided adequate cover. There was also a need to concentrate more launches along the south coast, and new ASR Units (ASRU) were formed at Plymouth, Poole and Portland. Together with the other 9 established units, a total of 76 high speed launches were available for the invasion, Operation 'Overlord'. In May the final redeployment of launches actually totalled 90. The Royal Navy also reinforced the area with RMLs drawn from other areas to provide an additional five flotillas; all were in place by 15 May. By the end of May the number of air sea rescue craft in the assault area totalled 136. The RNLI were approached to earmark 15 lifeboats for rescue work outside the assault area.

In the days leading up to the landings in Normandy, RAF and USAAF aircraft mounted concentrated attacks against coastal radar sites and to disrupt the French and German transportation system. Prominent amongst these attacks were the rocket- and bomb-carrying Typhoon squadrons flying from airfields on the south coast. The ordeal of a Canadian Typhoon pilot was remarkable, particularly since the rescue services had been so heavily reinforced and rescue could be expected to arrive quickly.

TYPHOON PILOT'S ORDEAL

Eight Typhoons of 440 (RCAF) Squadron took off from Hurn at 4 pm on 22 May to attack the radar site at Arromanche, which overlooked one of the beaches to be used by the British Army two weeks later. Piloting Typhoon MN 583 was Flying Officer Allen Watkins (see plate 30). As the fighters strafed the site with cannons and rockets, Watkins' aircraft was hit by ground fire and the engine of his aircraft was damaged. He turned out over the sea but he was soon forced to bale out. His colleagues saw him land in the sea and board his dinghy just 5 miles off the French coast. A search by a Walrus and Spitfires failed to find him before darkness fell.

The following morning the search was continued. Four Typhoons took off at dawn and they were relieved later in the morning by a further flight of four. By the end of the day, he had not been located and the squadron diarist noted 'we assume that he has been rescued by the Huns'.

The Sea Otter crews of 277 Squadron were not prepared to give up the search and over the next few days they flew regular patrols, but all to no avail.

On 28 May, the Spitfires and Sea Otters of 277 Squadron were busy checking numerous reports of aircraft ditchings and the sinking of a small vessel. At 9.30 am Warrant Officers W. Gadd and A. T. Bartels were airborne in their Spitfires, searching over a faded radar track 15 miles north of Fecamp, when they sighted a fighter pilot in a 'K' dinghy. Also airborne were Flight Lieutenant C.G. Robertson and his crew in a Sea Otter who were conducting a search nearer to their base at Shoreham. They immediately homed towards the circling Spitfires when the navigator, Flying Officer Len Healey, spotted the dinghy 8 miles west of Fecamp. Robertson immediately alighted and taxied towards the survivor.

As the Sea Otter came alongside, the survivor fell from his dinghy, but the Sea Otter crew managed to get him on board and discovered that it was Watkins, the man they had been searching for over the past week. He was in a very bad way, having had virtually no water or food and having been exposed to the sun and glare, which had made him virtually blind. He was covered in sores from his long exposure to the sea and sun, and the crew gently stripped him and wrapped him in Healey's uniform. They gave him just small sips of water.

Two Spitfires from 277 Squadron were scrambled to escort the Sea Otter, but whilst doing so they were vectored 75 miles southeast of Shoreham where a Spitfire was reported to be down. They found the pilot and orbited the position until relieved by two more who remained overhead until a Walrus arrived and picked up the Belgian pilot, Flying Officer Ester. He suffered no ill effects from his experience, which was his second ditching – he had been picked up off Margate a year earlier.

In the meantime, Robertson was heading for Shoreham where Watkins was handed over to the medical staff. He had suffered a terrible ordeal.

On the first night he had seen rescue aircraft being fired at by the shore batteries, but he was reluctant to use his flares. During the night he drifted into the Seine Estuary on the tide. A southerly wind carried him clear and he erected the sail and made his way north, but overnight he drifted back to the Seine. His efforts to sail and paddle away from the coast were constantly thwarted by the tides and fickle wind and he remained a few miles off Le Havre for the next two days. Remarkably, he was not seen from the coast, or perhaps no attempt was made to rescue him.

On 27 May he was too weak to paddle further and the dinghy started to drift northeast towards Fecamp. He was 8 miles off the coast when he saw two Spitfires – 30 minutes later the Sea Otter landed and picked him up.

This rescue illustrates the skill and perseverance of the air sea rescue crews and it brought 277 Squadron's total of lives saved to 505. The two Spitfire pilots had been tasked to search for the wreckage of a bomber, but they spotted the tiny dinghy in the meantime. The Sea Otter crew made a quick approach and rescue just a few miles off the enemy coast and other Spitfires were quickly scrambled to escort the rescue aircraft. But the most noteworthy aspect of this episode is the determination and courage of Watkins, who never gave up hope of rescue.

Watkins eventually recovered and was repatriated to Canada. In October 1944 it was announced that he had been awarded the DFC.

★

OPERATION 'OVERLORD'

As D-Day approached, a chart showing all the proposed routes for air operations was made and plans created for rescue launches to be positioned along these routes. They took up position on the night of 5 June to be available immediately should any of the crews and troops in the huge aerial armada of transport aircraft need rescuing. Two RAF high speed launches were attached to each of three fighter direction tenders allocated for the operation. The craft were alongside the tenders, to operate as directed by the senior RAF control officer within his area of responsibility. At first light on D-Day, after the first waves of transport aircraft had completed their tasks, the role for these launches was to search along the northern part of the track used by the transports, as the better armed boats of the Coastal Forces searched the southern part nearer the enemy coast.

All the aircrews were briefed on rescue arrangements, when it was emphasized that a successful pick-up depended more than ever upon correct actions. Pilots of single-seat aircraft were instructed to bale out, since a ditching alongside an Allied ship could easily be mistaken for a glider bomb attack. Crews of multi-engine aircraft were recommended to ditch heading in a northerly direction alongside a friendly ship. To assist surface craft, all aircraft were painted with black and white stripes on the wing and fuselage, and at night were to switch on the navigation lights in response to the aircraft recognition signal fired by the surface craft.

The plan for D-Day went according to schedule. There were so many naval ships filling the Channel that the chances of an aircrew being lost were remote. In the early hours of 6 June, the surface craft took up their rendezvous positions. Before dawn, the Spitfires, Walruses (see plate 31) and Sea Otters of the air sea rescue squadrons were out on patrol. The assault area, and the areas either side of it, were systematically covered, so it would have been difficult for any aircrew to bale out or ditch without being seen and rescued quickly. Of the many thousands of Allied aircrew operating on D-Day very few were lost. Unfortunately, no official records were kept although it is known that at least 60 were rescued.

On occasions distress signals were passed so efficiently to the control officers on the fighter direction tenders that they were able to send the rescue launches straight to the scene. One Spitfire pilot sent an SOS when he was about to bale out. A rescue launch was dispatched immediately and arrived to see the aircraft crash and the pilot descending in his parachute. They manoeuvred the launch so that they were alongside when he hit the water and he was picked up almost before he had the chance to get wet.

The crew of a USAAF Dakota carrying paratroops had to ditch in the early hours of D-Day after the aircraft had been hit by anti-aircraft fire. A destroyer was raised on the radio before a good ditching was made with the aid of the aircraft's landing light. On landing, the paratroops jumped into the water six at a time, clambered aboard the dinghies and were rescued 10 minutes later. This incident was only one of 14 successful ditchings of Dakotas during the 24 hours of D–Day.

The results of the special rescue arrangements for the initial period of the campaign surpassed all expectations. During the first 10 days of 'Overlord', the Air Sea Rescue Services alone picked up 163 aircrew, 58 others and 2 Germans in addition to other aircrew picked up by a variety of naval vessels and landing craft. The four rescue squadrons of ADGB flew a total of 1,471 operational sorties during June, and were involved in the rescue of many of the 355 lives saved during the period.

After the first few days, the number of calls for the rescue services started to decrease, due to the establishment of emergency landing strips in Normandy, which gave fighter pilots in particular an alternative to crossing the Channel with the attendant risk of having to ditch.

Once a firm foothold had been established on the continent, a number of the high speed launches used with the fighter direction tenders operated from the anchorages in the Seine Bay prior to the establishment of a mobile flotilla of marine craft being based in northern France. By early July, instructions to form two Mobile ASR Marine Craft Units (Nos 32 and 33) were given and Head-quarters Allied Expeditionary Air Forces assumed responsibility for the coastal area from Dieppe to Cherbourg. Three RAF launches were detached to the latter pending the formation of 32 Mobile ASRU. On 1 August, action was taken to base 'A' Flight of 276 Squadron, operating four Spitfires and four Walrus, near Cherbourg. It was visualized that more units would be based on the continent as the Allied armies advanced.

The progress of military operations on the continent during August and September resulted in a reduction of operational flying in the sea areas of the Western Channel and off the west coast of France. The rescue units based near Cherbourg moved eastwards. On 23 September the responsibility for air sea rescue passed back to ADGB. By October, with Allied forces well established in Belgium and penetrating into Holland, 32 and 33 ASRMCUs were based at Ostend with 13 high speed launches.

OPERATION 'MARKET'

The large-scale airborne operations against the bridges at Grave, Nijmegan and Arnhem in Holland, which commenced on 17 September, placed one of the heaviest tasks on the Air Sea Rescue Service. The need to reinforce the troops on the ground created a steady stream of gliders and transport aircraft each day until the 21st. RAF and naval rescue craft from Great Yarmouth, Gorleston, Felixstowe and Ramsgate were positioned in the North Sea in a double line under the air routes from the English coast up to the Dutch coast. Each launch was visible to its neighbour, thus minimizing the chance of any ditched aircraft or glider not being seen by at least one of them. There were 17 air sea rescue launches positioned to cover the northern route and 10 for the southern. Rescue aircraft flew constant patrols, with others on immediate standby.

On the first lift 358 gliders took off behind the tugs of the RAF's 38 and 46 Groups. Four were forced down in the North Sea; two of the Horsas ditched some 40 miles east of Harwich. The two had taken off from RAF Down Ampney behind Dakotas of 48 Squadron. Staff Sergeant Bruce Hobbs DFM in Glider 266 was carrying six men of the machine gun platoon of the 7th Battalion the King's Own Scottish Borderers. Halfway across the North Sea the tug suddenly cast off the glider and turned away with its starboard engine on fire. Hobbs and his co-pilot, Sergeant Tommy Moore MM, warned the soldiers to prepare for ditching and turned the glider into wind. The sea was calm and the glider remained afloat after hitting the sea, allowing the eight men to scramble out and clamber on to the wing. Flying Officer Dean and his crew of *HSL 2697* of 26 ASRMCU had seen the glider break away; Dean kept the launch under the glider and was alongside as soon as it ditched. The eight survivors hardly got their feet wet. As they were taken on board, the crew of *2697* saw another glider break away from its tug.

Sergeant Cyril Lane was carrying six men of the mortar platoon of 7th KOSB. He had just handed over the controls of his Horsa to his co-pilot, Sergeant Desmond Feather, when he watched with fascination a combination drop out of the stream and the glider (266) break away and make a leisurely descent to splash on the sea. As he turned to look ahead he saw the starboard propeller of his tug slow down and stop. As he started to overtake the Dakota he had to release and he too started a leisurely descent towards the sea. Feather made a good ditching and all the men eventually clambered on to the wing of the floating Horsa. A Walrus appeared overhead and *HSL 2697* soon arrived on the scene to pick up their second crew.

The eight men were taken on board to find Hobbs and his team wearing dry clothes and enjoying a mug of tea. The 16 men were transferred to other launches, but it was not until darkness that they eventually returned to Felixstowe, since their rescuers had to remain 'on station' until the day's flying operations were over.

During the four days of Operation 'Market' 205 personnel were rescued by the air sea rescue organization from 35 gliders and 1 Dakota tug aircraft, in addition to aircrew on support operations. A minesweeper and a lifeboat rescued a further 21. No fewer than 92 of those rescued were picked up on 19 September. Further patrols and searches were carried out over the next three days, but no further survivors were found. In supporting the operation a total of 251 sorties were made by the air sea rescue squadrons and 104 by the RAF's high speed launches. These launches were at sea for just under 900 hours and they saved 144 lives. Naval launches made 100 sorties and rescued 79 personnel.

The rescue arrangements for Operation 'Market' were a great success. When asked by HQ 11 Group if they were satisfied with the arrangements, HQ 38 Group expressed complete satisfaction. Indeed, the rescue operation had been so well planned and executed that 'the tug aircraft had no need to navigate, but had simply followed the track of the rescue launches spread along the route across the North Sea'.

★

As the Allies rapidly advanced into northwest Europe, the Germans moved their main U-boat bases from the Bay of Biscay to Norway. Coastal Command relocated some of its anti-submarine squadrons to the north of Scotland, with the consequent transfer of some of the air sea rescue effort to the north. The Coastal Command rescue squadrons

were reorganized and reformed as Nos 279 at Thornaby, 280 at
Beccles, 281 at Tiree and 282 at St Eval in Cornwall. Each squadron
maintained detachments at other airfields close to their main bases.
In this way, long-range air sea rescue cover with Warwick aircraft was
provided around the British coast.

Although fighter operations from Britain across the Channel had
virtually ceased following the advances on the continent, offensive
operations by Coastal Command's strike wings against convoys off
Holland and Norway increased when they often met fierce resistance
from armed escorts. The ordeal of one Beaufighter crew is a further
illustration of the determination of ditched aircrew to survive and of
the rescuers to find them.

BEAUFIGHTER CREW ADRIFT IN THE NORTH SEA

Throughout 1944, the Beaufighters of Coastal Command had taken
a heavy toll on the convoys sailing along the Dutch coast, forcing the
Germans to sail at night. In the afternoon of 2 October 1944, six crews
of 489 (RNZAF) Squadron based at Langham in Norfolk were tasked
to carry out night patrols down the coast of the Dutch Frisian Islands
and to attack any shipping they encountered. Flying Beaufighter NT
909 was New Zealand-born Warrant Officer Douglas Mann and his
21-year-old English navigator, Flight Sergeant Don Kennedy.

At midnight they took off for their twenty-ninth operation
together and headed for the island of Borkum. Shortly after arriving
in the area, they sighted a convoy and Mann prepared to make a
torpedo attack. The visibility was poor as the Beaufighter turned
towards the target. Suddenly, Mann saw something directly in front
of him – either a mast or a balloon cable – and there was a sudden
lurch as the starboard wing struck the object. The aircraft immediately
became difficult to control and Mann jettisoned the torpedo in the
direction of some escorting flak ships, which immediately opened fire
on the crippled aircraft.

Losing speed and height, Mann had no choice but to ditch the
Beaufighter in the heavy swell. As the aircraft hit the sea, his head

struck the gun sight and he momentarily lost consciousness. When he came to, he was waist deep in water and he scrambled through the top escape hatch, taking his 'K' dinghy with him. Looking around he saw Kennedy already in the circular 'L' dinghy, which had opened automatically from the port wing when the immersion switch activated.

Mann swam across and hauled himself into the larger dinghy, and was horrified when his foot went straight through the fabric floor. The two men had to sit on the rim of the waterlogged dinghy as it was tossed about in the rough sea. The convoy sailed by without seeing them. Mann had been injured in the ditching, both suffered from seasickness and they were very cold and wet in their uniforms. At first light they took stock of their situation but had to cling on to the rope as a 35-knot gale blew. They inflated the 'K' dinghy, which they tied to the bigger dinghy. They had a tin of water each and some Horlicks tablets, and decided to ration themselves to a mouthful of water three times a day together with two tablets.

During the afternoon, two USAAF Thunderbolts located them and their spirits rose, but night came without rescue. The two American fighters had been searching for the crew of a Fortress and had radioed the position of the dinghy to their base. A Hudson set off for the area and found a dinghy and successfully dropped a lifeboat. By coincidence, the Hudson had found the American crew, albeit 15 miles from the position passed by the Thunderbolts, and they were saved. Thinking that the Hudson had located the dinghy sighted by the fighters, the episode was closed and no further searches were made.

After a miserable second night, the two men saw the lighthouse on the island of Ameland and decided to paddle ashore at night and try to contact the Dutch Resistance. They paddled in the direction of the island all day, but their efforts failed and the dinghy drifted out into the North Sea. By 5 October their water had run out, and as their physical condition deteriorated they were barely aware of anything except the pain and the intense cold.

During the early morning of 7 October they were just still alive when two Warwicks of 280 Squadron, looking for USAAF crews, spotted their dinghy. A lifeboat was dropped but it was too far away for the two weak men to retrieve. The second Warwick, flown by Flying Officer L. Harvey, came lower and dropped a Lindholme Gear, which landed about 100 yards away. Mann realized that they must retrieve it if they were to survive, even though it appeared an impossible task. He tied a rope to Kennedy and to the single-seat dinghy and he started to paddle across to the large inflated dinghy. Willed on by the crew of the circling Warwick, Mann struggled to reach the dinghy, and after expending all his energy he flopped into the Lindholme dinghy and lashed his small dinghy to the side. Kennedy pulled on the rope and soon joined Mann.

The two men struggled into survival suits before hauling in the four containers packed with water, food and survival aids. They immediately drank a can of water and one of condensed milk as the Warwick continued to circle them until it had to return to base at 3 pm. The two men seemed dogged by bad luck. A further Warwick, which had taken off to relieve the first two, was shot down by German fighters and Flying Officer George Chesher and his crew had to ditch and take to their dinghy (see Chapter Six). Five hours later another Warwick arrived and dropped a lifeboat 100 yards downwind, but they were unable to reach it in the gathering gloom, and by the next morning it had drifted out of sight. The rescue aircraft also dropped flame floats around the dinghy and continued to orbit until midnight, when it left, having reached its limit of endurance.

The Warwicks resumed their search over the last known position and soon found a dinghy, but it was the crew of the Warwick that had ditched. A lifeboat was dropped to them as other aircraft continued to circle until they were picked up. In the meantime, Mann and Kennedy, whose dinghy had drifted a considerable distance overnight, were left alone. Their feet were very painful and became numb. They drifted past a mine but looked at it with indifference. As the eighth day dawned they were still alone in an empty sea; Mann's condition began to deteriorate and Kennedy had just enough strength to look after him. They had to spend another night at sea.

During the morning of 10 October, Flying Officer David Ross was the skipper of the duty launch of 24 ASRMCU at Gorleston-on-Sea.

He was ordered to take his *HSL 2679* to a position 50 miles west of Den Helder and be prepared to answer any request passed from the searching air sea rescue aircraft carrying out routine patrols. At midday he received a call from a Mustang escorting a 279 Squadron Hudson that had located a dinghy, and he was told to vector 130 degrees 30 miles where there was a dinghy with two occupants.

Two hours earlier Kennedy had seen the Hudson and Mustang and fired the last remaining signal flare – Mann was too weak. The launch spotted the orbiting aircraft and headed straight for the dinghy. The two men were unable to help themselves (see plate 32) and had to be carefully lifted on to the launch and carried to the warm sickbay, where they were stripped of their stinking clothing, washed and wrapped in warm blankets. Their nine-day ordeal was finally over.

Ross tried to take the Lindholme in tow, but this proved impossible in the heavy swell and the Mustang sank the dinghy with gunfire. As soon as the two survivors were landed at Gorleston-on-Sea at 6.30 pm they were taken to the naval hospital at Great Yarmouth. The two men were suffering from acute hypothermia and 'immersion foot'. As the circulation returned, their feet began to hurt badly and it was many weeks before they recovered fully. After a week in hospital, the two men returned to the squadron before going on a much-needed leave.

Kennedy and Mann were screened from further operations but Mann insisted on returning to his squadron. Although not fully recovered from his ordeal, he returned to 489 Squadron four months later and in May 1945 was awarded the DFC before returning to New Zealand (see plate 33). Kennedy remained in the RAF to complete 22 years' service.

★

By November, the lack of enemy activity over the Channel removed the need for Spitfires in the air sea rescue role and it was decided that amphibians, supported by the Warwicks with their airborne lifeboats, were capable of providing the necessary cover.

On 15 February 1945, responsibility for all air sea rescue in the British Isles was transferred to Coastal Command with five search squadrons, together with a flight in the Azores. Fighter Command ceased to com-mand any rescue squadrons when 278 Squadron transferred to Coastal Command and 275 and 277 Squadrons were disbanded. No. 276 Squadron remained on the Continent under the command of the Second Tactical Air Force (2 TAF), equipped with five Spitfires and six Walrus/Sea Otters.

Even with the Allied armies entering Germany the work of the air sea rescue organization continued. In Operation 'Varsity' – the Airborne Force's crossing of the Rhine – rescue aircraft and launches patrolled the routes followed by the gliders and transport aircraft. On 24 March Squadron Leader R.W.Wallens DFC and his crew patrolled the area between Folkestone and Cap Gris Nez. They located two gliders which had ditched and vectored high speed launches to pick up the pilots and soldiers. This was the last recorded wartime Walrus rescue.

In March 1945, 84 aircrew were rescued from a total of 291 down in the sea. By the end of the war, the air sea rescue organization had saved 5,658 aircrew. In addition, there were many non-aircrew personnel, both of the Allied forces and of the enemy, saved by the men who manned the aircraft and launches.

PART THREE

Mediterranean and West Africa

Chapter Eleven

The Early Years

T HE DEVELOPMENT OF the Air Sea Rescue Service in the Mediterranean and Middle East fell into two distinct phases. First were the campaigns associated with the defence of Malta and the desert war in North Africa, culminating in the final defeat of the Axis forces in Tunisia in May 1943. Second were the campaigns that saw the Allies return to Europe, first with the invasion of Sicily and Italy, then followed by operations in the Aegean and the re-occupation of southern France. From early difficulties and meagre resources, the organization and capabilities for air sea rescue expanded considerably, and ultimately it was developed on a large scale on similar lines to that in the United Kingdom.

EARLY DEVELOPMENT

At the outbreak of the war in Europe there were only four air sea rescue high speed launches overseas, and of these one was based at Malta with a second at Basrah in the Persian Gulf. There were no aircraft dedicated to air sea rescue based anywhere overseas. In June 1940 the entry of Italy into the war highlighted the need to augment the paltry resources in the Mediterranean. With so few resources available, and increasing demands to develop an air sea rescue organization in the United Kingdom, little could be spared for the overseas theatres. The launch (*HSL 110*) based at Basrah had been moved initially to Port Said in April 1940 and then to Hurghada at the entrance to the Gulf of Suez. At the end of the year, and in anticipation of the campaign in the Western Desert, the launch was moved again, this time to Mersa Matruh where it was assisted by a cabin cruiser improvised as a rescue boat.

As with marine craft, every aircraft that could be spared for rescue work was needed in the United Kingdom and the overseas Commands had to rely on aircraft drawn from operational and training units, when available, for search purposes. For the first year following the entry of Italy into the war, no formal system for rescue existed. It was the siege of Malta that highlighted the need to establish a sea rescue organization, although launches and specialist aircraft remained in desperately short supply.

It was in May 1941 that the Director ASR produced his re- quirements for worldwide commitments, and the establishment of high speed launches for the overseas Commands was authorized at 34 plus a reserve of 10. However, production rates were slow and it was obvious that it would be some time before this requirement could be met. Therefore, agreement was reached in June that six launches from existing stocks should be allotted immediately to the Middle East region, three of which were to be based at Malta and one each at Port Said, Aboukir and Mersa Matruh.

By the summer of 1941, the amount of flying in the eastern Mediterranean, most of it over the sea, had increased significantly and the need for air sea rescue facilities became more urgent. To meet this requirement, Middle East Command formed an Air Sea Rescue Flight in August under the operational control of 201 Group.

Early in November the two long-awaited high speed launches (*HSLs 121* and *141*) arrived at Port Said from the United Kingdom, On 14 November, fitted out, the launches sailed for Mersa Matruh. By the end of the year, five of the six additional launches allocated in the previous June had reached their overseas destinations and had been deployed to the operational areas. In the New Year, an air sea rescue officer arrived to co-ordinate the rescue organization throughout the Middle East. The air sea rescue organization in the Middle East and Mediterranean was effectively established, albeit on a very small scale.

THE AIR SEA RESCUE FLIGHT

The Flight was formed at Kabrit on 13 August 1941 under the command of Flight Lieutenant P.W. Dawson, and was equipped with three 'operationally tired' Wellington Ic aircraft based at Kabrit in the Canal Zone. The plan of action was for a Wellington to drop supplies to survivors, together with a dinghy if necessary, and shadow them until a surface craft could rescue them. About this time, 230 Squadron, operating Sunderlands, experimented with and perfected a type of supply container similar to the Thornaby Bag, and standardized methods of supply dropping were introduced.

The three Wellington Ic aircraft were modified to carry extra fuel, giving them an endurance of 15 hours. After moving in September to Burg-el-Arab in the Western Desert, the Flight was ready to commence operations on 26 September and three days later, Pilot Officer Ramsbottom and his crew took off to search for a missing Blenheim. Unfortunately, no trace of the bomber was found, but many lessons were learned, not least the need to speed up the time between receiving the first warning and getting the standby search aircraft airborne.

The Flight's first success came on 4 October when a reconnaissance aircraft sighted a ship's lifeboat. A Wellington took off and located it, dropped supplies and instructions on the course to steer and then remained shadowing the progress until dusk. It was found later that the boat carried escapees from Crete. In early November a Walrus was loaned to the Flight by the Royal Navy and established at Mersa Matruh. Later in the month two US amphibians, a Fairchild 91 and a Grumman, which had been presented by well-wishers in America, augmented the Flight, although in the event the Grumman proved unsuitable for sea pick-ups. The Flight's second success on 25 November ended in tragedy. One of its Wellingtons located a dinghy carrying three men and homed a Walrus to the scene, which completed a successful pick-up. The Wellington crashed on landing, killing most of the crew.

Over the next few months the Flight moved to the forward area to cover the advances of the ground forces, but by February the ground forces were in retreat and the unit moved east to Gambut. Squadron Leader S.W.R. Hughes took over command as the Flight was augmented with more Royal Navy Walrus amphibians and additional Wellingtons. Intensive training was carried out and the search and rescue procedures were improved and developed. Over the next six months 67 call outs were received, resulting in 16 successful rescues with 75 lives saved. In April the first overland rescue search was achieved and this was the prelude to many other similar sorties. One of the Flight's most successful sea searches occurred at the end of May 1942.

WELLINGTON DITCHING

At 11 pm on 28 May, Flight Sergeant Harry Nixon and his all-NCO crew of 221 Squadron took off from a landing ground near Sidi Barrani in their Wellington VIII (W 5732) to carry out an anti-submarine patrol in support of a convoy. After an uneventful patrol, Nixon set course for base at 3 am. After two hours he descended to 1,000 feet to stay below the enemy's coastal radar cover. When the Wellington was one hour from base it developed a tendency to swing to port. Soon an engine began to overheat and misfire and an emergency wireless message was sent as Nixon turned towards the coast. Despite using full power on the starboard engine, the aircraft could not maintain height and Nixon ordered the crew to take up their ditching positions.

The crew collected all the emergency equipment and signal flares, and the wireless operator transmitted a final SOS before clamping down his key. Nixon struggled to keep the Wellington level, but at 100 feet he throttled back the starboard engine and was able to make a good belly landing on the calm sea having assessed his height in the moonlight. Apart from minor abrasions the crew were uninjured and all managed to scramble clear of the aircraft, which sank after a few minutes. They were 45 miles northeast of Bardia.

The dinghy inflated upside down and the crew struggled to right it. In doing so, most of the emergency equipment and rations were lost. Eventually, all the crew scrambled aboard and Nixon took stock of the situation. Every man was wearing shorts and battle dress blouses. Their only rations were 80 Horlicks tablets, two bars of chocolate and some chewing gum. They had no water. Rations were fixed for the first two days at three Horlicks tablets per man each day.

Over the next four days the crew heard aircraft but none were sighted. Gunfire was also heard regularly along the coast (assumed to be Bardia) and bomb bursts and anti-aircraft fire were visible at night. The sun was hot during the day and the crew suffered sunburn, but the nights were cold.

On the fourth morning a Blenheim passed within a mile of the dinghy and during the afternoon another, piloted by Flying Officer Beresford-Pierce of 203 Squadron, approached within half a mile at 1,000 feet. Having no pyrotechnics the crew waved and used the Horlicks tins as a heliograph. The Blenheim came lower and circled the dinghy and the crew realized they had been sighted. Beresford-Pierce made a low pass and a parcel was dropped within 20 yards of the dinghy. The crew recovered it and found it contained some food and a note saying that help was on its way. Eventually the Blenheim left, but shortly afterwards a hospital ship appeared half a mile away and stopped. The crew shouted and waved, but inexplicably the ship sailed on and the survivors spent another night in the dinghy.

The Air Sea Rescue Flight was alerted and a Wellington took off to search the area, dropping flares throughout the night. They fell just 1 mile north of the dinghy but no sightings were made. Two more Wellingtons were airborne at first light and one soon located the dinghy. The two joined forces and circled the dinghy dropping flares before one made a low run to drop a bag of supplies, which the crew soon retrieved. One Wellington dropped a message telling the survivors that amphibians were on their way and remained on the scene for the next five hours. Two high speed launches also left for the scene.

During the afternoon, the Fairchild and a Walrus appeared, escorted by Hurricanes. They both landed safely and each took three men on board and returned to base, arriving late in the afternoon of 2 June. The Wellington crew had been in their dinghy for four and a half days.

Nixon and his crew were admitted to hospital at Sidi Barrani, but they were soon discharged and returned to their squadron. They were loud in their praise of the work of the Air Sea Rescue Flight, commenting in their report:'The story of their work on this occasion will inspire confidence in no small measure, to all airmen whose duty it is to fly over the Mediterranean.'

The crew returned to operations and in December 1942 Harry Nixon was awarded the DFM for completing 400 hours of operational flying. The citation also commented: 'During this ordeal [the ditching] he showed great resource and, as a result, his crew were in excellent condition when finally rescued.'

★

By late June, the military situation had become grave with the fall of Tobruk and Axis forces crossing the Egyptian frontier and threatening Sidi Barrani and Mersa Matruh. The Air Sea Rescue Flight moved back to Abu Sueir in the Canal Zone where it remained until November. The number of sea searches was limited owing to the small amount of air activity over the sea, but there was a dramatic increase in the number of land searches. A total of 44 aircrew were picked up or assisted after force-landing in the desert.

The number of aircraft was increased to nine Wellingtons, two amphibians and one Maryland. The latter proved particularly useful for making searches close to the enemy coastline or forward area where the Wellington would have been vulnerable to attack.

Following the victory at Alamein, and the 8th Army's subsequent advances in Cyrenaica, the Flight was able to move west to occupy Gambut and Berka with detachments further forward at advanced landing grounds. Two Wellingtons formed these detachments with a complement of ground crew and they were usually away for 10 days before being replaced by a new aircraft and crew. The Flight was responsible for an ever-increasing land and sea area and a new Blenheim Flight of six aircraft was formed in January 1943. By the end of March 1943, a move was made to Benghazi, and three months later the Axis forces had been swept out of Tunisia. In the two-year period up to June 1943 the Air Sea Rescue Flight had rescued or assisted 234 personnel, of whom 12 were enemy airmen; 142 had been rescued from the sea and 92 from the desert. The Flight had also carried out many anti-submarine patrols.

To support the Allied forces in northwest Africa following Operation 'Torch' on 8 November 1942, the first overseas air sea rescue squadron was formed in the following February. The Admiralty agreed to release six Walrus aircraft to form 283 Squadron as part of Eastern Air Command (which was afterwards absorbed into Mediterranean Air Command). The Squadron was formed at Algiers using the well-equipped former seaplane base. As the ground war advanced, it moved to Maison Blanche. The first customers were all Germans brought down over Allied ship convoys, but as the advance to Tunis continued, and the Squadron moved to La Sebala, those rescued were mostly Americans.

Whilst 283 Squadron was forming in the western Mediterranean, Headquarters Middle East were putting forward a request for composite air sea rescue squadrons of twin-engine land aircraft and amphibians for their sphere of operations in the eastern Mediterranean. They asked for 32 aircraft and 16 amphibians to cover their requirements for Tripoli, Malta, Iraq, Aden and East Africa. In London the air staff had been considering worldwide requirements and concluded that for the whole of the Mediterranean and Middle East there was a requirement for 40 long-range and 20 high-speed aircraft.

The HQ Middle East request could not be met in full and they were offered 20 Warwick and 10 Walrus aircraft to meet the total air sea rescue requirement, although some of these, particularly the Warwicks, would not be available for some time.

HIGH SPEED LAUNCHES

With the partial implementation of some of the decisions to allocate additional high speed launches to the Middle East taken in June 1941, a modest capability was in place by the end of November 1941. Three launches were based at Malta, with two at Mersa Matruh and one at

Aden. The launch *HSL 110* was back at Port Said, the cabin cruiser had returned to Alexandria, and an improvised rescue pinnace was stationed at Cyprus. Another step taken in the latter part of 1940 was the formation of a marine section at Port Said to deal with the refitting of the high speed launches and any other craft in the Canal area, the original master of *HSL 110* being put in charge.

It was the intense fighting over Malta during the summer of 1941 that had prompted the urgent review of air sea rescue capabilities in the area. Throughout this period, only the original launch, *HSL 107*, which was based at Kalafrana and would ultimately achieve considerable fame, was available for rescue work. The majority of pilots shot down inevitably landed in the sea, so improvised rescue arrangements were put in force with the aid of seaplane tenders and miscellaneous small craft. Although the Chiefs of Staff agreed to reinforce Malta as a matter of urgency, it was not until October that the two additional high speed launches and their crews arrived on the island.

Meanwhile the locally improvised rescue unit of 1 rescue launch, 3 seaplane tenders and 12 miscellaneous craft did their best under the most hazardous conditions. Although no accurate records were kept prior to November 1941, 30 British pilots were rescued from the sea by this collection of craft with *HSL 107* picking up 17 of them.

After the arrival of the two new launches in November 1941 a combined Marine and High Speed Launch section was formed with two high speed launches and the headquarters at Kalafrana, and the third rescue launch and a seaplane tender at St Paul's Bay. By the end of the year 34 allied and 12 enemy aircrew had been rescued. On 4 February 1942 Messerschmitt 109s attacked one of the new launches, *HSL 129*, as it went to the aid of a Hurricane pilot. The enemy fighters strafed the launch, killing two of the crew and severely wounding others, including the master, Flying Officer Nicholls. Despite serious wounds and the loss of a hand, the second coxswain, Corporal Cooper, managed to get the launch back to Kalafrana where a third member of the crew died. *HSL 129* had suffered major damage and it was hauled out of the water for repairs. A few days later it was destroyed in the hangar during a bombing raid.

The two surviving rescue launches were hard pressed to keep pace with the demands, and serviceability became a severe problem, as spare parts were virtually non-existent during the siege. The Army had a high speed target-towing launch, HMAV *Clive*, which was loaned to the RAF for a year from August when it was adapted and assumed the identity of *HSL 100* and was normally based at Sliema. By the end of 1942, *HSL 166* had arrived at Kalafrana from Alexandria under her own power. During 1942, Malta's rescue launches rescued 85 Allied and 40 enemy aircrew.

By the autumn of 1942 the general policy of marine craft provisioning had been sufficiently clarified to permit the forward planning of Air Sea Rescue Units (ASRU) overseas. Unlike many of the RAF's marine units that had a wider task than simply air sea rescue work, the new ASRUs were exclusively established for air sea rescue. It was decided to allot 135 craft to overseas commands and this number permitted the formation of 47 ASRUs, of which 13 had already formed.

The plan for Operation 'Torch' did not include any ASRUs in the assault phase, but as soon as the Allied forces had gained a foothold after the 8 November landing in northwest Africa, there was an immediate need for rescue craft. Six launch crews arrived in Algiers four days after the landings and a further six a week later. The high speed launches began to arrive by the end of the month. During January 1943, three ASRUs formed at Algiers, Bone and Philippeville, each unit with four 63-foot launches.

The operational record of the first five months of 1943 was largely one of abortive sorties, normally for ditched fighters. Control was poor and the information was often vague. Nevertheless, in spite of a lack of spares, there was always one launch available. The help of the Royal Navy in providing slipping facilities at the three bases and the full use of workshops was of immense value in the early days.

As the Allies advanced so the launches followed, first to Tabarka and then to Bizerte, which became the focal point for air sea rescue work, and to Sousse and Sfax. Pinnaces were left behind to cover Algiers and Bougie. In preparation for the invasion of Sicily, a new unit, No. 254 ASRU, was formed in the United Kingdom with eight 68-foot

21 *Eric Hartley and his crew at the point of rescue by HMS Mahratta (via Norman Franks).*

22 *Three of Nelms' crew. Left to right: Graham Richardson (killed), Robert Gregory and 'Slim' Sommerville (R. Gregory).*

23 *Roderick Gray, who died during his ordeal and was posthumously awarded the George Cross (ACA Archives).*

24 *G.E. Whiteley and John Ford draped in the single-seat dinghy with Gordon Bulley clinging to the side where he had remained throughout the ordeal (TNA: PRO AIR 27/150).*

25 *A Walrus of 277 Squadron and aircrew at Martlesham (via Norman Franks).*

26 LEFT: *The crew of a Fortress sail their lifeboat with their dinghy in tow on 26 July 1943 (TNA: PRO AIR 20/4710).*

27 ABOVE: *Noel Belford (right) and his wireless operator, Sergeant T. Trinder (Wickenby Register).*

28 RIGHT: *Noel Langdon (right) and a fellow officer serving on 278 Squadron (Noel Langdon).*

29 ABOVE: *Vic Motherwell (left) with his bomb aimer, A. Macdonald, and his navigator, Ian McGown (Vic Motherwell).*

30 *Allen Watkins DFC RCAF, who drifted off the enemy coast for seven days (via Chris Thomas).*

31 *A 278 Squadron Walrus on patrol over the English Channel (Noel Langdon).*

32 *Douglas Mann and Don Kennedy are brought alongside HSL 2679 totally exhausted after their nine-day ordeal (via Roy Nesbit).* **33** INSET: *New Zealander Douglas Mann DFC pictured at the end of the war (via Roy Nesbit).*

34 *ABOVE: The veteran Malta skipper Eric Price in the wheelhouse of HSL 107 with the launch's 'scoreboard' prominent (Ted Shute).*

35 *Canadian Terence Moore (T. Moore).*

36 *Peter Carver (right) and a squadron colleague (P. Carver).*

37 *Jack Rogers (extreme right) and Eric Parham (top left) and crew of HSL 2543 (Eric Parham).*

38 *A Wellington crew takes advantage of the heavy flooding on their airfield at Foggia in the winter of 1945 to carry out a dinghy drill. A Halifax is in the background (photograph courtesy of the Imperial War Museum, London CAN 2724),*

39 *Pinnace P 1304 tows Sunderland K/204 towards Bathurst (TNA: PRO AIR 29/449).*

40 *A 'Hants and Dorset' launch, callsign 'Seagull 34', at speed in the Bay of Bengal (photograph courtesy of the Imperial War Museum, London CI 1477).*

launches and, together with its crews and support and servicing equipment, it sailed for North Africa arriving just before the invasion.

The advance of the 8th Army from the east and the availability of port facilities for the rescue launches had allowed *HSL 2518* to sail from Benghazi to Tripoli on 5 February 1943. With the eastward advance of the units from Algiers, there was a continuous chain of ASRUs along the whole of the North African coast by June. Gradually, more of the spacious and powerful 'Hants and Dorsets' and American-built 'Miami' launches began to arrive.

Three rescues of Spitfire pilots by high speed launch early in 1943 are typical of very many made by the Malta-based rescue crews over a long period of time and they illustrate well the skill and courage of these men.

MALTA'S LAUNCHES RESCUE SPITFIRE PILOTS

During January 1943, 11 Spitfire Vs took off from Krendi on the island of Malta to attack warehouses in Sicily. Forty-five minutes after take off, the engine of one of the Spitfires started to misfire and the pilot turned back towards Malta, but he was forced to bale out 30 miles northeast of the island.

As he hit the sea he attempted to inflate his dinghy before releasing his parachute, which soon began to sink. He let go of his dinghy in order to release the parachute, which he successfully achieved, but he was not quick enough to grab the dinghy before it too sank. He made several dives in an attempt to recover the dinghy, but they all failed. He swallowed a lot of sea water. Two of his colleagues set up an orbit overhead as others transmitted a distress call.

The ASRU at St Paul's Bay received a call out at 11.35 am and *HSL 107*, with Pilot Officer K. Baker as master, headed for the reported position. As it approached the area a Spitfire was seen flying very low on the horizon; although radio contact was made, the reception was poor and the fighter failed to respond to the request for directions from the launch. The Spitfire passed another unintelligible message and departed the scene. The launch closed to the last position of the Spitfire, but nothing was seen and it returned to the original datum. A second Spitfire appeared, waggled its wings and veered off; the launch immediately followed but, once again, VHF contact could not be established.

Shortly afterwards contact was made with the Spitfire and Baker asked it to dive over the position. Within minutes more Spitfires were seen, all orbiting and diving, and the launch closed on the area rapidly. After a brief search, a pilot was seen in the water and the launch was alongside at 1 pm. The pilot was in an exhausted condition, suffering severely from cramp. He was unable to help himself, but was eventually got aboard with difficulty. The crew stripped off his Mae West and jacket and carried him below. The remainder of his clothes were cut away and work commenced on his body to try and get his circulation going as rapidly as possible. The launch crew commented that the pilot's resistance seemed to be very low. A few drops of brandy were forced down his throat, and fortunately this caused him to be sick and bring up sea water.

After about 45 minutes of hard rubbing and massage, the pilot said he felt warmer and wanted to sleep. He was covered with blankets and kept warm. One hour after being picked up, he was landed and received attention from the medical staff who were waiting for him. He made a full recovery.

The report on this incident is very critical of the pilot, commenting that 'there was so much wrong with everything that the pilot did, it is hard to know where to begin'. He had never practised a dinghy drill and was not wearing his own Mae West. He had not checked to see if any distress flares were in the lifejacket but he 'thought there were some'. In the event he made no attempt to look once he was in the sea. Had he done so, he would have found three and the use of them would undoubtedly have resulted in him being rescued earlier. His parachute and dinghy release procedures were also incorrect, resulting in the loss of his dinghy. On recovery, he admitted that he had virtually given up hope after being in the sea for just 90 minutes.

Fortune favoured this pilot. Some of his comrades were able to remain overhead and keep him in sight. The operations staff ensured that other Spitfires were launched in time to maintain a constant patrol over him. Had there been a break in the continuity, it is almost certain that aircraft arriving late would never have spotted a bobbing head. The skill of the launch lookouts in spotting him allowed the rescue to be effected before he succumbed to exposure and weakness. Finally, by chance, a nursing orderly was aboard the launch when the call out was received, and there can be no doubt that his presence was crucial. As the report of this incident comments, 'It is to be hoped that he is a wiser man now. He is certainly a lucky one.'

This pilot went on to become a very successful fighter leader and was twice decorated for gallantry for operations in northwest Europe.

The actions of Canadian Pilot Officer Robert Taggart of 1435 Squadron on 3 March made a potentially difficult rescue close to the enemy coast relatively straightforward because he knew his drills and carried them out perfectly. He was flying a Spitfire V (BR 161) as part of a four-aircraft formation tasked to carry out a sweep of southern Sicily. The German radar station at Bono reported their approach and six Messerschmitt 109s were scrambled to intercept them.

Six miles south of Comiso the German fighters attacked and quickly sent one of the Spitfires crashing into the sea. Taggart's aircraft was hit in the oil cooler, but instead of breaking away he pursued his attacker. At 16,000 feet his engine showed signs of seizing and he belatedly turned towards Malta.

He was still over Sicily when he realized that he would have to bale out. He headed for the sea, transmitted for an emergency fix and stopped the Spitfire's engine. He allowed the fighter to glide out over the sea, then he prepared to bale out. He finally abandoned the Spitfire at 6,000 feet when he was 2 miles out to sea. During his parachute descent, he was able to drift further from the coast.

When Taggart hit the sea, he was unable to release his parachute so he rolled over on to his back, pressed the release box and the parachute floated free. He had no trouble inflating his dinghy and climbed aboard. It was 8.50 am.

Within minutes of receiving Taggart's SOS, *HSL 107* sailed from St Paul's Bay under the command of Malta's veteran master, Flight

Lieutenant Eric Price (see plate 34). He was told to head 013 degrees for 41 miles. Shortly afterwards, four Spitfires of 249 Squadron led by Pilot Officer B.J. Oliver scrambled to locate and protect Taggart in his dinghy. Thirty minutes after baling out, Taggart saw them approaching; he fired his emergency flares and they turned towards him and set up a patrol. A Junkers 88 appeared and was chased away, and when a second appeared, the Spitfires engaged it and shot it down.

Price soon made radio contact with the patrolling fighters and he was able to head straight for the survivor. Within one hour he saw two Spitfires orbiting and he altered course and was soon alongside the dinghy. Taggart was able to clamber aboard *HSL 107,* which was soon heading for Malta. Price reported that he was 'fit and cheerful and following a rub down, and a change of clothes he was quite fit'.

Twenty minutes after setting course for Malta, Price received a radio call that another Spitfire pilot was in the sea and he was directed to a position 25 miles north of Grand Harbour. At 11.20 am he sighted two Spitfires to the south and he headed towards them. He established radio contact with them and discovered that they were orbiting over a pilot who had no dinghy. Price closed rapidly and at 11.45 am his lookouts spotted the pilot.

Sergeant W. Stark of 249 Squadron was flying one of the Spitfires sent to assist Taggart, but he had to bale out of his Spitfire after it had been hit by return fire from the Junkers 88 and his aircraft suffered an engine failure. His right foot became entangled in his parachute harness and he lost his dinghy during his attempt to get free. Two Spitfire pilots dropped their dinghies but Stark was unable to recover them. He inflated his Mae West, fired three of his emergency flares and discharged the fluorescene, which was visible 3 miles away. He had been in the water for 45 minutes when the crew of *HSL 107* pulled him aboard. He rapidly revived after being wrapped in warm blankets and hot water bottles and being given a dose of brandy. More Spitfires arrived to escort the rescue launch and at 12.40 pm the two pilots were landed at St Paul's Bay.

This rescue operation may appear undramatic and straightforward. In many aspects it was, but only because everyone involved played their part correctly. The first rescue took place just 8 miles off the enemy coast and two enemy aircraft were sent to disrupt the operation, both failing. The reporting officer commenting on Taggart's rescue summarized the event perfectly when he concluded, 'a most efficient rescue. The pilot knew his drill, carried it out effectively and made his full contribution to ASR. A big hand to fighter control, the escorting Spitfires and *HSL 107*.' With regard to Stark he commented, 'The pilot seems to have done his stuff, but was unlucky.'

Later that afternoon, the Malta ASRU made its two-hundredth rescue when *HSL 166* rescued another Spitfire pilot.

★

On 29 July 1942, *HSL 107* played a minor role in a remarkable episode, which resulted in the return of the four-man crew of a Beaufort aircraft shot down the previous day

HIJACK TO FREEDOM

Following a reconnaissance report of a large merchant ship escorted by destroyers creeping down the Greek coast with supplies for Rommel's army, nine Malta-based Beaufort torpedo bombers of 217 Squadron were tasked to launch an attack. South African Lieutenant Ted Strever captained one of the crews and they took off in Beaufort L 9820 at 9.10 am. The convoy was found and, in the face of intense anti-aircraft fire, Strever dropped his torpedo. As he turned away, his aircraft was hit repeatedly and both engines started to fail. With little time to prepare, he was forced to ditch parallel to the swell.

The first contact with the sea was slight but the second was a bone-shaking crash. As soon as the aircraft settled, the New Zealand air gunner, Sergeant John Wilkinson, clambered on to the port wing and operated the dinghy toggle. The CO_2 bottle functioned correctly and the 'H' dinghy inflated. The wireless operator, another New Zealander, Sergeant Alex Brown, and Wilkinson stepped into the dinghy without getting wet. Strever and the English navigator, Pilot Officer Bill Dunsmore, eventually struggled free of the submerged cockpit and joined their two colleagues in the dinghy.

The aircraft had ditched 5 miles off the coast but all the crew's efforts to paddle ashore were in vain. An Italian fighter circled overhead and it was soon joined by a tri-motor Cant Z 506 float-plane, which landed a few yards away from the dinghy. Strever swam over to the aircraft and was received courteously by the Italian crew, who soon had the rest of the Beaufort crew on board. The Italian pilot indicated that the heavy swell prevented a take off and the Cant was taxied to the lee of some small islands where conditions were calmer and it was able to take off. The Beaufort crew took the opportunity to visually examine the aircraft and note the operating procedures. The aircraft flew north for two hours and landed at its base where the crew were escorted to the officers' mess and given dry clothing.

The Italians proved hospitable and Strever and his crew were well looked after and fed. They were given rooms for the night and politely asked not to run away. A map on the wall of one of the rooms indicated that they were on the island of Corfu. After a good breakfast and a series of photographs with their captors, they were told that they would be transferred by air to a POW camp. They had expected to be sent by road and rail, which could have offered an opportunity for escape, but they soon discovered that they would be flying in the Cant that had rescued them.

The Cant's crew consisted of two pilots, an engineer and a wireless operator, with a corporal acting as an armed escort. Strever and his colleagues had only the briefest time to discuss the possibility of capturing the aircraft. After take off the aircraft headed west and the Beaufort crew assessed that it was heading for Taranto.

Once the aircraft had settled on course and all was quiet, the powerfully built Wilkinson attracted the wireless operator's attention and then smashed his large fist into the unsuspecting Italian's face. He then leaped over the falling man and grabbed the astonished escort, seizing his revolver and throwing it to Strever. Taking their cue from Wilkinson's actions, the other two Beaufort men overpowered the engineer. As the second pilot left his seat to recover a gun, Wilkinson used the corporal as a shield. By forcing him on to the second pilot, he was able to grab the gun in the scrimmage. In the meantime, the Cant pilot had descended towards the sea, but under the immediate threat of the revolver he levelled out and handed the controls to Strever.

The other members of the Beaufort crew armed themselves with wrenches, and heavy spanners from the toolbox, but the Italians soon submitted and allowed themselves to be tied up. The British felt embarrassed at returning the Italians' kindness in such a way and soon eased their bonds and made them comfortable.

Strever descended to very low level to remain under radar cover as Dunsmore hunted for maps. They decided to head west and pick up the coastline of Italy and then turn for Malta. Brown familiarized himself with the guns and remained on the alert in the turret. Once the Italians were aware that the Cant was heading for Malta, they became very excitable shouting, 'Spitfire, Spitfire!' This issue had also concerned Strever as they approached the toe of Italy and turned towards the well-defended island. Just north of Malta three Spitfires intercepted the floatplane and set up a series of attacks. Strever was flying just above the sea and Brown swivelled the turret in an attempt to indicate that they were friendly. Dunsmore took off his vest and trailed it outside the cockpit as a sign of surrender. These efforts did not deter the Spitfire pilots and when bullets struck the wing Strever ordered the Italian pilot, Tenente Mastrodrasa, to land. As they landed the engines stopped, starved of fuel.

The nine men quickly climbed on to the wing and started waving Dunsmore's vest. The Spitfires pulled away, recognizing that the 'Italians' were surrendering. Within minutes, *HSL 107* was alongside and Strever was able to convince the launch's gunner that they were members of the RAF. Amongst much jubilation, the launch crew tried to take the Cant in tow. Eventually, the aircraft was towed to St Paul's Bay where an excited crowd had gathered. Strever and his colleagues took the Italians to the mess in an attempt to repay their hospitality before they escorted them to the POW cage, where they all shook hands. In due course they were transferred to England where they spent the rest of the war.

All four of the crew of the Beaufort survived the war. For their actions they were all decorated, Strever and Dunsmore receiving the DFC and the two New Zealanders, Wilkinson and Brown, receiving the DFM. For security reasons, the citations made no mention of their escape. Strever retired as a lieutenant colonel having been badly injured in an air crash. He later had a successful career and retired to Northern Transvaal.

★

RESCUE BY MALTA-BASED SUNDERLAND

Flight Lieutenant G.B.S. Coleman and his navigator Sergeant L. Lyne-Hale took off in their Beaufighter (T 5112) from Takali on Malta on 17 January 1943 at 9.30 am to carry out an offensive sweep off the North African coast. Leading the formation of four aircraft was the commanding officer of 272 Squadron, Wing Commander J.K. Buchanan DSO. The experienced Coleman and his navigator had joined the squadron the previous afternoon, so this was their first operation with the unit. South of Cape Mahadia three small schooners were sighted and attacked with cannons. Shortly after, T 5112 developed engine trouble and one of the accompanying Beaufighters called to say that the aircraft was on fire.

Coleman selected 20 degrees of flap and prepared to ditch. He descended to a few feet above the sea and throttled back the serviceable engine, released the escape hatch above his head, undid his parachute, but remained strapped into his seat. By this time the cockpit was full of fumes and Coleman ditched the Beaufighter with little impact. He undid his harness and climbed out on to the wing, which was just awash. He saw his navigator opening the rear hatch and throw out his 'K' dinghy. He was a non-swimmer and Coleman inflated the dinghy and ushered Lyne-Hale aboard. In the meantime one of the three Beaufighters circling overhead dropped dinghies, but it was impossible to recover them. Coleman swam to retrieve his own 'K' dinghy, inflated it and climbed aboard. The two men salvaged items that were floating around them, including an escape kit. Shortly afterwards the Beaufighter sank.

One of the three accompanying Beaufighters sent a distress message and immediately returned to Malta to report the position of the dinghies as the other two circled overhead. They remained until their fuel state dictated the need to depart, leaving the two ditched airmen some 100 miles to the west of Malta and 30 miles off the Tunisian coast.

The distress call sent by one of the Beaufighters had been received at Malta and a Sunderland (EJ 131) of 230 Squadron on detachment to Luqa was alerted at 12.50 pm. The captain, Flight Lieutenant Todd, took off from Kalafrana 50 minutes later and jettisoned his depth charges as soon as he was airborne. Had the depth charges been off-loaded before take off, he would have been delayed by a further hour. Eight Spitfires escorted the Sunderland as it headed for the survivors.

On reaching the datum, Todd set up a square search of the area with the four Spitfires line abreast either side of him. After an hour, one of the Spitfires on the edge of the area fired a flare and started to circle. The Sunderland, flying at 150 feet, turned for the position and the crew spotted the two dinghies at very short range. The Beaufighter crew had lost their distress flares and the Spitfire pilot had seen the red flag waved by the pilot. Todd dropped a flame float to assess the wind direction, and then went in to land on the calm sea. There was only a slight swell and Todd had no difficulty with the landing or taxiing to the dinghies.

After landing, Todd taxied well downwind before turning into wind, cutting the two inner engines and putting out the drogues. He taxied slowly forward until the flying boat was 20 yards away, then cut the two remaining engines and put down the flaps. The Sunderland lost way as it came alongside the two men, and by opening the front hatch they were brought on board. The Spitfires called to say that they were very short of fuel and must depart.

Just as Todd was preparing to take off, his crew saw a Spitfire dive into the sea about half a mile away with the pilot floating down in his parachute. He taxied over to the area and the billowing parachute on the water provided a good guide. However, once it sank, they could see nothing of the pilot. It was getting dark and the swell made it difficult to see a head in the water. The Sunderland taxied around for some minutes, when one of the crew saw the Spitfire pilot waving. Todd commented later that they would never have seen him in the poor light if he had not been on top of the swell, even though they were just 30 yards from him.

Todd repeated the earlier procedure of taxiing downwind before turning and cutting his engines and allowing the Sunderland to drift up to the survivor. The crew had great difficulty getting him on board since he had been unable to release his parachute, which had become completely waterlogged. As soon as all three survivors were on board, they were stripped and put into sleeping bags and given hot tea.

Todd was able to take off without trouble and return to Kalafrana. The reporting officer commented on the luck of the Spitfire pilot, Sergeant Tony Williams, who would not have survived if the Sunderland had not been in the immediate area and then made a chance sighting. Sadly, one of the escorting Spitfires failed to return and the pilot was posted as missing.

★

The accounts of rescues related so far highlight the many varied ways aircrew came to be rescued at sea. Two incidents in the spring of 1943 in the sea areas around the central Mediterranean had a German influence. The first involves the crew of a Wellington aircraft flying on an anti-shipping patrol near Sicily.

INTERCEPTED WIRELESS MESSAGE

As the operations in Tunisia were drawing to a close in the spring of 1943, a great deal of Axis shipping was transiting between North Africa and the ports in Sicily, and on the west coast of Italy. Out searching for them were the Wellington anti-shipping aircraft of 221 Squadron based at Luqa on the island of Malta. Many narratives and reports of ditchings start with the words, 'It was just another routine operation.'These were the words used by Flight Sergeant Terry Moore RCAF (see plate 35) from Toronto in his report.

Moore was the navigator of a torpedo-dropping Wellington VIII G/221 (LB 134) captained by Flight Sergeant James Hemsworth. They had been on patrol north of Sicily on the night of 14 April 1943, and the aircraft was heading back to Malta at 2,000 feet when Moore was jerked from his work at his navigator's plotting table by an exclamation that the propeller from one of the two engines had broken free. He next heard Hemsworth calling the crew to jettison all loose articles, but as soon as he and the wireless operator had started to throw equipment down the flare chute, Hemsworth shouted that he was ditching. A brief SOS was sent before the aircraft hit the water in a slight turn, ripping off one of the wings. The impact was less than expected and Moore quickly activated the dinghy release, left via the astro dome and climbed on to the wing and into the dinghy. Three of the crew were soon aboard and were taking stock of the situation when they saw the captain still in the cockpit. He was dragged through the emergency hatch and into the dinghy just as the aircraft sank. He had sustained a deep gash in his leg; the rest of the crew broke open the first aid kit and soon had his leg bandaged. The second pilot and one of the three wireless operators were lost.

It was soon dawn and the four survivors were all wet and suffering from seasickness. A few hours later they were feeling much better as the heat of the sun started to dry out their clothes, but by noon it was almost unbearably hot and the survivors could get little relief except by constantly soaking their heads in sea water, taking care not to swallow any.

During the morning they examined their survival aids and discovered that they had 12 tins of water and six packs of emergency flying rations. In addition, they found two paddles, a sea anchor, a flag and some hand-held signal flares. They also had the Verey pistol and cartridges, together with two packs of fluorescene dye.

Back on Malta, the Wellington's SOS was picked up by Headquarters 248 Wing giving a position 60 miles due west of Malta. Within an hour, the operations room at Luqa had sent a Swordfish to search the likely area, and a high speed launch was brought to immediate readiness. A Beaufort of 39 Squadron was prepared and left at 10.30 am to relieve the Swordfish. This was in turn replaced by two Baltimores of 69 Squadron, which carried out a creeping line ahead search until relieved by a Beaufort at 6.30 pm. Over the next two days, a steady stream of aircraft searched the area without success.

During the first afternoon, two aircraft (almost certainly the two Baltimores) passed close to the dinghy but failed to see the flares and the sea markers. One aircraft (the Beaufort) appeared just before dark, but flew on. Most of the crew slept fitfully, but at one point all must have been asleep as one of the crew woke to find the dinghy filling with water and the side chambers deflating. They all hastily started to bale and the pump was found, and soon afterwards normality had been resorted. However, it was a good lesson and after this at least one of the crew remained on watch as the others dozed.

The next day they had an encounter with a large turtle that circled before diving away. A mine was the next object to occupy their attention and, as it appeared to be bearing down on them, they paddled away and evaded it before settling down to await events. To occupy themselves they resorted to childish games and stunts. Moore was carrying a copy of Alexander Woolcott's *While Rome Burns*, which he was able to partially read as he dried out each page on the side of the dinghy. The four men were also able to muster six usable cigarettes among them and these were passed around.

By the third day, the crew decided that their only hope of getting back to land was by their own exertions. They had two choices, paddle east for Malta or west for the North African coast. They decided on the latter as it was nearer and the currents appeared to be carrying them in that direction. They also decided to cut down their water ration by half to a quarter pint each and to limit the Horlicks tablets to six a day for each man. A sail of sorts was improvised from the signalling flag and they got under way with the paddles. With the aid of their small 'escape' compass, they attempted to maintain a westerly heading.

Their progress was discouragingly slow. When they dropped a piece of paper and timed its disappearance, they calculated that it would take two weeks to reach the coast. Spirits rose at dusk when they heard an aircraft, and this turned to elation when it turned towards them after spotting their signal cartridges fired from the Verey pistol. As they speculated on the identity of the aircraft, they suddenly realized that it was not the anticipated Wellington but a Luftwaffe Junkers Ju 88. They stopped waving their flag and felt very conspicuous. There seemed to be two options: the aircraft could either dispose of them or send a message for a German motor torpedo boat from Pantelleria to come and take them off to captivity. The aircraft passed over the dinghy twice and then, with a flash of its navigation lights, it flew off.

The morning of 18 April dawned with the expectation that they they would shortly be picked up and would be 'put in the bag' by evening, so they destroyed any papers and prepared themselves for captivity. Unknown to the four men, Headquarters 248 Wing were informed at 6.47 am that an 'international broadcast' had been intercepted, giving the position of a dinghy. Luqa operations immediately launched a Baltimore to head for the position and at 9.40 am the crew sighted a dinghy with four men. A high speed launch left for the area with a fighter escort. Later during the morning of their fifth day in the dinghy, a Royal Navy Walrus aircraft appeared with an escort of eight Spitfires. The fluoroscene was released into the water and the Walrus alighted shortly after and picked up the four men. Their last view of the dinghy was a sad one as the Spitfires dived on it and sank it with gunfire.

The crew spent a few days in hospital before a spell of 'survivor's leave' in Egypt. A few weeks later, Moore met an army corporal working in the signals section of the Malta Headquarters. He was on duty when a signal arrived with the news that a dinghy had been sighted. Apparently the International Red Cross had established a wireless net in the Vatican for humanitarian purposes and had intercepted a wireless signal on the international distress frequency giving the position of a dinghy containing four men. It could only have come from the Luftwaffe bomber. It was the crew's only encounter with the enemy.

Terry Moore returned to complete a tour of operations before becoming an instructor. He was commissioned and returned to Canada where he studied law. He retired as a judge.

*

The second incident concerns a fighter pilot who owed his rescue, in the first instance, to an escaping German boat before the Royal Navy appeared on the scene to complete the rescue of the RAF pilot and his German rescuers.

RESCUED BY GERMAN ESCAPERS

As the final remnants of the German Army evacuated Tunisia, RAF fighter-bombers flew patrols aiming to cut off any shipping attempting to escape. At 5 pm on 8 May 1943, 11 Kittyhawks of 260 Squadron took off from Kairouan, south of Tunis, to provide top cover to 24 Kittyhawk bombers of 3 (RAAF) and 250 Squadrons carrying out a shipping search off Cape Bon. Providing extra high cover for the Kittyhawks was a flight of Spitfires, and piloting one of the 260 Squadron fighters was Sergeant Peter Carver.

Climbing to 14,000 feet, the formation was engaged by medium flak as it crossed the peninsula. Once clear of the coast 12 Messerschmitt 109s attacked the Kittyhawks. Carver became separated from the rest of the formation at 12,000 feet, and seeing a lone aircraft, he turned towards it thinking it was a Spitfire. Moments later cannon shells hit the engine of his Kittyhawk, which burst into flames and stopped.

Carver had no alternative but to bale out, and as he drifted down under his parachute, the German fighter turned towards him and fired at him twice before turning away. The sea was a flat calm and he had difficulty assessing his height as he descended. Remembering his training to 'discard your parachute when you are 12 feet from the water', he dropped his helmet in an attempt to assess his height, but soon lost sight of it. Minutes later he hit the water and had no difficulty releasing his parachute and inflating the dinghy.

Carver had not been able to send a distress message, and since he had been alone the rest of his formation had not seen him shot down. Until he failed to return to Kairouan his squadron was unaware that he was missing, and thus no search and rescue attempt was mounted.

Darkness soon fell and he had to sit out the night in his dinghy. He saw gun flashes on the horizon and estimated that he was some 12 miles off the coast.

Just after dawn he saw what appeared to be a small sailing boat and he started to blow his whistle to attract the attention of the crew. The boat, which was towing a dinghy with two men aboard, came alongside. It contained a German officer and seven men who had commandeered a small wooden harbour boat; two Italians were sitting disconsolately in the dinghy. The officer spoke English and told Carver that they were escaping to Sicily, making it clear to Carver that he would soon be in Germany as a POW. The small boat made slow progress throughout the day. At 5 pm smoke was seen on the horizon and it was not long before three warships appeared.

They turned out to be British destroyers in line astern and the Germans immediately threw their guns overboard. The officer gave his Luger to Carver. Ten minutes later the destroyers sailed by and Carver thought the small boat was going to be ignored. However, the third destroyer stopped and threw a line, which fell short and a German had to swim to retrieve it. The men were soon climbing aboard, where the warship's crew immediately recognized the German uniforms but were astonished when Carver scrambled aboard and identified himself with some choice Anglo-Saxon words.

The men had been picked up by HMS *Paladin*, and the captain commented that they had been very lucky since he had been given orders to sink any vessel he came into contact with. Carver was given 'five-star treatment' by the destroyer's crew and was eventually landed at Malta three days later, when the Germans were taken to the POW camp. Within a few days, Carver was back with his squadron.

Peter Carver (see plate 36) went straight back on to operations and fought over Sicily and Italy and completed his tour as the squadron approached Rome.

Chapter Twelve

Invasion of Sicily and Italy

OPERATION 'HUSKY'

Following the capture of Tunisia and the clearance of Axis forces from North Africa in May 1943, there was a period of consolidation by the Allies as plans to gain a foothold in southern Europe were developed. By early July, a new air sea rescue control had been set up at Bizerte on the Tunisian north coast to co-ordinate all rescue efforts in the area, and the high speed launches were based at various ports to meet the expected commitments. Two days before Operation 'Husky', the invasion of Sicily, 32 rescue launches were available in support with more due to arrive in the theatre of operations over the next few weeks.

Following the formation of 283 Squadron in the western Mediterranean in February 1943, the planned invasion of Sicily created the need for a second squadron. No. 284 Squadron, which had been formed on 7 May 1943 from various detachments of other air sea rescue units in the United Kingdom, left for the Mediterranean at the beginning of June. It began operating Walruses from Hal Far on 12 July before moving to Sicily in mid-August.

The capture of Tunisia also affected the organization of the Air Sea Rescue Flight, which continued to operate in the eastern Mediterranean. With its headquarters at Berka detachments were established at Mellaha, Misurata, Gambut and at a landing ground in the Amriya area. These detachments were by July more in the nature of permanent formations rather than the mobile units they had been during the 8th Army's advance. Between them they covered the area up to the Tripolitanian–Tunisian border, the rescue to the west being the responsibility of North West African Coastal Air Force. The invasion of Sicily called for a strengthening of the Flight's detachment at Misurata and in August, owing to the impending offensive operations in the Aegean area, further detachments were formed at St Jean in Palestine, at Limassol in Cyprus, and at a landing ground near Mersah Matruh. At the beginning of September, the Cyprus detachment comprised nearly half the Flight.

During the air offensive, which preceded the assault on Sicily, frequent calls were made upon the rescue services and there were a number of successful incidents. On 2 July, a torpedo-carrying Beaufighter of 47 Squadron, piloted by Flight Sergeant J.E. Carroll, ditched 80 miles off the Tunisian coast. A Walrus of 283 Squadron flown by the commanding officer, Squadron Leader W. Sterne, was scrambled. The crew found the two Beaufighter men in their dinghy. The sea was very rough but Sterne managed to land and pick up the two survivors. With the extra load and the state of the sea, he was unable to take off again and he started to taxi home. He was met by a high speed launch and the Beaufighter crew was transferred before the Walrus was taken in tow. Sterne made another attempt to take off, but he was unsuccessful and he taxied on through the night. Eventually the engine ran out of fuel and the amphibian was finally towed back to Bizerte by a motor torpedo boat.

The following day another crew of 47 Squadron needed the services of 283 Squadron. Flying Officer C.A. Ogilvie's Beaufighter was hit by flak during a shipping strike and he was forced to ditch. New Zealander Sergeant Arnold Divers and his crew took off in a Walrus from Maison Blanche, and after landing to refuel at Bone they found the missing crew following a brief search 15 miles south of Sardinia. They were unable to take off and for the next nine hours taxied back in a very rough sea before the Walrus ran out of fuel. The next afternoon, *HSL 176*, arrived and took off the survivors and two of the Walrus crew who were suffering badly with seasickness. Divers remained at the controls of the Walrus and *HSL 182* arrived to tow him back to Bone harbour.

For the invasion of Sicily, Wellingtons of the Air Sea Rescue Flight and Catalinas of the United States Navy were based at Bizerte for deep searches and rescues in conditions unsuitable for the Walrus crews. A detachment of Sunderland flying boats of 230 Squadron was made available for the first two weeks. The newly forming 284 Squadron at Hal Far augmented the Walrus detachments based on the North African coast.

The ASRU at Malta was temporarily reinforced to a total of 8 high speed launches, 4 pinnaces and 6 seaplane tenders, and during the first 7 days of the assault of 'Husky' serviceability was maintained at 100 per cent. It was in this period that the peak of rescue work at Malta was reached.

On Saturday 10 July, the invasion of Sicily began, and by 17 August the whole island was in Allied hands. Throughout the period air sea rescue launches and aircraft, reinforced by the Sunderlands and Catalinas, searched continuously for missing aircrews.

GALLANT RESCUE OFF SARDINIA

On 2 August a USN Catalina was scrambled to search for a Beaufighter crew who had radioed that they were baling out close to the Sardinian coast. Lieutenant Roger Bishop and his crew located the two dinghies 2 miles off the enemy coast near Cagliari and the Catalina alighted in rough seas and picked up the two men. In attempting to take off, the starboard propeller was damaged by the mounting seas. Bishop attempted to taxi away but the enemy shore batteries opened fire each time he tried. Enemy fighters then appeared on the scene, but the Catalina's fighter escort managed to shoot down three before the amphibian was set on fire. So soon after being rescued, the two Beaufighter aircrew found themselves in the sea for the second time as they abandoned the blazing aircraft with the Catalina's six-man crew, three of them wounded. They all took to the amphibian's large dinghy, which they soon discovered had been damaged by bullets.

The eight men fought to keep the half-submerged dinghy afloat as it drifted towards the enemy coast. For four hours they took it in turns to bale out the sea water and inflate the surviving chambers of the dinghy. They watched as battles continued to rage overhead, with P 38 fighters seeing off the enemy.

Shortly before this episode started to unfold, *HSL 2595* of 254 ASRU left Bizerte to search for a US Warhawk pilot. Two hours into the search, the master, Flight Lieutenant James Lang, picked up a VHF radio call from one of the P 38 fighter escorts alerting him to the perilous situation of the eight men off the Sardinian coast. He immediately ordered his coxswain, Flight Sergeant John Edwards BEM, to head for the position. After two more hours they reached the scene and soon located the swamped dinghy, which had drifted nearer to the enemy coast. The high speed launch immediately came under heavy fire from coastal batteries and salvoes landed around it. Lang calmly directed the launch, and Edwards' expert handling in the difficult sea conditions allowed the survivors to be taken from the dinghy. The launch was just 2 miles off the coast when the fighter escort had to leave, short of fuel, just as the rescue was being completed. Throughout the 40-minute operation the launch was under constant enemy shellfire. Eventually *HSL 2595* was able to withdraw without sustaining damage. Six hours later it reached Bizerte after completing a round trip of 250 miles. Edwards remained at the wheel throughout the 14-hour operation, including the night passage back to port.

For their actions during this daylight rescue close to the enemy coast, Lang was awarded the DSC for his 'cool judgement, great dash and leadership', and Edwards was awarded the DSM for 'his coolness and judgement, which were an inspiration to all on board'.

★

Amongst the considerable assets supporting the invasion and subsequent operations to occupy Sicily were the Wellington squadrons operating in the anti-shipping role, flying patrols, mostly at night, in the sea areas around Sicily and western Italy. On the night of 4/5 August six Wellingtons of 458 (RAAF) Squadron took off from Protville in Tunisia to carry out armed reconnaissance sorties off the coast of Sardinia and Corsica, the Elba Islands and the approaches to Leghorn.

SOLE SURVIVOR AFTER EIGHT DAYS ADRIFT

Captain of one of the six Wellingtons was 27-year-old Australian Flight Sergeant Roy Spencer. His wireless operator was fellow Australian Sergeant B.A. Watson, who was working on the ASV radar. Just after midnight the port engine of the Wellington failed 50 miles east of Sardinia. The torpedo was jettisoned as the Wellington was turned south to head for base and as a distress message was transmitted. Suddenly, Spencer called out 'Stand by for ditching.'

None of the crew had time to take up their ditching positions as the aircraft hit the sea almost immediately after the captain's warning shout. Watson had, however, just managed to get the astro hatch open and believes that he was catapulted through it and into the sea. He could only remember struggling underwater. On surfacing he saw burning fuel on the sea, but no sign of the aircraft. An uninflated dinghy was floating 20 yards away. Heavily bruised and unable to use his arms fully, Watson struggled across to the dinghy and after 30 minutes' effort he was able to inflate it and scramble aboard. By this time the fire had virtually gone out and it was a pitch-black night.

Watson started shouting for the remainder of the crew and was answered by Sergeant Clifford Ebbage, the other wireless operator, who said he was floating but was blinded. The two kept calling to each other as Watson tried to paddle around until he came across his colleague and pulled him aboard the dinghy. Ebbage appeared to be in great pain, could not see and was vomiting. Watson found the survival and ration box and tried to open it to get out the morphine. However, before he could do so, he fainted as a result of his exertions, and when he awoke two hours later Ebbage had died.

At dawn Watson started to paddle west but made no progress and abandoned the idea. He finally managed to open the ration box that contained 12 half-pint tins of water, 5 tins of Horlicks tablets with 50 tablets in each and some barley sugars. He also found a Verey signal pistol with 54 red cartridges, and a red flag, which was hauled. He decided to ration himself to one tin of water every two days, sipped at dawn and dusk, and six Horlicks tablets a day made into three 'meals'. He maintained this severe rationing throughout his ordeal.

During the first afternoon two Baltimores passed 4 miles away and Watson fired two reds, but they were not seen. Later, one of the aircraft returned, but another red failed to attract its attention. Watson felt weak but did not experience hunger or thirst and he revived quickly once the sun's heat died. He spent a cold, wet and sleepless night. He heard an aircraft at 4 pm the following day, but nothing was seen, and at sunset he committed Ebbage to the sea.

During the night a storm blew up creating a very rough sea and he spent the long night baling out the dinghy with one of the expended cartridge cases. The storm continued all day with 20-foot waves. At 2 pm a three-engine German flying boat flew overhead and Watson fired six reds. The aircraft circled the dinghy and after 30 minutes it alighted, but was unable to approach because of the sea state. It then tried to take off, but after 50 yards it was hit by a large wave and the flying boat appeared to break in two. Six men clambered out and got into two dinghies, which remained visible for the rest of the day.

Late that night an aircraft appeared, exchanged signals with the flying-boat survivors and circled throughout the night. At dawn Watson saw that it was a white twin-engine flying boat with Red Cross markings. The storm was still blowing hard and the rescue aircraft was unable to alight. No other aircraft appeared that day and Watson was kept occupied baling out the water from his dinghy. Just as the previous night, another aircraft appeared, exchanged signals and then flew off, probably to pick up the ditched crew.

On the fourth day the sea was calm and the sun hot. Watson had a swim and kept cool all day by dipping his clothes in the sea. He was feeling quite well but thirsty and hungry – his attempts at fishing with coloured paper as bait failed – and he stuck to his rigid rationing plan. His left arm was better but he was still troubled by heavy bruising to his right one. He heard aircraft in the night, but none came close, and he had only a broken sleep.

For the next two days he maintained his routine of a swim, dipping his clothes and strict rationing and had his first night of unbroken sleep. He kept his water cool by keeping the tins away from the sun and wrapping them in a sock, which he kept wetting. At 9 am on the seventh day a Baltimore flew within 100 yards at low level, but the Verey pistol jammed and the crew of the Baltimore inexplicably failed to see the dinghy and his waving. Such an event would have broken many men, but Watson maintained his routine and later commented that he was determined not to let his morale be broken.

After another good night's sleep, he had just had his swim when a USN Catalina appeared with a fighter escort of P 38 Lightnings. With the Verey pistol still jammed, he stood up and waved the red flag. The Catalina circled him before alighting and taxiing across to the dinghy. Watson was soon on board and being fed coffee and tomato juice. He was taken to Bizerte and admitted to the 56th Evacuation Hospital where he recovered from his eight-day ordeal.

Watson's survival was due to his tremendous willpower in sticking rigidly to an excellent plan, added to his great determination. The official report commented on 'his persistent confidence and refusal to give up hope'. Throughout his ordeal he kept himself occupied during the day by singing and talking to himself. When he was rescued, he still had 5 tins of water left, 4 tins of Horlicks tablets and 3 tins of cartridges.

★

The heavy fighting during the invasion and occupation of Sicily placed heavy demands on the crews of the Walrus rescue squadrons. The capture of airfields on the island allowed the forward deployment of rescue aircraft. By the end of July, 284 Squadron was operating from Cassibile and in the first three weeks of August it had picked up eight Allied and one German aircrew. As soon as Palermo was in Allied hands, a flight of 283 Squadron moved to occupy the airfield, and two days after arriving on 5 August, a Walrus rescued three enemy soldiers trying to escape from Sicily in an open boat. Unable to take off because of rough seas, the pilot, Flight Sergeant L.H. Newman, started to taxi to Sicily, but approaching darkness and shortage of fuel forced him to head for Salina Island. The rescuers were in luck since Allied forces had just occupied the island. However, communications had not been established and it was not until 10 August, when a launch arrived with supplies, that the mystery of the disappearance of the Walrus and its crew was solved.

The careful preparation of the search and rescue organization to meet the anticipated demands of the Sicilian campaign was well repaid. From 8 July to 17 August, when the campaign was closed, 4,527 sorties were flown on air sea rescue missions. A breakdown of the rescue figures is not available, but in the first 14 days of the assault 45 lives were saved.

A real test of the air sea rescue capability occurred on 17 August when USAAF heavy bombers took off from airfields in England to bomb the Messerschmitt aircraft works at Regensburg before heading south to land at airfields in North Africa. Seven Fortresses came down in the sea north of Bone, having run out of fuel. Over the next three days over 65 aircraft of all types, assisted by several RAF high speed launches were involved in the rescue of 42 aircrew.

Following the successful occupation of Sicily, Mediterranean Air Command were immediately involved in preparations for an assault on a much bigger scale directed towards the mainland of Italy. To meet the increased requirements to cover the next phase of operations, and the continuing tasks in the eastern Mediterranean, authority was sought for the formation of four air sea rescue squadrons from the existing two. On 30 August, the two existing squadrons were split, allowing two additional units, Nos 293 and 294 Squadrons, to be formed. Each squadron was a composite one of landplanes and amphibians. The plan was to equip each with Warwick aircraft but constant delays prevented their arrival before the invasion of Italy. Lindholme-equipped Bisleys of 614 Squadron, assisted by Wellingtons and Sunderlands, supplemented the squadron's Walrus.

By the end of August, a redeployment of ASRUs became necessary. With Sicily clear of the enemy, Palermo was used for covering the Tyrrhenian Sea while Augusta and Catania became the bases for launches brought forward from 253 ASRU at Malta. No. 223 ASRU covered the Bizerte area, 224 ASRU covered Sousse and 225 ASRU was at Bone. To provide cover for the Salerno landings, launches were deployed along the north Sicilian coast.

From 3 September, when the Allied forces crossed in strength to the toe of Italy, to 8 September, when the assault at Salerno began, the air sea rescue units were constantly in action but the results of long and exhausting searches were often disappointing. With so much activity at sea, many aircrew were rescued by passing convoys and naval patrols. Nevertheless, 27 lives were saved by the search and rescue organization. However, some aircrew forced to ditch in the sea returned by unconventional means.

MEDITERRANEAN ADVENTURE FOR BEAUFIGHTER CREW

Just before 11 am on 15 September 1944, 11 Beaufighters of 39 Squadron took off from Protville in Tunisia to attack shipping off the east coast of Corsica. Leading the five aircraft that made up the anti-flak section were Flying Officer J.C. Yorke and his navigator, Pilot Officer W.B. Mathias, in their Beaufighter X (JM 386). Two hours after take off a 10,000-ton tanker was sighted between the small islands of Capraia and Elba. Yorke dived to attack one of the two escorts slightly astern of the tanker and came under concentrated and accurate anti-aircraft fire. A large hole appeared in the starboard wing and within moments the entire wing was on fire.

Attempts to put the fire out and feather the propeller failed and so Yorke immediately ditched, having closed both throttles. With so little time to prepare, the Beaufighter hit the water hard, but both men were able to get clear of the aircraft before it sank. The 'H' dinghy immediately inflated the right way up and the crew retrieved it. They were also able to retrieve both 'K' dinghies, which were floating nearby, together with the aircraft water tank containing 30 pints of water. In addition to the water they had six tins of emergency rations, two escape kits and an escape purse, which contained local currency and instructions in numerous languages to aid conversations with potential captors.

After baling out the dinghy, Yorke and Mathias started to paddle towards an island some 7 miles away as the enemy convoy sailed on. An hour later a boat was seen heading for them, and shortly after an Italian F-Boat came alongside. The Italian crew cheered when Yorke informed them that they were '*Inglesi*'. Once on board the two survivors were given dry clothes and told that the Germans had left the island of Capraia where the F-Boat was based.

Once ashore, an Italian lieutenant who spoke good English met the crew and took down their personal details before escorting them to meet the island's commandant, an excitable army lieutenant. After more questions the two men were taken to the officers' quarters and given a dank but clean room. They were well fed and spent the next three days in reasonable comfort, able to wander round the small town. The Italian armistice had only recently come into effect and the commandant was unsure whether to remain a free Italian or revert to the Fascists. With German forces still holding nearby Corsica, Elba and the Italian mainland, he was waiting to see developments before deciding.

There was one radio on the island; every evening the whole population gathered to listen to the news, and Yorke and Mathias were later able to pick up the BBC news, which confirmed that Allied forces had arrived at Ponza, the most northerly point so far reached on the Italian mainland. The two men took their Verey pistol and the dinghy flag, with the intention of sitting on a nearby hill to attract an Allied aircraft. In the meantime, the Italian sailors wanted to leave for Sicily, and after some wrangling with the commandant, they were told they could depart under the cover of darkness. Yorke and Mathias were given permission to accompany them on the F-Boat. They recovered most of their survival equipment and used some of their money to pay for the hospitality they had received.

At 8 pm on the fourth day, the boat was ready to leave. Most of the islanders came to wish them 'bon voyage'. The naval lieutenant briefed the Beaufighter crew that they would be the captain and navigator of the boat since they were the only officers on board, an interesting appointment since neither of the two airmen had sailed before. With only two of the three engines serviceable, the boat nosed out of the harbour an hour later on a very black, moonless night. The plan was to reach Monte Cristo during darkness and spend the day sheltering before attempting to make Ponza overnight.

There was an alarm as soon as the boat left the harbour when a number of German ships sailed by. Eventually, a course was set for Monte Cristo and the lack of cloud allowed Mathias to steer by taking very rough bearings on the Pole Star. At 4 am the crew saw Monte Cristo in the moonlight and found a small cove for shelter during the daytime. At dawn one of the Italian sailors swam ashore and discovered that the Germans had left.

At nightfall the boat sailed for Ponza, 150 miles away, although a dogleg had to be steered to avoid getting too close to the coast. At 7 knots, they estimated, the journey would take 22 hours so they had to leave at 3 pm, giving a few hours of daylight to negotiate. The boat was very overcrowded when they set sail – they had left Capraia with 45 Italians and had acquired another seven. They steered a southeasterly course and the five hours until darkness were 'the most tortuous we had ever encountered'. The boat was in full view of Giglio and the mainland throughout, and had they been sighted life could have been very difficult – and short.

Eventually darkness fell and they sailed through the night. Fortunately, the sky remained clear and Mathias was able to steer a rough course. At dawn they estimated that they were south of Rome and turned on to an easterly heading hoping to hit the coast near Ponza. At 10.15 am they sighted the coast and soon identified their destination. They arrived during the afternoon to find that the Germans had left, but the Allies were still 30 miles away. They found some English-speaking Italians and were taken to the naval commander's house, where they were able to wash. During the evening a US Navy launch arrived and at 7 pm it sailed with the Beaufighter crew, four German aircrew prisoners and an Italian aristocrat and his daughter who had been held prisoner.

At midnight the launch reached Capri, where Yorke tried to radio the RAF authorities, but the message was not intercepted. After a bath, a meal and the first decent sleep for three days, the two men spent the next day relaxing and making arrangements for the next stage of their journey. Late on the evening of 22 September, a week after they had ditched, they left for Malta on the Royal Navy *MTB 636*, which together with *MTB 634* was acting as an escort for three Italian E-Boats carrying two Italian admirals. After an overnight stop at Messina, the two boats arrived at Grand Harbour, Malta at 6 pm on 23 September. Twenty-four hours later, after getting new clothes and being interviewed by the intelligence staff, they left by air, arriving back at Protville after an absence of almost 10 days.

Chapter Thirteen

The Italian and Balkans Campaign

A T THE BEGINNING OF October 1943 Mediterranean Air Command's search and rescue service was reorganized to meet the changing operational needs following the Allied advance in Italy. Air Headquarters Malta was made responsible for all air sea rescue operations in Sicily and the toe of Italy. With the exception of detached Walrus Flights, the rescue squadrons were non-operational as they were withdrawn to re-equip with the Warwick. To provide cover in the meantime, all general reconnaissance squadrons were required to keep one aircraft fitted with Lindholme Gear and be at readiness for deep search duties. Where possible, fighter squadrons had aircraft on call for close search.

To meet the increased requirements for a rescue service around Corsica and Sardinia, and to provide cover for the armies advancing up Italy on both the east and west coasts, the Walrus aircraft were spread over as wide a field as possible with detachments at Palermo, Ajaccio, Monte Corvino, Brindisi, Catania and Malta. Those from 283 Squadron operated on the west side of Italy and 294 Squadron covered the Adriatic. There was also a reorganization of the deployment of high speed launches. By the end of the year Nos 252 and 253 ASRUs had absorbed launches from other units and were responsible for west Italy and the Adriatic respectively. No. 254 had responsibility for Corsica and Sardinia, 251 covered the North African coast from Algiers to Bizerte and 204 took over Sicily and Malta.

By these redeployments, protection was given to the key operational areas in the Ligurian, Tyrrhenian and Adriatic Seas, and in the
Mediterranean between Cap Bon and Sicily.

The occupation of Corsica, Sardinia and southern Italy had doubled
the operational area of the rescue services, and long-range aircraft were
badly needed. The continuing delays in the delivery of Warwicks,
together with the wretched serviceability state of the aircraft, created
major difficulties. By the middle of November only 13 Warwicks had
been delivered and representations were made to the highest level in
the Air Ministry. In January 1944 Mediterranean Air Command (which
had become Mediterranean Allied Air Forces) was in a parlous state for
air sea rescue aircraft. They still had received only 16 Warwicks, all of
them 'Bastard Bombers' and unable to carry the airborne lifeboat. All
through the winter of 1943 and spring of 1944, the lack of Warwick
aircraft put a severe strain on the organization and this put added
pressure on the outstanding Walrus aircraft, which had to shoulder
some of the search responsibilities in addition to conducting rescues.

USAAF aircraft were in constant action in the Mediterranean area
and RAF rescue aircraft were often called out when an American
aircraft got into difficulties. A Walrus of 283 Squadron based at
Palermo was scrambled on 3 November 1943 to search for a USAAF
bomber crew who had baled out over the sea.

WALRUS TO THE RESCUE OF USAAF BOMBER CREW

The crew of a USAAF B-25 Mitchell from the 82nd Squadron of the
12th Bomb Group returning to Gerbini in central Sicily sent a distress
message that they were baling out over the sea after an engine failure.
At 3.45 pm Flight Sergeant Arnold Divers RNZAF and his gunner,
Sergeant E.F. Keeble, were scrambled to 'search for five dinghies' 30
miles south of Salerno, and 20 minutes later they were airborne and
heading for the area.

The bomber was part of a 12-aircraft formation detailed to bomb
Ceprano in Italy. Piloting the aircraft was First Lieutenant Paul Devlin,
who was flying his fiftieth and final operation before returning home;

his co-pilot, Second Lieutenant Bill McGonigle, was flying on his first. Over the target the Mitchell was hit by anti-aircraft fire but Devlin was able to complete his bombing run before turning for home. On the return journey the starboard engine started to lose power and the bomber was unable to maintain height. Unable to feather the propeller, and with the aircraft becoming very difficult to control, Devlin ordered the five-man crew to prepare to bale out.

As the aircraft started to spin, Devlin told the crew to jump. Three of the crew left before McGonigle vacated his seat, when he stood holding the controls to allow Devlin to unstrap and leave his seat. The two pilots baled out within seconds of each other. The crew were wearing lifejackets but had no individual dinghies. As the aircraft hit the sea, McGonigle noticed that the aircraft's five-man dinghy had released and inflated. During the descent he took the precaution of aligning the floating aircraft with a cloud, and as soon as he had hit the water and released his parachute, he started to swim in the direction of the wreckage. The sea was rough, but each time he crested a wave he realigned his swimming and he soon came alongside the dinghy, which he immediately cut free of the sinking aircraft.

McGonigle saw another member of the crew, so took off his clothes and started to swim with the dinghy in tow. Making little progress he boarded the dinghy and used the broken stump of one of the paddles. Shortly afterwards, he pulled Devlin on board. Hearing shouts, the two men headed in their direction and picked up the gunner. Over the next two hours the other two men were located and pulled into the dinghy. A B-25 from their formation had noted the position of the dinghy and alerted the air sea rescue organization.

During the afternoon a searching Mitchell appeared and the survivors fired a flare. The aircraft spotted them and dropped another dinghy, which McGonigle recovered, and the two dinghies were lashed together.

In the meantime, Divers and Keeble in their Walrus were on their way to the scene. At 5.35 pm they spotted a red flare some 6 miles away. The light was fading fast and there was a moderate swell. Divers alighted, and with the aid of the aircraft's searchlight he saw the two dinghies and taxied over. In 10 minutes he had all five men on board and then attempted to take off. The Walrus porpoised violently and the take off was abandoned due to the swell, darkness and excessive weight. Divers decided to stay on the water overnight, so the drogues were thrown out and the bilge pumps were manned every hour.

The sea and wind increased and the aircraft started to roll badly. Divers started the engine to keep the aircraft into wind but he soon noticed a list to port, which rapidly became more pronounced. The port float was leaking, causing the mainplane to bend under the weight of the sea, and there was a danger that the Walrus would break up. Just before midnight, Keeble moved out on to the starboard wing to counteract the list, but this was only partially successful. After an hour, Divers relieved him.

For the next two hours the two men alternated for shorter periods because of the cold. Soon the seas began to break over the Walrus. A light was sighted on the horizon so a two-star green-red flare was fired and the Aldis lamp was used to signal for help. After 30 minutes a ship trained a light on the Walrus before drawing alongside. The five survivors of the B-25 were taken on board, but Divers and Keeble were determined to stay with the aircraft in the hope that they could salvage it. By this time the aircraft was almost heeling over and the captain of the launch ordered the Walrus crew to leave it. The two men were thrown ropes and were dragged on board the US Navy hospital ship *Seminole*, which took the seven men to Naples. After two nights recovering, the RAF crew returned to Palermo.

Neither was injured, but it is worth recording that Arnold Divers had only been released from hospital that day after recovering from malaria and was unfit for flying. When the emergency call came to scramble, all the other pilots were unavailable and, without reference to any senior officer, Divers immediately took off despite his weakened state. For his outstanding devotion to duty, Divers was awarded the DFM.

Arnold Divers continued to fly with 283 Squadron and answer rescue calls, and he will appear again later in this chapter. Bill McGonigle returned to his squadron and completed 66 bombing operations. For his selfless gallantry and determination in assisting his colleagues in the water, who admitted that they were too weak to help themselves and would not have survived without his help, he was awarded the American DFC.

★

The late months of 1943 and the early ones of 1944 were relatively quiet, but 253 ASRU did some busy periods in the Adriatic picking up bomber crews and giving valuable aid in Bari harbour during the enemy raids in December. During the Anzio operations in January, 252 ASRU saved many lives, often under shellfire and air attack, losing one launch to enemy air action. They remained while the fight for the beachhead continued before moving to advanced bases on the west coast of Italy.

Many calls were made on the Corsica detachment, including one of particular note on 8 March.

LAUNCH RESCUE UNDER SHELLFIRE

Four Spitfire Vs of 253 Squadron, one piloted by Canadian Flying Officer J.W. Munro, took off from Borgo, Corsica at 7.20 am and headed for the north of the island of Elba to carry out a shipping reconnaissance. Two F-Boats were sighted escorting a schooner and the Spitfires dived to attack with cannons. Munro's Spitfire (MA 691) was hit by flak and he was forced to bale out. His dinghy failed to inflate and he was left floating in his Mae West 5 miles off the north coast of Elba.

A Walrus (W 2788) of 293 Squadron piloted by the now Warrant Officer Arnold Divers DFM, with Warrant Officer P. Graham as his crew, was directed to the area. A large oil patch and fluorescene were seen and Munro was soon located floating in his lifejacket. After dropping a smoke float to assess the wind, Divers landed on the rough sea and taxied up to Munro, who was exhausted. As Graham started to drag him on board the shore batteries opened fire with salvoes of four shells. Divers attempted to take off, but shrapnel hit the engine of the Walrus and also damaged the propeller. Despite taking evasive action, the amphibian was again hit and badly damaged. An SOS was sent and Divers decided to abandon the Walrus.

After destroying the equipment and maps on board the Walrus, Graham inflated the 'M' dinghy into which he dragged the injured Munro. Divers inflated a 'K' dinghy and loaded it with rations, the Verey pistol and cartridges. Graham attended to Munro as the dinghies drifted away from the Walrus.

At Bastia on Corsica, Flying Officer Jack Rogers, the master of the Miami class launch *HSL 2543*, was alerted at 9.35 am by his operating authority, 'Blacktop', that a Spitfire pilot was in the sea. He and his very experienced crew (see plate 37) were holding at a waiting position midway between Corsica and the Italian coast and immediately headed for Elba. Two Spitfires of Munro's squadron, led by Squadron Leader H. Hopkinson, took off and provided an escort for the launch, maintaining excellent radio communications and remaining with it for almost two hours.

Shortly afterwards, a Walrus rescue aircraft flew overhead en route to the scene and came up on the VHF radio with the following message: 'We will leave the dinghy for you, chum,' a typically friendly remark from airborne rescuers when passing a rescue launch. In the event, they spoke too soon.

Rogers was told that the Walrus had picked up the Spitfire pilot. Just as he turned for base, he was informed that the Walrus had been hit and was unable to take off so he continued to the scene at 30 knots.

As the launch approached the north side of the island he spotted the shells falling ahead, and a smoke signal from the survivors, and he directed the launch towards the dinghies at full speed. The shore batteries opened fire on the rescue launch at 11.05 am and for the next 20 minutes gave their undivided attention to it as the coxswain, Corporal Eric Parham, took evasive action and manoeuvred towards the survivors. Despite the intense bombardment, the three men were taken on board the launch, which miraculously remained undamaged. Before setting course, Rogers asked if he should take the Walrus under tow, although this would have meant remaining stationary as the tow lines were made fast. He was ordered to abandon the amphibian and leave the area.

Hopkinson, who was circling overhead, gave a dramatic running commentary which was relayed into the operations room at Bastia. He reported later that he could not believe that the launch would survive the shelling. On numerous occasions it completely disappeared under a cloud of spray.

Rogers escaped at high speed, still under the protection of RAF and USAAF fighters that escorted him out of the area. The shelling continued until the launch was 10 miles north of Elba. On return to Bastia, the launch was refuelled and the crew returned to immediate readiness to be available to respond within 3 minutes should another call come for their assistance.

To prevent the Walrus falling into enemy hands, it was destroyed by a 37 mm shell fired by one of the escorting P-39 Airacobras of the USAAF's 345th Fighter Squadron.

This rescue speaks highly of the courage and determination of the men of the Air Sea Rescue Services. Rogers had previously given valuable service in the English Channel. After this particularly hazardous and gallant rescue, he was awarded the DSC. His coxswain, Eric Parham, received the DSM and the rest of the crew received commendations. For Arnold Divers, it was the third time he had been in such straits. He had been towed to safety in July 1943 and forced to abandon another Walrus in November.

★

At the end of February 1944 there was a remarkable rescue south of Crete, which further demonstrated the tenacity and skill of those who manned the air sea rescue aircraft and launches. Wellingtons of 294 Squadron (formerly the Air Sea Rescue Flight) played a key role in the eventual rescue, which was at the absolute range of the high speed launches operating from North African berths. To supplement the specialist rescue crews, many aircraft from other squadrons were co-opted to assist.

LONG-RANGE RESCUE

At 1 pm on 25 February 1944 four Beaufighter Xs of 47 Squadron took off from Gambut III to conduct a sweep around the island of Scarpanto to the east of Crete. Flying as number three in the formation was Flying Officer R. Euler and his navigator, Flight Sergeant C. Boffin. As the formation headed down the west coast of the island, a schooner and a caique were seen and attacked. Light flak was encountered and Euler's aircraft was hit. Ten minutes later he reported an oil leak from the port engine, and after jettisoning his bombs and some fuel he ditched the aircraft on a relatively calm sea.

Two of the Beaufighters remained in the area and their crews saw Euler and Boffin get into the aircraft's dinghy. One of the aircraft climbed to send a ditching report as the other remained circling the position, where it remained for the next hour before having to leave, short of fuel, at 4.40 pm.

As soon as the report was received, the standby air sea rescue crew of 294 Squadron at Gambut was called to the operations headquarters and briefed to fly to the position, make contact and shadow the dinghy. Twenty minutes later, Flight Sergeant G.D. Lister RNZAF and his crew were airborne in their Wellington Ic 'O' (W5620) and heading north. Since the circling Beaufighter had departed, Lister had to relocate the dinghy. At 6.20 pm the dinghy was sighted and a report was transmitted to Gambut operations, who ordered a high speed launch to be sent out from Tobruk. Lister dropped a Lindholme Rescue Gear, which Euler and Boffin retrieved. They clambered aboard the larger dinghy, taking their own in tow. Lister remained circling until darkness when he returned to Gambut.

On his return Lister briefed his commanding officer, Squadron Leader G. Thomas, who had taken on the responsibility of co-ordinating the squadron's rescue efforts. At first light the following morning Thomas took off in Wellington 'N' HX 510 to resume the search. His crew included two extra men to act as additional lookouts. He arrived in the area at 8 am and immediately commenced a square search, and on the eighth leg he located the dinghy 10 miles north of the position given by Lister. A Verey flare fired by the survivors had attracted the rescue crew's attention. Thomas dropped further supplies and remained shadowing the dinghy for the next six hours. Sighting reports were sent but a high speed launch failed to make radio contact with the Wellington and had to return to Tobruk.

As the day advanced the weather conditions deteriorated. The sea grew rougher and an increasing haze made it very difficult to keep the dinghy in sight. One man was permanently stationed in the Wellington's astro dome with instructions to keep the dinghy in sight at all costs, and to direct Thomas as he made his turns after diving to drop flame floats and further supplies. Thomas later claimed that it was the presence of the lookout in the astro dome for six hours that enabled the crew to maintain contact with the survivors. The Wellington had to leave the scene before the relief aircraft arrived.

With the visibility reduced to just over a mile, the relief Wellington was unable to relocate the dinghy. At 6.50 pm Wellington 'U' appeared on the scene and soon gained a brief sighting of the dinghy. A sighting report was passed but the crew were unable to maintain contact in the poor visibility and increasing darkness. By plotting the positions given by the searching crews, it was clear that the dinghy was drifting to the north in the direction of Crete. Throughout the night, two more Wellingtons attempted to relocate the dinghy, but without success.

After the disappointments of the night searches, it became clear that more resources must be made available for searching. No. 237 Wing was detailed to provide Baltimore and Ventura aircraft to support the searching Wellingtons, and 47 Squadron sent out Beaufighters throughout the morning of 27 February. Squadron Leader Thomas took off in Wellington 'O' at first light and headed for the small island of Gaidouronesi off the south coast of Crete, where his navigator fixed the aircraft's position. Thomas then commenced a creeping line ahead search pattern, and at 12.10 pm he located the dinghy, which had continued its northerly drift. The position was passed to three high speed launches, which had moved to waiting positions to the south of the area. The Wellington's wireless operator contacted one of the launches and attempted to 'home' it on to the dinghy, but the launch was unable to gain an accurate bearing.

At lunchtime, two Wellingtons and two Beaufighters took off to relieve Thomas. Wellington 'Y', flown by Flying Officer Berry, arrived over the scene and also tried to 'home' the launch, but without success. Eventually, the launch had to return to Tobruk to refuel. Berry remained with the dinghy until dusk but his relief suffered engine problems and had to return to base. Two Hudsons were sent to try and relocate the dinghy, but they were defeated by poor visibility. Contact with the dinghy had been lost again. However, Euler and Boffin had plenty of supplies and water, sufficient to sustain them for many days.

Once Thomas had returned to Gambut, a conference was convened to make arrangements for the night of the 27th and morning of the 28th. The following was decided:

Two Hudsons or Venturas of 459 Squadron to be over the dinghy together throughout the hours of darkness. Three high speed launches to take up waiting positions at sea. One Wellington to take off at 3 am to arrive over the dinghy two hours before first light. Beaufighters in pairs to take off from Gambut at first light continuing throughout the day. Four Baltimores from 237 Wing to arrive at position at first light, and to be relieved by further Baltimores during the day. Two more high speed launches to be at position one hour before first light and to heave to looking out for pyrotechnics and endeavouring to home on search aircraft. One destroyer to leave Alexandria for position, with instructions to home aircraft if necessary. Beaufighter cover for destroyer to be carried out by 235 Wing. Two Wellingtons to standby at Gambut. All aircraft to be given full details of homing procedure to be carried out.

Later that evening Air Headquarters Eastern Mediterranean took over responsibility for the rescue action.

During the night a Ventura obtained a contact on a dinghy responder but flares failed to identify it. At 7 am on 28 February, Wellington 'M' arrived on the scene, soon located the dinghy and reported its position. An hour later the Wellington sent an SOS reporting that the port engine was failing but it was remaining over the dinghy. After 30 minutes it departed to the south in an attempt to reach North Africa, but a further message 20 minutes later said it was ditching. The two Beaufighters of 47 Squadron providing cover for the destroyer, the *Krakowiak*, headed for the ditched Wellington's position. After a brief search the survivors were located; the Beaufighters homed the destroyer to the position and the seven crew members were picked up.

Throughout 28 February, Baltimores of 15 (SAAF) Squadron maintained a continuous patrol over the dinghy. They passed bearings and distances to the destroyer and to the high speed launches, but attempts to 'home' them to the dinghy failed. One Baltimore dived on the surface craft to show them the direction of the dinghy, but neither vessel complied. The high speed launches were operating at their maximum range, and unless they were successful early in their search they had no option but to return due to fuel shortage. Nevertheless, the failure to home them on to the dinghy was very frustrating.

Throughout the afternoon and evening of the 28th, no sightings of the dinghy were made. Venturas continued to search through the night and *HSL 2622* was ordered from Matruh to be at the datum at first light when a Wellington and Baltimores would take over the search. At first light the dinghy was relocated by the last of the night Venturas. In the meantime Wellington 'Y' took off at 5 am with Squadron Leader Thomas at the controls and Flight Sergeant Lister acting as second pilot. On the outward leg the *Krakowiak* was located, and Thomas pressed on to arrive at the estimated position at 7 am, when he commenced a square search.

Conditions for searching were excellent, and on the third leg Lister sighted the dinghy about 4 miles away. The Wellington set up an orbit over the two survivors, who appeared to be well. Thomas was conscious of the previous sightings and subsequent failures to maintain visual contact with the dinghy, so he dropped a long burning flame float to mark the position. He then dropped more supplies, which Euler and Boffin recovered.

After sending a sighting report, the wireless operator, Flight Sergeant Dean, sent a message asking for an immediate relief. Thomas did not want to lose sight of the survivors but was anxious to locate the destroyer and guide it to the dinghy; a second aircraft would allow him to do this. Dean also made contact with *HSL 2622* and transmitted to allow the launch to 'home' to the position, as the launch had failed to see the dinghy or the flares fired by the Wellington. Thomas could see the island of Gaidouronesi in the distance and his navigator obtained a bearing and distance, which were passed to the launch and the destroyer. Dean continued to use a number of frequencies in an attempt to home the two vessels.

At 9 am a Ventura arrived on the scene and immediately set off to locate the high speed launch. Dean continued to transmit the position of the dinghy to the destroyer, which was soon located by two Baltimores that had just arrived on the scene. At 10.45 am Thomas, who was still circling overhead, saw the destroyer, which had been joined by *HSL 2622,* steaming towards the dinghy at full speed. Within minutes the two survivors had been taken on board the launch and were soon transferred to the destroyer, where they met the survivors of the ditched Wellington. Euler and Boffin were uninjured but weak. At 11.12 am Thomas was able to signal that the long rescue had been completed successfully as he turned for Gambut, where he landed two hours later.

During the four days Euler and Boffin were in their dinghy, they drifted 60 miles north and were just 20 miles off the enemy-held southeast coast of Crete by the time they were rescued. Interestingly, no enemy aircraft or shipping was seen despite the extensive air activity generated by the searching aircraft. The rescue amply demonstrated that no effort would be spared to rescue a crew whilst ever a remote chance of success remained. No fewer than 44 aircraft flew during this rescue, generating 229 hours of flying time; one aircraft was lost. Five high speed launches were almost constantly at sea, operating at maximum range. The failure of the launches to 'home' successfully attracted some criticism, but no one could fault the tenacity of the crews.

In a signal to AHQ Eastern Mediterranean, the group captain at Gambut commended the work of the Wellington search aircraft. He concluded his signal with: 'I wish to highly commend the work of

Squadron Leader Thomas whose efforts in finding the dinghy on several occasions after it had been lost touch with were nothing short of amazing and it is due to his unstinting efforts that the operations was brought to a successful conclusion.'

A few weeks later it was announced that Squadron Leader G.D.M.Thomas had been awarded the DFC.

★

By the spring of 1944 Mediterranean Allied Air Forces' three air sea rescue squadrons had all become operational on Warwick aircraft and were redeployed to cover the increasingly large area of operations in the western Mediterranean. No. 283 Squadron was stationed at Hal Far, Malta, and from April 284 Squadron was at Alghero and 293 at Pomligliano, where they provided cover for the Sardinian, Corsican and Italian coasts. Detached flights of Warwicks and Walrus amphibians were created as operations dictated. From mid-March air sea rescue activity over the Adriatic increased considerably. Two flights of United States Catalinas based at Foggia and Grottaglie assisted detachments covering this area. In May 1944, 97 rescue incidents were recorded in the Adriatic, of which 33 were successful.

No. 283 Squadron received its first three lifeboats in May, but the first operational drop did not take place until 22 July, and it was not a success. Further drops by 283 and 284 Squadrons were all equally unsuccessful. It appeared that the parachute release gear was not functioning correctly, contrasting with the success of the lifeboats around the United Kingdom, where the fault was not encountered.

Apart from the airborne lifeboat failures, Mediterranean Allied Air Forces' rescue service had very successful results during June and July 1944, recording 80 successful incidents out of 143, which represented the saving of 235 Allied aircrew as well as 4 of the enemy.

On 6 June 1944 a Walrus of 284 Squadron was lost, but not before the crew had rescued a South African pilot. Lieutenant Peter Louw was flying one of six Spitfires of 242 Squadron engaged on a fighter sweep over Florence. The aircraft's engine temperature started to rise and the Spitfire leader told Louw to return to base with his section leader escorting him. Not long afterwards, the Spitfire's engine caught fire and Louw baled out, landing in the sea 2 miles off the coast at Grossetto. His leader remained overhead until a Walrus appeared, escorted by two USAAF P-39s.

Flying the Walrus (Z 1784) were Warrant Officer C. Paterson and Flight Sergeant E.F. Keeble. They found Louw in his dinghy waving his red flag, and after they alighted safely the South African was hauled on board. What had so far been a straightforward pick-up suddenly took a turn for the worse. The sea was moderately rough and the hull of the amphibian had been damaged when it alighted. As the Walrus prepared to take off, water started to pour in, and Keeble and Louw manned the bilge pumps as Paterson moved inshore to seek calmer water for take off.

As the Walrus approached the coastline, some men appeared to be handling a large calibre cannon so Paterson veered away. The escorting fighters made a pass at the men, who immediately departed, leaving their weapon behind. Paterson made a number of attempts to take off but each failed, and once the pump broke more water poured in and the amphibian started to sink.

The three men clambered into the 'M'dinghy and waited for a high speed launch, which they had summoned. Not long afterwards, Flight Lieutenant Lindsell appeared with his launch *HSL 2597*. The men were soon taken on board and returned to Bastia. This was the second occasion that Keeble had completed a successful rescue, only to lose his Walrus and return by sea (3 November 1943). Sadly, six weeks after being rescued, Peter Louw was lost when his Spitfire crashed into the sea.

OPERATION 'DRAGOON'

Whilst the landings in Normandy were meeting with success, Mediterranean Allied Air Forces were preparing for the invasion of southern France, Operation 'Dragoon'. Based on the experience gained at the landings in Sicily and Italy, a full air sea rescue plan was drawn up for this operation.

A fighter direction ship was provided with a flying control team and two high speed launches, whilst HMS *Antwerp*, equipped as an air sea rescue ship with full VHF control and homing facilities, was stationed between Corsica and the assault area. Aboard the fighter direction ship the air sea rescue flying control team was responsible for initiating any immediate action necessary to effect a rescue and for requesting *Antwerp's* facilities if required, including use of her two pinnaces. Special refuelling facilities were also provided for the air sea rescue launches. Outside the assault area high speed launches, Warwick aircraft and Walrus amphibians were positioned at bases in Corsica and Sardinia.

The landings commenced on 16 August but met with light opposition and the rescue service had little call for its expertise. As soon as Mediterranean Allied Tactical Air Forces was established ashore it took over rescue responsibilities up to 40 miles from the coast, with the aid of three high speed launches and three Walrus aircraft from Calvi.

Few aircraft were lost during the landings in southern France, and the advance inland became so rapid that there was little flying over the sea. Three launches were established at St Tropez, and at the beginning of September the force was joined by the Headquarters of 254 ASRU. From September the Mediterranean Allied Air Force's rescue squadrons (with the exception of 293 Squadron based in Italy) had little operational rescue work to do, and they provided cover mainly for non-operational areas and transit and ferry routes. As a result, four launches were transferred from Corsica to Taranto to cover the intense operations over the Adriatic.

★

The main air sea rescue commitment of the Mediterranean Allied Air Forces from September was in support of operations by the 15th Air Force against some of the most heavily defended targets in Europe. No. 323 Wing of Mediterranean Allied Coastal Air Forces, stationed at Foggia (see plate 38), had control of the major part of the rescue aircraft and rescue launches, with a flight of Catalina amphibians of the 1st United States Emergency Rescue Squadron, a Warwick detachment of 293 Squadron, and an ASRU of high speed launches at Manfredonia. In addition, this Wing could call upon Cants of the Italian Seaplane Wing, USAAF bombers and Walrus of 293 Squadron, which had detachments on the Italian east coast, as well as fighter escorts from the many fighter units in the theatre.

The 293 Squadron detachments on the west coast of Italy were kept busy in October when 32 aircrews were rescued by, or with the assistance of, the squadron's Walrus and Warwick aircraft. By the end of the year, calls on the rescue squadrons and launches began to reduce significantly. Both 283 and 284 Squadrons had little rescue work to do, and it was the same story in the eastern Mediterranean, where the reduced amount of operational flying in the Middle East area continued to decrease and the services of 294 Squadron were rarely required.

Although the airborne lifeboat was little used in the Mediterranean for its initial purpose of bringing survivors into friendly waters, it proved its worth in the heavily mined seas of the northern Adriatic, where rescue launches and amphibians dared not venture.

On the evening of 10 March 1945 Warrant Officer R.E. Chamberlain and his navigator, Flight Sergeant N. Goodyear, of 256 Squadron, dived to attack a barge northeast of Venice. As Chamberlain opened fire with the 20 mm cannons, the nose of his Mosquito XIII (MM527) exploded. The starboard engine was damaged and the aircraft started to lose height, and Chamberlain was forced to ditch at 7.05 pm. Just before the Mosquito touched down, it exploded, throwing the pilot clear but killing his navigator.

Despite suffering from burns and a broken ankle, Chamberlain was able to scramble into his dinghy. The Mosquito crew had managed to transmit a 'Mayday' call alerting the air sea rescue organization. A Warwick took off to search for the dinghy, escorted by a Boston and a Baltimore. With enemy night fighters reported in the area, the search was called off at dusk.

Soon after dawn a Walrus took off, but low cloud hampered the search and it was not until early in the afternoon that a 293 Squadron Warwick (BV 415), flown by Flight Lieutenant A. Rawlings RAAF and escorted by Spitfires, located the dinghy. Rawlings called up a

Walrus (L 2207) and shortly afterwards Flight Sergeant R.J. Bickle and his crew arrived on the scene. Rawlings dropped a series of smoke floats to guide the Walrus to the survivor. Bickle flew over the dinghy and realized that Chamberlain was sitting in the middle of a minefield. He landed the Walrus as near to the edge of the minefield as possible and stopped the engine.

His two crewmen, Flight Sergeants A.S. Goldstein and W. Burnett, inflated the 'M' dinghy and attempted to row across to the injured Mosquito pilot. The current proved to be too strong and the attempt had to be abandoned. Bickle called up the Warwick and Rawlings made a perfect drop of the airborne lifeboat, which landed just 50 yards up wind of the Walrus. Goldstein and Burnett paddled across and boarded the lifeboat. They started the engines and then very carefully picked their way through the minefield and recovered Chamberlain. They then made the equally hazardous journey back to the Walrus. This was almost certainly the only time that an airborne lifeboat was dropped to the rescuers, who then completed a daring rescue.

Bickle took off at 3.45 pm after spending almost two hours on the water and was escorted back to base after the Spitfires had sunk the lifeboat and dinghies.

The month of April brought more success for the airborne lifeboat, including what many believe to be the most remarkable sequence of events in the history of air sea rescue, the rescue of the same pilot on three separate occasions in less than four weeks.

THREE LIFEBOAT RESCUES

On 2 April, Lieutenant R.H. Veitch, a South African pilot of 260 Squadron, was flying his Mustang (KH 592) as part of a formation of 10 aircraft attacking trains in the Maribor–Graz area on the borders of Yugoslavia and Austria. During the rocket attack, Veitch's aircraft was hit by light anti-aircraft fire and the engine started to leak glycol. With Lieutenant K. Foster escorting him, he immediately turned southwest and started to climb. At 7,000 feet he had just crossed the coast of the Istrian peninsula when the engine finally failed.

Veitch baled out and landed in the sea 4 miles from the shore. He climbed aboard his dinghy and waited. Foster had alerted the rescue services and he remained over his colleague until a Walrus, piloted by Flight Sergeant L. Newsome, appeared. It soon became apparent that Veitch was in a minefield and it was impossible for Newsome to alight. A Warwick (HF968), piloted by Flying Officer F.G. Weaver, was scrambled from Foggia and arrived over the dinghy at 11.23 am, escorted by Spitfires. After assessing the situation, Weaver dropped his lifeboat 50 yards from Veitch, who had no difficulty paddling towards it and climbing on board.

A boat appeared from the enemy coast to investigate, but Mustangs drove it off. Veitch, who had no sailing experience, followed the written operating instructions and soon had one of the engines of the lifeboat working. Weaver had included a note telling Veitch to steer for the open sea, where he would be picked up. A Catalina of the US 1st Emergency Rescue Squadron appeared and put down a line of smoke floats for Veitch to follow. When he reached the end of the line, the Catalina was waiting to pick him up. So ended the first of a remarkable trilogy.

Two days later, Veitch was flying as number two to Flight Lieutenant R. Brown on an armed reconnaissance operation near the Yugoslav border when his aircraft was hit by 20 mm ground fire. His aircraft was badly damaged, but he managed to get back to base. The following day he was not so fortunate.

At first light on 5 April, six Mustangs took off to attack road and rail transport in the Ljubliana area. Veitch was flying FB 315 as the formation dived on a train in Kamnik station. Small arms fire hit the engine of his Mustang and he pulled away with the ominous stream of glycol coolant from the engine. With Lieutenant Nelson in company, he climbed to 7,000 feet and headed for the coast, which he crossed at Trieste. Shortly afterwards the engine seized and he was forced to bale out. Nelson watched him descend, hit the water and clamber into his dinghy.

Veitch had landed just 2 miles off the enemy coast and Nelson had to drive off an approaching motor torpedo boat, which he damaged with his rockets. As Nelson was forced to leave through lack of fuel,

Spitfires and Mustangs arrived to relieve him and they were soon in action driving off enemy aircraft and boats. Throughout the morning a succession of Spitfires and Mustangs kept watch over the dinghy. A US Catalina arrived, piloted by Lieutenant Kaminski, but it was soon apparent that a combination of mines and gunfire from ashore made it too dangerous to attempt a landing. It was decided the only chance of rescuing Veitch was to adopt a similar method to the one used successfully three days earlier. A Warwick (BV 449) was scrambled from Foggia and Flying Officer Goldspink and his crew headed north.

Escorted by five Mustangs, the Warwick arrived at 4.15 pm and was at once engaged by anti-aircraft fire from the shore batteries. Despite this interference, Goldspink made a perfect drop and Veitch was soon aboard the lifeboat. He started the engines and immediately set off on a heading of 210 degrees. As the Warwick left, the shore batteries turned their attention to the lifeboat, one salvo landing 200 yards away, and as Veitch sailed out of range of the guns, enemy naval vessels appeared in an attempt to capture the lifeboat. Mustangs and Mosquitos, the latter having just arrived on the scene to provide cover as Veitch sailed away from the coast, drove them off. Undeterred, one returned and a Mosquito was forced to sink it.

Veitch sailed on, stopping the engines as night fell for fear of alerting patrol boats. He donned one of the survival suits, had a meal and was able to get some sleep. At first light he got under way and at 8 am his colleagues on 260 Squadron spotted him. Kaminski and his Catalina appeared with an escort; wary of mines, he dropped a series of smoke floats leading to a clear area and a note was dropped instructing Veitch to follow the smoke.

In poor visibility the Catalina crew and escorting Mustang pilots watched the lifeboat reach the open sea when Kaminski alighted on the choppy water. Veitch had difficulty coming alongside, so one of the Catalina crewmen jumped into the sea and helped the South African swim to the flying boat where he was greeted with the inevitable 'Haven't we met before?' A few days later it was announced that Ray Veitch had been awarded the DFC.

At 6 pm on 30 April the Australian Flight Lieutenant A. Rawlings was scrambled to a position at the north of the Adriatic where a Mustang pilot was in a dinghy. It was Roy Veitch. During an attack near Udine, his Mustang had been hit by ground fire, and shortly after crossing the coast near Trieste he had been forced to bale out. His number two climbed to allow the shore radar stations to take a fix before returning to the dinghy, where he remained until relieved.

The weather was bad and the Warwick was forced to crawl up the coast, reaching the area just before dark and in the midst of an electrical storm. The aircraft came under heavy, erratic flak and in the virtually impossible conditions Rawlings had to abandon the search. Veitch's colleagues, who had been trying to keep the dinghy in sight until the arrival of the Warwick, also had to abandon their vigil due to the weather.

Veitch spent a very uncomfortable night on the rough sea just a few miles off the coast. At dawn, his squadron commander, Squadron Leader Peter Blomfield DFC, with another Mustang in company, appeared overhead and immediately called for assistance. A US Catalina appeared but the sea conditions were too bad for it to alight. It appeared that the dinghy was in a minefield, so a call was put out for an airborne lifeboat. First to arrive on the scene was a Fortress of the 1st Emergency Rescue Squadron. Lieutenant McMurdio dropped the American A-1 lifeboat in the correct position, the squadron's first successful lifeboat drop.

Veitch managed to board the lifeboat and start the engines after some difficulty, but eventually he got under way and headed away from the coast. Since the sea state still prevented the Catalina from completing the rescue, a high speed launch was called and at 11.15 am Roy Veitch was pulled from the water for the third time in four weeks, having survived with the aid of an airborne lifeboat on each occasion.

This remarkable sequence of events was unprecedented in the history of air sea rescue. It prompted his Air Officer Commanding, Air Vice-Marshal 'Pussy' Foster, to suggest that Roy Veitch should become the Honorary Commodore of the Desert Air Force Sailing Club.

*

The rescue of Roy Veitch is an appropriate way to conclude the descriptions of air sea rescue in the European theatre of operations. His experience highlights the lengths that the men of the Air Sea Rescue Services were prepared to go to when one of their colleagues was in distress. It also highlights the likely success of those unfortunate to come down in the sea if they kept their heads and knew the correct drills and the capabilities of their survival and rescue equipment. Above all, it was a desire and resolve to survive that was the fundamental and key factor for a successful outcome after coming down in the sea.

Chapter Fourteen

West Africa

ALTHOUGH WEST AFRICA was never an active theatre of operations, it formed an important part of the southern reinforcement route for aircraft from Britain, and later the United States, to the Middle East. It was also a base for general reconnaissance squadrons tracking down the U-boats attacking convoys in the South Atlantic and those steaming from South Africa to Europe and the Mediterranean. These extensive activities generated a considerable amount of flying from the earliest days of the war and created a clear need for an air sea rescue organization

In August 1941, when the first overseas requirements for rescue craft were presented to the air staff by the Director of Air Sea Rescue, West Africa was allotted four high speed launches for use at Freetown in Sierra Leone and Bathurst in the Gambia. Owing to the overall shortage of marine craft, however, the first two launches did not arrive in West Africa until October 1942, and no more until July 1943.

The first air sea rescue officer was appointed to Air Headquarters, West Africa, in October 1942. A certain amount of rescue work had already been performed by the Sunderland flying boats stationed at Jui, a base situated in a mangrove swamp 15 miles up-river from Freetown, one aircraft being detailed for rescue work as required. These were equipped with locally improvised rescue kits modelled on the Thornaby Bag, made from kit bags or parachute bags filled with food, first aid kits, signal and distress flares, the whole packed round with kapok and secured in a ship's lifebelt.

One of the early rescues accomplished by these Sunderlands was recorded in October 1942 when the passengers of the SS *Oransay* were rescued through the efforts of a searching Sunderland equipped with the makeshift rescue packs. The *Oransay* was torpedoed 300 miles off the coast of Liberia. The next morning a Sunderland sighted six lifeboats, and after dropping supplies, called up a naval vessel to their aid. The following day the Sunderland found nine more lifeboats, and on the third day the remaining three were located. As a result of this effort, all the passengers and crew were saved.

In December 1942, supplies of Lindholme Rescue Gear arrived for use with the Hudson aircraft of 200 Squadron. West Africa was thus the first overseas Command to receive and use official rescue equipment. Whilst the supply of this specialist equipment was of assistance, the efficiency of the rescue service was still hampered by shortage of marine craft. Naval launches provided the bulk of assistance in sea rescue when they could be spared from their established operational duties.

In July 1943, the Air Ministry raised the establishment of air sea rescue units in West Africa to five, each with an allocation of two rescue craft. During July four pinnaces arrived to be added to the two high speed launches already in the Command. This enabled a unit to be formed at Takoradi in the Gold Coast, in addition to those already at Freetown and Bathurst. It was intended that the other two units should be stationed at Pointe Noire and Port Etienne as soon as more launches arrived in the theatre. This still left a large area of the coastline without a service, but the USAAF in Dakar were provided with two rescue launches which could be called on, and the French naval authorities indicated their willingness to co-operate whenever possible.

A most unusual event occurred on 11 August 1943. A Liberator of 200 Squadron failed to return after sending a brief message that it was attacking a submarine. Early the following morning two Sunderland flying boats were searching in the likely area looking for survivors. Flight Sergeant C.H. Wilkinson of 204 Squadron located a dinghy and dropped a Lindholme Gear. Shortly afterwards, the commanding officer of 95 Squadron, Wing Commander Percy Hatfield DFC, arrived on the scene and dropped further supplies. The two Sunderlands 'homed' HMS *Clarkia* to the spot and seven men were taken on board. It transpired that they were the captain, two officers and four ratings from the German submarine *U-468*.

During his interrogation, Oberleutnant zur See Clemens Schamong related how he was transiting on the surface when a Liberator approaching out of the sun surprised him. The submarine's twin 20 mm cannons put up a withering fire but it did not deter the pilot, Flying Officer Lloyd Trigg DFC, RNZAF, from continuing with his attack. The Liberator was set on fire, but Trigg pressed on and straddled the U-boat with his depth charges just before the big bomber crashed in flames into the sea. He had delivered a perfect attack and the submarine sank 10 minutes later, after some 20 members of the crew had jumped into the sea; most perished. Nothing more was seen of Trigg and his crew.

The impact of the Liberator hitting the sea sprung the wing panel releasing one of the aircraft's dinghies. One of the German ratings recovered the dinghy and was able to inflate it. Over the next hour he was able to recover six other survivors from the U-boat.

The seven German survivors were eventually sent to England, where Schamong and his first lieutenant expressed their greatest admiration for the courage of the pilot who continued with the attack when it was already clear that his aircraft was doomed. Based on these testimonies, Lloyd Trigg was posthumously awarded the Victoria Cross, the only occasion it has been awarded based exclusively on the evidence of the enemy.

By January 1944, the final disposition of rescue launches in West Africa had been settled and the total allocation received. Two high speed launches were stationed at Port Etienne, a further two at Freetown, and two pinnaces were at Bathurst. Takoradi and Banana, a Belgian possession, each had one high speed launch and a pinnace. By August, the service had been augmented sufficiently to cover the whole of the West African coast from Port Etienne to Lagos in Nigeria.

SUNDERLAND TOWED HOME

At 11.30 am on 9 April 1944, Bathurst operations ordered pinnace *P 1304* to come to readiness. A Sunderland of 204 Squadron had reported that it was returning with engine trouble and the pinnace was to position along its route in case of further problems. Flying Officer A. Chitty took the pinnace to sea one hour later and proceeded to the African Knoll buoy to await further instructions. At 1.50 pm the Sunderland was seen heading for Bathurst, and Chitty prepared to return. Shortly afterwards, Sunderland K/204 (DW 104) of 204 Squadron on an anti-submarine sweep also reported that it had engine trouble and was returning. Fifty minutes later, the captain, Flight Lieutenant D.W. Pallett, was forced to alight on the sea after jettisoning fuel and the depth charges. In the next message, he reported that the flying boat was drifting south at 2 knots.

Chitty was ordered to proceed to the Sunderland. After plotting the flying boat's position, he calculated that he needed to set a course of 150 degrees to make an interception at 1 am the following day. At 6.45 pm *HSL 2545*, under the command of Pilot Officer Tom Carroll, set sail from Dakar and also headed for the estimated position of the Sunderland. Six hours later, with its greater speed, it overtook *P 1304*. The pinnace then lost radio contact with the high speed launch and with Bathurst Operations, but continued to head for the estimated position.

By dawn, radio contact had not been restored with *P 1304* so Bathurst decided to launch a 95 Squadron Sunderland D/95 to locate the downed Sunderland and home the pinnace *P 1311,* which sailed under the command of Flying Officer R.H. Unkles, the commanding officer of 202 ASRU. On board the pinnace were Sergeant Berrett and Flight Sergeant Edwards, a pilot and wireless operator of 95 Squadron.

In the meantime *HSL 2545* had located the Sunderland; 10 of the 12-man crew were transferred to the launch before the flying boat was taken in tow, but not before the bows had been damaged. Sunderland D/95 arrived on the scene and passed orders to transfer the remainder of the crew to the launch. *HSL 2545* abandoned the tow at 9.45 am through shortage of fuel and headed for Bathurst with the downed crew.

Sunderland D/95 remained on the scene and *P 1304,* listening on 500 kc/s, obtained a bearing and homed to the scene, finally arriving at 2 pm. A tow was established within 30 minutes and the pinnace headed north at 5 knots (see plate 39). Fifteen minutes later *P1311* arrived on the scene and the tow was halted while Berrett and Edwards were transferred by dinghy to Sunderland K/204. The aircraft was successfully boarded through the forward turret despite the heavy swell running at the time. By 4.30 pm the tow was resumed, with *P 1311* in company.

By 7.30 pm the weather had deteriorated and the sea was moderate to rough; speed was reduced to 3 knots. The tow continued at this slow speed for the next 15 hours when *P 1304* was requested to heave to in order that hot drinks could be taken over to the two men in the Sunderland. The tow was resumed and the African Knoll was reached at 3 pm. With a following sea and wind, both Sergeant Berrett on the Sunderland and Chitty had considerable difficulty controlling the tow. The harbour was eventually reached at 5 pm on 11 April and Sunderland K/204 was finally moored 30 minutes later.

Both masters were fulsome in their praise for Berrett and Edwards. Berrett had spent much of the time at the controls of Sunderland K/204 during the difficult 26-hour tow. During the night, the water pump failed and both men had to constantly bale out the water entering the damaged bows by hand under extremely adverse conditions.

Chitty and his crew of *P 1304* had been at sea for 54 hours, but within five hours, at 10.30 pm, they were again ordered to sea as a 95 Squadron Sunderland was returning with engine trouble. Twenty minutes later, the Sunderland crashed as it approached the flare path and *P 1304* spent the next eight hours securing the wreckage and placing marker buoys.

★

This operation to recover the Sunderland reflected great credit on the masters and crews of the two pinnaces. Their efforts spread over a long and arduous period at sea resulted in the saving of a valuable aircraft. A few months later, another Sunderland came down on the sea as a result of engine failure, but the efforts to tow it safely to port met with less success, although the crew were rescued.

AN UNSUCCESSFUL ATTEMPT TO TOW

In July 1944, Flight Lieutenant Tom Harvey and his crew had just completed a short course at 302 Ferry Training Unit when they took off from Oban in Scotland to deliver Sunderland ML 860 to 490 (RNZAF) Squadron based at Jui in Sierra Leone. The 13-hour transit to Gibraltar passed without incident. A few days later, Harvey and his crew were airborne for Bathurst, passing down the coasts of French and Spanish Morocco. Seven hours into the flight, oil was noticed pouring from the port inner engine. The navigator, Flight Sergeant Peter Lee, fixed the aircraft's position off Cape Jurbi in Spanish Rio de Oro where the sea was calm. Harvey decided to alight to investigate the problem, and Bathurst operations were told of his intentions and the position of the aircraft.

The flight engineer, Sergeant Ron Flockhart, inspected the engine and found the oil filter was blocked; after he cleaned it, the Sunderland took off again. However, within minutes the other three engines were similarly afflicted and the big flying boat was landed near the beach. Flockhart set to work to clear the three filters, which were all full of a gummy substance, but it proved impossible to replace one of them. The crew were faced with attempting a take off on three engines and Harvey decided to make for Port Etienne, two hours' flight away and the nearest suitable port.

Several abortive attempts were made to take off from the calm sea in the windless conditions. A request for a spare filter was sent to Bathurst but the crew were informed that a motorboat would arrive from Agadir the next morning to tow the Sunderland into the port for repairs.

To avoid the risk of running aground on Spanish territory, Harvey decided to taxi away from the beach. With the engines at low power to avoid overheating, the Sunderland was taxied out to sea through the night. By the morning, the sea state had deteriorated but the

Sunderland crew were pleased to see a French Catalina appear on the scene and the two aircraft exchanged messages. A boat was expected to arrive later in the day and the Catalina signalled that a Canadian Sunderland, which had taken off from Gibraltar one hour after ML 860, was also down 30 miles to the north with the same symptoms of an oil blockage.

Towards evening, a French motor gunboat arrived on the scene just as the second Sunderland arrived, having taxied to join Harvey and his crew. Tow ropes were passed to each flying boat and secured to the bollards in the bows. Unfortunately, the captain of the gunboat set off too quickly and the two flying boats collided despite swift action by their crews to chop through the ropes. A larger American patrol boat appeared and took the Canadian aircraft in tow, and the French boat resumed the tow of ML 860. Throughout the night, Harvey and his co-pilot, Flying Officer Bert Houtheusen, had nothing but the white light on the mast of the gunboat for reference.

By dawn the sea had become rough with waves of 20 feet from the port beam causing the Sunderland to heel over to starboard. The starboard float took a battering and all the loose kit was stowed to try and reduce the list. Eventually, all the crew except the captain moved to the port wing tip in an attempt to ease Harvey's problem of keeping the flying boat on an even keel. Throughout the day, the crew remained in their precarious position on the port wing.

The next day the wind rose again and it was soon obvious that the starboard float was filling with water, losing its buoyancy and becoming reluctant to lift the wing. With the rising wind, there was a serious risk that the starboard wing would dig into the water and throw the crew off the port wing. Flockhart volunteered to lash himself to the float and pump it out manually, which he did for several hours in spite of being battered by the waves and frequently submerged.

With darkness approaching, it was decided that he must return and he was helped back on board, exhausted by his valiant efforts. The situation worsened during the night; it was clear that it was only a matter of time before the flying boat capsized, and Harvey took the reluctant decision to abandon the aircraft. The dinghy was inflated and the crew transferred to the French gunboat. The Sunderland had been towed for 150 miles in worsening sea conditions, but Agadir was still 50 miles away. Instructions were received to sink the Sunderland and this was eventually achieved using the gunboat's 40 mm cannon.

The Canadian crew had experienced similar difficulties in the bad weather and they too had to abandon the tow with the American patrol boat. Both crews met up with each other at Agadir where they exchanged views on their almost identical experiences. After returning to Gibraltar, investigations into the cause of the two incidents failed to fully explain the mysterious cause of the oil leaks, although there was a strong suspicion of sabotage. Neither crew had been able to obtain a sample from their aircraft so the mystery remained unsolved.

Four weeks after setting off for Jui, Harvey and his crew finally arrived on 490 Squadron where they eventually completed a successful tour of operations.

For his valiant efforts in trying to pump out the starboard float, Sergeant Ron Flockhart was awarded the BEM. Flight Lieutenant Bert Houtheusen remained in the RAF and flew Sunderlands during the Korean War when he was awarded the DFC.

PART FOUR

India and the Far East

Chapter Fifteen

Air Sea Rescue Organization

IN OCTOBER 1941, the first air sea rescue officer was appointed to Air Headquarters, Far East. He managed to create a basic rescue service in Malaya to cover the approaches to Singapore using the only high speed launch sent to Singapore before the outbreak of war, together with a pinnace and a marine tender. In spite of the few resources available, this rescue service did achieve some success and in December 1941, the service's first full month of operations, it rescued or assisted in rescuing 11 pilots from the sea.

In January 1942, 12 pilots were rescued with the aid of Moth aircraft of the Malaya Volunteer Air Force, equipped with smoke floats and lifejackets to drop to aircrew in the sea. On 23 January the service recorded its first rescue of a Hurricane pilot from a 'K' dinghy. After the Moth had kept the dinghy in sight for 30 minutes in poor visibility, a high speed launch picked up the survivor. The January report was the last received before the fall of Singapore, which saw the end of the embryo rescue service.

Early in 1942, Air Headquarters, India, asked for assistance in both surface craft and aircraft for rescue purposes, but the overall shortage in the more active theatres of war made it impossible to give India any immediate assistance. The Air Ministry approached the Admiralty for assistance but it was unable to provide any dedicated resources. However, in April, authority was given to make Royal Navy Walrus amphibians available for rescue purposes by local arrangements, provided other operational requirements could still be met.

There were similar problems with the provision of rescue launches. It was hoped that the first rescue craft would be available early in 1943. In the meantime, the rescue organization had to rely on naval assistance when an emergency arose and the diversion of ships and operational aircraft when the tactical situation allowed.

Until the spring of 1943, the needs of India and the Far East remained the lowest priority, and the scale and availability of equipment and facilities was almost negligible due to the greater activity in the Home Commands and the Mediterranean. Eventually, during the summer of 1943, authority was given for the establishment of India's first Air Sea Rescue Unit (No. 203) with an allotment of two launches. This was followed in October by the establishment of a second unit.

Owing to the diversion of craft for the invasion of North Africa and other operations in the Mediterranean, there were constant alterations to the original allocations, and by the beginning of July 1943 only five high speed launches had reached India. Four more arrived during that month, but from then until January 1944, no further launches arrived and no additional ASRUs could be formed. The situation with the provision of rescue aircraft was equally poor and it was not anticipated that the first Warwick aircraft would be available until June 1944.

Although an air sea rescue officer was at last appointed for the Indian theatre of operations in March 1943, he could do little with the few facilities available in the Command to put a rescue organization into working order. On the whole, the demands for air sea rescue assistance were very light, except in the Chittagong area, where the original 63-foot Miami launches were based. These were called out from time to time to search for aircraft in distress off the neighbouring enemy-held coasts and on their first operational sorties were successful in rescuing three members of a ditched Wellington.

An air sea rescue organization based on the system in force in the United Kingdom, adapted to local conditions, was formed in India by November 1943. During the same month, the first consignment of rescue equipment was sent to India, supplies of both Lindholme Gear and the Bircham Barrel being dispatched. Whilst the lack of specialist aircraft still hampered the development of a full rescue service, the supply of this survival gear enabled any operational aircraft employed on search duties to make a worthwhile contribution in the search for survivors. The successful rescue of a USAAF crew with the aid of a Lindholme Gear was recorded within the same month.

Plans were made to form 292 Squadron in February 1944 with 16 Warwick aircraft and 5 Walrus. It was soon decided that the latter would be supplemented with five Sea Otter amphibians. However, at the end of January came the sad story of the delivery delays for the Warwick, already so familiar to the Mediterranean Air Forces. Eventually, the long-awaited flow of Warwicks began in April, when the first Sea Otters also started to arrive. With these two aircraft types 292 Squadron formed at Jessore. Plans were developed to base detached flights of Warwicks at Bombay and in Ceylon, with the Walrus based in Ceylon. The Sea Otters were to be based at Chittagong to provide a service for aircraft operating along the west coast of Burma. Until sufficient air sea rescue aircraft became available for all these demands, searches continued to be carried out by operational aircraft, carrying the Lindholme Gear whenever possible.

During the early part of 1944, when the Warwick Flight of 292 Squadron was still forming and training, most of the air sea rescue searches around the coast of India continued to be carried out by aircraft of No. 231 Group, mainly Wellington aircraft. In several cases United States Catalina amphibians of the Eastern Air Command assisted in several successful rescues. Both types of aircraft co-operated on 17 April when a Beaufighter crew sent out a distress call in the Chittagong area.

Two Wellingtons were successful in locating the Beaufighter's two-man crew in their dinghy before dropping a Lindholme Gear to them. The survivors clambered into the dinghy and trailed a fluorescene marker behind them to assist the shadowing aircraft throughout the rest of the day as they drifted in a southeasterly direction. Next morning a Wellington relocated them and called up a US Catalina to the rescue. The amphibian alighted alongside the dinghy, took off the survivors and returned them safely to base.

Once 292 Squadron was fully established with rescue aircraft, the rescue organization in South East Asia Command (SEAC) began to improve. By June 1944 more air sea rescue launches had become available and were now based all round the coasts of India and Ceylon from Karachi to Chittagong, with a total of 45 craft. Plans had been established to create two ASRUs in the Persian Gulf and these became operational at the beginning of August. The supply position of ancillary rescue equipment had also improved slowly. The arrival of a number of safety equipment workers greatly eased, and improved, the maintenance of the specialist rescue equipment. Air sea rescue liaison officers were appointed to the staffs of Eastern Air Command, the 3rd Tactical Air Force and the various Group Headquarters. The two major difficulties for the efficient control of the organization were the vast distances involved and the lack of telephone and wireless communication facilities.

Throughout the summer and autumn of 1944, the air sea rescue organization continued to build up. However, the Warwick aircraft were proving very unreliable. Added to the maintenance troubles, which gave this aircraft a high rate of unserviceability in all theatres, the climate of India caused rapid deterioration of the fabric, a trouble that had already been experienced with the Wellington. A replacement was needed urgently, and the need to retain Lancasters in the European theatre forced the authorities to turn to the very long-range Consolidated Liberator, which already equipped the RAF's strategic bomber force in SEAC.

To offset the unserviceable Warwicks, general reconnaissance Liberators and Catalinas were called on for search and rescue work as a temporary measure. In December it was agreed that the Catalinas of 212 Squadron would cover the west coast of India from Karachi, together with detachments at Red Hills Lake near Madras and Bally near Calcutta for operations over the Bay of Bengal in support of the US 20th Bomb Group. In January 1945 this was followed by the move from Italy of two flights of the USAAF 1st Emergency Rescue Squadron, to form the 7th Squadron, equipped with Catalinas and Fortress aircraft capable of carrying the airborne lifeboat. The availability of this squadron and 212 Squadron gave SEAC a long-range rescue capability in the Indian Ocean and Bay of Bengal over a greater distance than the troublesome Warwick could provide. From the beginning of 1945, most of the Warwicks of 292 Squadron were replaced by Liberators.

With the rapid ground advances by the Army in Burma, and the subsequent development of many airstrips to support the ground offensive, the area to be covered by the air sea rescue organization increased dramatically. This created command and control difficulties, having just the one very large squadron operating in the rescue role. It was decided to disband 292 Squadron at the beginning of June 1945 and create seven separate independent Flights based throughout India and Burma. Some of the Flights were equipped with the Warwick or Liberator and others with the Sea Otter.

With the rapid increase of long-range bombing operations by the RAF's Liberator squadrons and the USAAF B-29 Superfortress squadrons, the range limitations of the RAF's air sea rescue launches (see plate 40) became very apparent. As early as May 1944, the Deputy Director ASR had identified the need for a new type of rescue craft for the Indian Ocean and Far East theatre. A specification for a long-range rescue craft, with a range of up to 2,500 miles at 35 knots, was promulgated. It was soon evident that considerable time would elapse before any could be made available so the Admiralty agreed to release a number of Type 'D' Fairmile launches fitted with Packard engines. Arrangements were made to send some to the theatre early in 1945, but serious delays were encountered in a number of critical areas and these were not resolved until August, when the requirement virtually ceased as the war in the Far East came to an end.

As the ground war in Burma moved south, more ports in Assam and Burma became available, allowing the redeployment of some ASRUs or the creation of new ones. Some locations lacked the appropriate facilities, and at Chittagong 229 ASRU operated from a 'mobile' base. The 900-ton barge *Henzarda*, armed with one Oerlikon cannon and a two twin Browning turrets, was moored in the middle of the River Karnaphuli and provided a base for four 68-foot high speed launches. A second barge, *Hatiali*, was on station at Akyab in July 1945. The plan was to move these barges forward as the ground war advanced until reaching the Malayan peninsula. However, as with the plans to establish more Fairmile launches, the end of the war with Japan came before the need to move the barges forward.

Chapter Sixteen

Rescues

FROM THE EVIDENCE of the previous chapter, it will be clear that the scale of air sea rescue operations was significantly less than in the other two main theatres of the Second World War. There were a number of reasons for this. War did not come to the Far East until some 20 months after the outbreak of war in Europe, and after the rapid advance of the Japanese forces it was some months before intensive air operations commenced. Although considerable, air operations were on a much smaller scale than elsewhere and, with such large land masses, transport, fighter and close support operations involved very little flying over the sea, particularly during the years of campaigning in Burma. Unlike northwest Europe and the Mediterranean theatres, there was virtually no war against surface warships and submarines. Also, the rescue services were slow to develop and their capabilities were limited, so there was less chance of aircrew being rescued. Notwithstanding these factors, there were some spectacular and valiant rescues.

BEAUFIGHTERS IN THE SEA

The Beaufighter squadrons of the RAF based in Assam and Burma provided the primary capability to attack Japanese lines of communication during the early years of the Burma campaign. Many sorties flew deep into occupied territory, when as much of the route as possible was flown over the sea to avoid anti-aircraft fire. This introduced its own problems, particularly for aircraft that had suffered damage due to enemy action. However, it was always felt that crews had a better chance of survival if they came down in the sea rather than baling out or crash landing behind the Japanese lines, where capture or death was the most likely outcome. Whenever possible, the crews of damaged aircraft almost always immediately headed for the sea.

Two crews of 177 Squadron were forced to ditch. Both resulted in a successful outcome, but the methods of rescue were very different.

The morning of 16 April 1944 was a big occasion for Sergeant D.H. Smith and his navigator, Sergeant W.A. Storey. They had recently joined the squadron, and just before 8 am they took off from Feni in East Bengal for their first operational sortie. Leading the pair of aircraft on a low-level patrol was Warrant Officer Don Anderson. The two Beaufighters were tasked to attack enemy transports along the Japanese supply route from the coastal town of Sandoway to Prome in the Arakan Yomas.

On arrival at Sandoway, both aircraft attacked the coastal gun battery with cannons. The Japanese were alert and immediately returned fire. The next recollection Smith had was heading out to sea with the starboard engine of his Beaufighter on fire. Unable to maintain height, Smith had little time to prepare for a ditching, but he successfully put the aircraft down on the calm sea. Smith scrambled clear without difficulty but Storey struggled to release his cupola, which had become jammed against the machine gun. He squeezed clear just as the Beaufighter sank. Meanwhile, the dinghy had inflated and Smith was able to pull his navigator on board.

Don Anderson circled overhead and transmitted a distress call. He also appreciated that the dinghy was uncomfortably close to Japanese-occupied territory, with the risk that the crew might drift ashore and be forced to try and walk home. So, by a remarkable piece of flying and physical contortions, he managed to take off his own jungle survival suit, which contained additional escape aids and supplies, wrap it in his Mae West and drop it to the men in the dinghy.

Eventually, with fuel running low, Anderson had to depart, landing to refuel at Ramu, the nearest Allied airfield. Smith and Storey settled down to wait for help. While waiting, they decided to try and paddle to Foul Island, which was visible 6 or 7 miles away. A cache of food and supplies had been placed on the uninhabited island and Royal Navy submarines often patrolled the area. They thought it was just possible that rescue might come from that quarter. However, they had reckoned without the strong current, which seemed to be taking them in the opposite direction. Throughout the rest of the day, Beaufighters of 177 searched for the missing crew, but without success.

Night came and the two men welcomed some respite from the heat. They could hear sounds from ashore and they realized that they were still close to the enemy coast, so much of the night was spent paddling westwards interspersed with periods baling out the dinghy.

At dawn the following morning, two Beaufighters took off to search for the men. They rendezvoused with a US Catalina at Foul Island and searched the area without success. Due to the range from Feni, the Beaufighters had limited time to search, and this undoubtedly hindered progress. At 11 am another Beaufighter took off to continue the search, and four hours later the crew sighted the dinghy and dropped a map marking their present position and a course for Foul Island. Thirty minutes later a Wellington appeared on the scene and dropped a Bircham Barrel with supplies. The sea had become moderately choppy and Smith and Storey had some difficulty retrieving the valuable survival aids.

At 4 pm, 177 Squadron sent another Beaufighter to provide cover for the dinghy and relieve the Wellington, but the aircraft's front hatch blew open and it was forced to land at Chittagong. The aircraft did not finally reach the search area until it was nearly dark, and the crew failed to locate the dinghy.

As soon it was light the next morning, two Beaufighters took off to resume the search. After an uncomfortable night, Smith and Storey had started to consider heading for the coast, which was still well within reach, and taking their chance of an overland journey. Before they had reached a decision, Flying Officer George Taylor and his navigator, Gordon Pirie, appeared on the scene, attracted by the flares fired from the dinghy. Taylor immediately set up an orbit and sent a wireless message back to base. He remained overhead for the next two hours until a US Catalina appeared. The aircraft alighted and successfully picked up the two survivors, but managed to get airborne only after considerable difficulties due to the rough sea state.

Taylor escorted the rescue aircraft out of the area before returning to base. The Catalina took Smith and Storey to Alipore near Calcutta where they were admitted to hospital suffering from severe sunburn and exposure after 45 hours in their dinghy. Both made a full recovery.

The successful rescue of this Beaufighter crew illustrates the relatively 'ad hoc' arrangements for air sea rescue at this stage of the war in India Command. Most of the effort was made by the individual squadron and by using a Wellington from an operational squadron to drop basic survival aids.

★

Three months after the successful rescue of Smith and Storey, another crew of 177 Squadron were forced to ditch and take to their dinghy. Although their subsequent rescue was not as a result of the efforts of the air sea rescue organization, their four-day ordeal in a dinghy fully justifies a place in the annals of survival at sea.

During August 1944, 177 Squadron had moved to Chiringa, south of Chittagong and some 200 miles further south than Feni. This allowed the Beaufighters to attack the vital Japanese lines of communications targets in southern Burma and on the Siam railway – the infamous railway of death.

On 27 August the squadron mounted its first operation against the Siam railway since arriving at Chiringa. Four Beaufighters were tasked, including one flown by Pilot Officer Rupe Horwood RAAF and his navigator, Warrant Officer Chas Bateman. The four aircraft flew in a loose formation at sea level, keeping well out to sea before turning eastwards across the Gulf of Martaban to hit the target at 2 pm. The Beaufighters flew in line astern as they strafed two trains in a wooded cutting near Anankwin, south of Moulmein. Horwood and Bateman were bringing up the rear and the defences were ready for them. As they pulled off the target a large hole appeared in the starboard wing as the Beaufighter came under heavy anti-aircraft fire.

Horwood pulled the Beaufighter into a climbing turn and immediately took up a westerly heading to reach the coast. Over the Gulf
of Martaban the starboard engine failed and with it the wireless, which
was powered by a generator on that engine. They rejected the idea of
ditching off Elephant Point, where there was a cache of food and
survival equipment, and decided to press on. On reaching the Bay of
Bengal a new course was set for Oyster Island, near Akyab.

Abeam Ramree Island the weather started to deteriorate with a
low cloud base and a squally wind. With fuel running out, the two
men took off their parachute harnesses and loosened the latches on
the upper hatch above the pilot's seat and the navigator's cupola, in
preparation for ditching the Beaufighter. At about 6 pm Horwood
ditched the aircraft 15 miles southwest of Oyster Island. The aircraft
settled on the water quickly and both men jumped into the sea and
soon got into the dinghy, which had self-inflated as the immersion
switches were activated. The dinghy was cut loose from the aircraft,
and the drogue was paid out and the packet of fluorescene marker
trailed.

Both men had been slightly injured during the ditching, but this
did not hamper them. Both were wearing the jungle survival suit with
.38 revolvers and Bateman had brought his navigator's bag with maps,
a Verey pistol and cartridges. The standard dinghy rations with
Horlicks tablets were attached to the dinghy. It was soon dark and the
weather had worsened, with waves breaking over the dinghy and
waterproof covering making paddling impossible.

There was little improvement the next day. As they crested the
waves, they could see land in the distance, and throughout the day it
became obvious that they were drifting towards the coast near Akyab.
At dusk a heavy squall changed the direction of drift, and during the
night they were conscious of the dinghy scraping across shoals of
submerged rocks.

The weather on the following day was still poor and the two men
took it in turns to bale out the dinghy as waves kept coming aboard.
On two occasions they heard aircraft above the clouds and they fired
the Verey pistol, more in hope than expectation. They did see a
Beaufighter late in the day but their final cartridge failed to ignite.

The squadron had mounted patrols throughout the three days, but the awful weather thwarted all their attempts to locate their two colleagues.

On 30 August, their fourth day in the dinghy, the weather improved and the sea was calmer. Both men were exhausted and they slept through most of the day. Towards midnight, under a clear sky, the dinghy drifted on to a beach. Unsure whether they were still behind enemy lines, they realized that they must get ashore quickly. Although with very stiff muscles and finding it difficult to stand, they dragged the dinghy up the beach to some sand dunes. Finding a hollow, they pulled the dinghy over themselves to form a shelter and rested.

The next morning they were awakened by the excited voices of natives, who soon made it clear that the Japanese were inland and close by. They quickly deflated the dinghy and buried it with their Mae Wests before the natives – local fishermen – showed them a more suitable hiding place. Bateman was able to pinpoint their position near Alethangyaw on the border between India and Burma. The dinghy had drifted almost 60 miles north during the monsoon. The men hid and the natives disappeared, promising to return at dusk. This presented them with a difficult dilemma since it was always possible that the Japanese could be alerted. However, the natives returned as promised and brought food and water.

After Horwood and Bateman had finished a small meal, the party set off northwards along the beach. The Beaufighter crew had discarded their boots in the dinghy for fear of damaging it so they had to walk in their stocking feet. After 2 miles they turned inland and soon arrived at a village, where the headman was clearly nervous of their presence. At dawn the two men, with three native guides, set off north for the River Naf. As they approached, two Gurkha soldiers stepped out of the jungle and challenged them with rifles. The two men soon established their identity and were led to the river where a camouflaged rowing boat was anchored. They boarded and were taken to a small island where they found themselves at an advanced Allied army camp.

A British captain met them, and soon they were eating a meal and, after a rudimentary bath, given clean clothing and footwear. In the meantime, the three native fishermen had been waiting patiently on the riverbank. The captain invited them over; he sat at a small table and divided the Burmese silver coins from the money belts carried by Horwood and Bateman into three equal piles. Each native stepped forward, shook hands and received his share with the profound thanks of the Beaufighter crew. Later in the morning, a landing craft arrived from Maungdaw, collected the two survivors and took them to safety.

Both men returned to operations and Rupe Horwood was awarded the DFC in January 1945.

★

RESCUE HAMPERED BY TURTLES

Three Liberators of 354 Squadron took off from Cuttack, 120 miles south of Calcutta, at midday on 22 April 1945 to carry out an anti-shipping sweep off the lower Burma coast south of Moulmein. Captain of aircraft 'J' (EV 863) was Canadian Flight Lieutenant F.E. Taylor with a mixed crew of RAF and RCAF aircrew. The Liberators attacked a coaster and severely damaged it, putting the steering gear out of action, and causing the crew to jump overboard.

The aircraft set off on the long return journey but Liberator J/354 failed to return and Cuttack operations staff informed ASR Control. The aircraft had earlier passed a message giving an estimated time of arrival at base as midnight, but a faint SOS was picked up by Cuttack at 10.48 pm. The aircraft had been heading 307 degrees and on the assumption that the aircraft had ditched shortly after sending the SOS, a probable position of ditching was calculated. At 3 am Flight Lieutenant A. Yoxon and his 354 Squadron crew took off in their Liberator to head for the area and set up a square search. The squadron launched three more Liberators at first light to join the search.

A large-scale effort was mounted throughout 23 April when a 212 Squadron Catalina, three from the 7th USAAF Emergency Rescue Squadron and the RAF HSL J41 of 227 ASRU all headed for the area.

Late in the afternoon a 354 Squadron Liberator reported seeing seven survivors in the sea. The rescue Catalinas and the high speed launch were ordered to the area, and the Navy Office at Calcutta diverted a corvette to the position.

In the event that the Catalinas could not alight due to the sea state, a 292 Squadron Liberator was placed on standby ready to drop a Lindholme Gear to the survivors to assist in their survival until the high speed launch could reach their position. With no further news from any of the searching aircraft, this Liberator was ordered to take off to maintain contact with the survivors. At 6.30 pm the Liberator that had made the first sighting returned to base and the crew were interrogated. They reported seeing six survivors in 'K' dinghies with one man in the water. As they left the position, one of the Catalinas arrived and flew low over the scene. The relief Liberator soon joined it. Messages were received from both aircraft that no survivors had been seen in the area. As the official report commented, this was 'an amazing state of affairs'. At first light on 24 April, three US Catalinas took off to set up a parallel track search of the area.

HSL 341 had sailed from Maiskal Island, near Calcutta, at 10.15 am on the first morning and taken up a waiting position by the Western Channel Light Vessel. Ten hours later it received the message that the Liberator was circling a group of survivors and it immediately headed for the area. After seven hours of sailing, the launch crew spotted the Liberator and closed to a position marked by flares. A landing craft, *LST 163,* was also on the scene and the aircraft reported that this vessel had picked up a survivor. The captain was questioned and he confirmed that there were no survivors, but he had picked up a barrel. The *LST* then proceeded on its way and *HSL 341* hove to in order to conserve fuel and to await further instructions from the searching aircraft.

As daylight broke, the launch crew sighted a yellow object and recovered a partially inflated 'K' dinghy. Another dinghy was sighted, and en route to retrieve it, a Bircham Barrel was found. The dinghy proved to be a Lindholme Gear. Three Catalinas appeared on the scene and the launch remained in the area ready to assist.

During the day, the captain of the 354 Squadron Liberator, which had made the initial sighting, was questioned again. He remained positive that survivors had definitely been spotted, some of them waving. Two 'K' dinghies and two Bircham Barrels had been dropped and had fallen about 20 yards from the survivors. This heightened the mystery, because these dinghies and the Bircham Barrels were those picked up by *HSL 341* earlier in the day.

Despite the determined efforts of the searching aircraft, no sightings had been made during the day and an offer from HQ No. 222 Group to provide a further three Catalinas based at Redhills Lake for the search on the following day was accepted. An air sea rescue Liberator took off to be in the search area at dawn, when four Catalinas of 7th Emergency Rescue Squadron took off. This gave a total of eight aircraft in the area, but no sightings were made throughout the day.

The captain of one of the Catalinas sent a message at 5.30 pm informing his headquarters that he had completed his search and was returning to base. Flight Lieutenant W. Shackel and his 191 Squadron crew, flying JX 355, had been airborne from Redhills Lake for almost 18 hours. Flying at 1,000 feet they had searched all day but seen nothing. They had flown 60 miles away from the search area and were on the return flight when two dinghies with survivors were sighted. The aircraft dropped a sea marker and some emergency rations and sent a signal to base seeking approval to land. However, before receiving a reply, Shackel decided to alight and pick up the survivors. The aircraft was nearing its limit of endurance and he felt that the survivors could not be left for another night at sea. He landed safely and was airborne again 24 minutes later with five survivors on board. A signal was sent asking for an ambulance to meet the aircraft, which landed at Coconada at midnight after being airborne for 22 hours. All the survivors had been injured during the ditching and were suffering from exposure.

Rescue control was informed that only five of the 10-man crew had left the aircraft and so the search was called off. The Liberator captain, Flight Lieutenant Taylor RCAF, his navigator, Pilot Officer B. Bjarnason RCAF, and three RAF gunners, Sergeants R. Leonard, L. Whalen and R. Baril perished and were posted as missing.

A possible explanation of the sighting of seven 'survivors' was found later, when a Catalina pilot visiting the search and rescue cell at Headquarters Strategic Air Force reported a number of false sightings being made by crews. These had all turned out to be turtles. Some hundreds of them were seen in the area, many lying on their backs and exposing a large expanse of yellow belly and waving their flippers. It is not unusual for some of these creatures to measure up to 8 feet by 5. A number grouped together could easily have been mistaken for a group of survivors when seen from 200 feet.

There is no doubt the sighting of the seven 'survivors' entailed considerable wasted effort, since all the aircraft and launches available were concentrated into this small area. In the event, it was a chance sighting that led to the rescue of the five men. Fifteen long-range search sorties were flown during the three-day period, some of almost 24 hours' duration. In addition, a high speed launch and a corvette were employed, together with a number of merchant ships. The rescue launch had been at sea for almost three days. Once again, the details of this search and rescue operation graphically highlight the prodigious efforts the rescue organization was prepared to go to whilst ever there was the remotest possibility of finding survivors.

★

TWO CRASHED USAAF BOMBERS

Just after midnight on 25 March 1945, crews returning from bombing operations with the USAAF 7th Bombardment Group reported seeing a B-24 Liberator, No. 28, pull out of the formation with one engine feathered and head for the coast. The formation had taken off four hours earlier for a 16-hour mission. No radio calls were intercepted from the bomber and by the time the returning crews had made their reports, the Liberator had been missing for 12 hours.

It transpired that 6 of the 10-man crew had baled out of the bomber over the sea with the remainder staying on board. The aircraft was ditched in calm water; three of the men got clear but one died of multiple injuries. The captain went down with the aircraft.

Two Catalinas of the USAAF 7th Emergency Rescue Squadron took off for the scene and after a two-hour search four men and one body were recovered. At 11.20 am one of the rescue aircraft spotted some survivors ashore. It alighted in a river to the west of their position and the captain and one other crew member went ashore to contact them. They were away for nine hours due to the almost impenetrable undergrowth.

As the search was continuing, reports were received that a B-29 Superfortress had crashed at 9.40 am 30 miles from the scene of the search for the Liberator. From subsequent reports it appeared that two bombers had collided. One lost 4 feet from a wing but was able to return to base for an emergency landing. However, four of the crew had baled out into the sea. The second Superfortress lost a complete wing and went into a spin. Only two parachutes were seen before the aircraft hit the water.

Two Catalinas of 212 Squadron were scrambled to search for the Superfortress crews, and two high speed launches from 227 ASRU immediately put to sea. With this latest incident happening near the scene of the Liberator episode, and men scattered after baling out, a considerable amount of confusion arose about the location of the survivors and to which aircraft they belonged.

Shortly after taking off, Squadron Leader P. Rumbold, captain of Catalina H/212 (JX 282), received a message that survivors had been seen in the water and he immediately headed for the area. He arrived off the coast to find that the second Catalina, B/212 (JX 324), captained by Flight Lieutenant Cecil Bradford RCAF, had located wreckage scattered over a large area and two parachutes spread on a nearby beach. Soon afterwards two survivors and four natives were seen on the beach and Bradford dropped a flare to mark their position. Rumbold decided to land and anchored a half-mile offshore in a moderate sea. A dinghy was launched and Flight Sergeant M. O'Dell and Corporal Morris set off for the shore, where they recovered the two survivors (Sergeant McLeary and Corporal Gray), who were soon transferred to the Catalina and given first aid treatment. Bradford carried out a search of the area while Rumbold remained on the sea, but no further survivors were located so H/212 took off at 4 pm.

Bradford was ordered to search further to the north. His crew soon located two more survivors, one on land and another in a dinghy a short distance off the coast. B/212 landed and the two survivors (First Lieutenant Coulter and Second Lieutenant Walls) were picked up. Bradford resumed the search and soon located the USAAF Catalina anchored in shallow water. He landed again and two members of the US aircraft rowed out to brief him that the aircraft's captain and one other had set off to locate a parachute a mile inland. Bradford decided to take off and look for them and B/212 was airborne again at 5.20 pm. The Catalina crew soon located a native boat with five white men in it (three survivors and the two Catalina men) and they were directed to the anchored US Catalina. Bradford continued his search, but no other survivors were found.

In the meantime, a searching Superfortress had intercepted Rumbold, and the US crew beckoned him to follow. Another survivor was spotted inland and B/212 was waterborne at 5.10 pm. The Australian navigator, Warrant Officer J. Burke, swam ashore and made his way to the survivor. Pilot Officer C. Lloyd and Sergeant C. Stanley manned a dinghy and paddled ashore, where they recovered Burke and USAAF Sergeant Hyde. After a further search, both 212 Squadron Catalinas returned to Bally as darkness fell. At the end of the first day, it was assessed that two men who had baled out of the Liberator and one from the Superfortress were still missing.

Throughout the next day, two RAF Catalinas, a Liberator and six USAAF aircraft continued the search. One or two parachutes were seen and an abandoned dinghy, but no survivors. At first light on 27 March, a 292 Squadron Liberator took off followed shortly after by Squadron Leader Rumbold and his crew in Catalina H/212. At 11 am the Liberator crew spotted a survivor on the beach and dropped Bircham Barrels to him. Rumbold was directed to the scene where he saw the Liberator circling. He alighted and soon had Lieutenant W.J. Davies of the 678th Bomb Squadron on board. This accounted for all the men who had baled out of the Superfortress, and Rumbold continued to search for those still missing from the Liberator. That evening, pinnace P 60 reported hearing whistles in response to the launch's siren, but only discarded parachutes were seen.

The search continued for the next two days but no survivors were seen. At interrogation, those who had been picked up reported that the two men still missing had baled out at a very low altitude and their parachutes had not been seen to open. Four days after the Liberator had crashed, the search for survivors was called off.

This complex operation in a particularly difficult area near the Sundarbans in the Ganges Delta resulted in the rescue of 12 survivors and the recovery of one body. The air sea rescue aircraft flew 17 sorties and three RAF rescue launches were employed.

Three weeks before this rescue, Bradford and his crew had been involved in another dramatic rescue. Late in the afternoon of 2 March, he and his Canadian navigator, Flight Lieutenant Maurice Shnider, were called to the operations room to be briefed for a 'special sortie'. A B-29 Superfortress had sent a distress call after which nothing further was heard. Catalina B/212 was airborne from Bally at 9.30 pm, heading for the area 920 miles away. It reached the position given by the USAAF bomber after a flight of seven hours, and a search pattern was established. At 7.30 am the following morning, a distress flare was seen by the second pilot and, on investigation, a large dinghy was sighted with six survivors. While this dinghy was being circled, two other men were seen in the water a mile from the dinghy. Bradford immediately landed and picked up the two exhausted men before taxiing to the dinghy to recover the other six survivors.

Soon after the aircraft was airborne, a Liberator of 292 Squadron was seen circling and dropping a smoke float. On investigation, two more men were seen in the sea. Initially Bradford decided not to land since the aircraft was overloaded, but attempts to contact a nearby Allied submarine failed. The men had been in the water for many hours and Bradford decided to risk a landing, which was successful. The Catalina crew pulled the two men on board. Once airborne again, the search was resumed and a message sent to base, 'Ten B-29 hitch-hikers aboard. One still missing.'

The survivors were fed on bacon and eggs and hot tea, and Bradford and his crew set off on the long return journey through the night. Bradford landed the Catalina at Bally after a flight of a few minutes under 24 hours, and with only a few gallons of fuel left in the aircraft's tanks.

Following their parts in the two complex rescues, both Bradford and Shnider were awarded the DFC.

★

SAVED BY FLOATING WRECKAGE

By the middle of July 1945, the 14th Army had advanced to the south of Burma and Rangoon had been captured. The Japanese forces retained control of a small area on the eastern side of the Gulf of Martaban where they relied almost entirely for re-supply on the railway from Siam.

On the morning of 17 July, four Mosquito fighter bombers of 110 Squadron were tasked to attack the railway with delay-fused 500 lb bombs at Apalon, 50 miles to the south of Moulmein, in the narrow coastal strip of lower Burma that borders Siam, now Thailand. The aircraft took off from an airstrip south of Mandalay for the 500-mile route to the target. Flying Mosquito 'N' (RF 705) as number two in the formation were Flying Officer Chas Locke and his navigator, Warrant Officer Nick Nicolson.

The crew were wearing their bulky 'Beadon' jungle survival suits, with side arms, and their parachutes. This left little room in the cramped cockpit, and with only a very short part of the route over the sea they elected not to wear their Mae West lifejackets.

After two hours' flying, the four aircraft turned towards the target and opened the bomb doors. The station and sidings at Apalon came into view and Locke commenced his shallow dive. As he released the four bombs, there was a loud explosion in the bomb bay and the aircraft staggered over the trees with both engines misfiring. Almost certainly, the delay fuse on one of the bombs had malfunctioned and the bomb had exploded instantaneously, immediately below the Mosquito.

Locke pulled up as the fuel pressure warning lights glowed red, and Nicolson immediately switched to the wing fuel tanks as one of the formation called that fuel was pouring from the fuselage. Most of the fuel in the wing tanks had been used during the transit to the target and Locke estimated that he had barely 20 minutes left. He was unable to close the damaged bomb doors as he turned immediately to return by the shortest route to Allied occupied territory, but this involved a 100-mile crossing of the Gulf towards Rangoon.

The other Mosquitos flew in formation with Locke and one climbed to transmit a distress call to allow ground radars to obtain a fix of the position. With land appearing on the horizon after 20 minutes, the fuel was finally exhausted and the engines spluttered and stopped. Holding the tail well down, Locke put the plywood bomber down on the sea, but when the nose dipped the open bomb doors churned into the waves and the aircraft split open, leaving two large jagged pieces floating on the surface. The other crews watched in dismay as a tragedy appeared to unfold.

As the aircraft broke up, Locke found himself underwater with wreckage striking him. He pushed towards the lighter patch above but his cumbersome parachute and survival suit hampered him. He eventually managed to struggle free and, with lungs bursting, he finally broke the surface. Dazed with concussion and shock, he saw the rear fuselage and tail a short distance away with the automatically inflated dinghy drifting away. With broken limbs and a serious head wound, he was in no state to recover the dinghy. There was no sign of Nicolson.

As he struck out for a large piece of wrecked Mosquito, he found that his legs were useless. He eventually managed to flop on to a piece of wreckage and pull himself up into the shelter of the broken fuselage. He was in great pain and knew that if he fainted again, he could fall into the water and drown. He wedged himself inside the fuselage and waited as the water lapped around him. After 40 minutes the last Mosquito left, having seen no signs of movement, and the squadron diarist commented, 'It is feared that we have lost another fine crew.'

Locke took stock of his situation and realized that both legs were broken; he was also in intense pain from his back. He managed to ram some sulphonomide tablets into a gaping wound in his leg, which appeared to stop the bleeding, and he crushed the last tablet and rubbed the powder into his head wound. Within an hour two Spitfires appeared overhead at 1,000 feet, but made no indication that they had seen him before finally flying off.

He soon became aware that the fuselage was gently sinking as water seeped into the empty fuel tanks, which were keeping the wreckage buoyant. Slowly the water rose up to his armpits and he noticed that the sea was getting rougher. The two Spitfires suddenly reappeared and started to dive towards him, waggling their wings. Now it was a race against time as the water level continued to rise. A Lysander appeared and dropped a dinghy close by, but his injuries prevented him from leaving the fuselage to recover it.

With the water up to his neck and the wavelets splashing his face, a Sea Otter arrived and started to circle in preparation to land. It finally alighted 100 yards from the wreckage and began to taxi towards the dinghy before stopping 30 yards away. The gunner appeared in the open nose position and threw a rope, which fell well short. The Sea Otter taxied round again and made a number of attempts without success. The amphibian had roughened the water and Locke was in danger of drowning when, at the eighth attempt, he was able to grasp the rope and was hauled in. The two crew members got him aboard and he was given first aid as the Sea Otter made a number of attempts to take off before finally succeeding. Just as the Sea Otter recovered Locke, a high speed launch appeared on the scene, but it was decided to try and get him to hospital as quickly as possible.

Locke had been in the sea without any life-saving equipment for almost six hours and he could not have lasted much longer. He was landed at Mingaladon and taken to a mobile field hospital in Rangoon where it was discovered that he had a fractured spine, a broken right ankle, a smashed left knee and concussion. He later made a full recovery, but his navigator was never found and was listed as killed in action.

★

With the Japanese surrender on 15 August, the plans for the amphibious landings on the Malayan coast, Operation 'Zipper', were shelved. Also, plans to deploy a long-range bomber force for the final onslaught on the Japanese mainland, 'Tiger Force', together with Lancaster and Catalina air sea rescue squadrons to support it, were also overtaken by events. Thus the rescue of Locke was one of the final episodes for the Air Sea Rescue Services in the Far East.

In keeping with so many other military aspects of the war in the forgotten theatre of the Far East, the air sea rescue organization was low on the list of priorities and it had to take the necessary equipment only when the demands of other theatres had been met. It was a constant struggle to develop and maintain an efficient rescue service in a theatre of operations that many officials, sat in the United Kingdom, simply did not understand. They found it difficult to comprehend the influence of the weather and the vast scale and distances involved, and the allied problems these created for the communication systems, which were such a vital link in the timely rescue of aircrew in distress. It says much for those involved that the rescue organization was able to function at all.

Before the formation of the Air Sea Rescue Service in SEAC in June 1943, no record was maintained of rescue operations in that area. From June 1943 until the end of the campaign in August 1945, 150 aircraft, involving 700 aircrew, were recorded in distress over the sea. In 88 of these incidents successful rescues were effected with 327 aircrew saved, representing 50 per cent success. Interestingly, the majority of the successful rescues were completed with the aid of operational rather than air sea rescue aircraft. Although not forming part of the rescue services, credit must be given to the rescue work undertaken by the general reconnaissance Catalinas. In co-operation with naval and merchant vessels, 1,304 shipwrecked mariners were saved during the 27 months leading to the end of hostilities in the area.

Epilogue

The manner in which aircrew found themselves suddenly in the alien environment of the sea, and the methods used for their subsequent rescue, were very varied. The men who manned the numerous air sea rescue units rescued the majority; others owed their rescue to operational aircraft, RNLI lifeboats, fishing trawlers and passing ships. The enemy rescued some. However, the survivors all share a common experience and unique bond that the very great majority of others cannot, understandably, appreciate or relate to from the comfort of serviceable aircraft or their armchairs.

A universal feeling experienced by survivors was an immense gratitude to the countless people who were both directly and indirectly involved in their rescue. Many were conscious that they would never have been saved had they not been able to survive in the sea before rescue arrived. For this they owed their lives to the efficiency of their lifejackets and dinghies.

The firm of P.B. Cow & Co., rubber and plastic engineers, specialized in the manufacture of dinghies and other air sea rescue apparatus. Scores of aircrew wrote to the firm expressing their heartfelt thanks, and many others called in to the factory just outside London where they met the chief designer, Charles Robertson, and his staff. It was clear to him that most of them had suffered terrible ordeals without gaining any form of recognition. He suggested that an exclusive club should be formed, and so the company's managing director, Lieutenant Colonel F. Baden-Powell, founded the Goldfish Club in November 1942. Gold represented the value of life; fish, the sea. Baden-Powell became club president and Charles Robertson agreed to be the honorary secretary.

Initially, membership was restricted to RAF aircrews, but applications flooded in from all over the world and all members of the Allied air forces and naval air arms became eligible. The office staff handled administration in their own time. They observed that there was a considerable increase in applications a few days after a major air operation. The club became so popular during the later years of the war that applications were handled officially through embassies and dominion offices, and special divisions were formed in Australia, Canada and the United States.

Robertson designed a waterproof membership card and a badge. The badge consisted of a small goldfish, with an upswept wing attached, set above two blue wavy bars to represent the sea, with space to add a third bar to denote a second ditching. Metal or other raw materials were too scarce so the badge was made of cloth. In response to an appeal in the *Daily Express*, 23 redundant dinner suits were sent in and the material was cut into small rectangles with the club's badge embroidered, the gold and silver thread being supplied by the girls in the factory. USAAF personnel who qualified were allowed to wear the badge on their uniforms. Air Ministry could only approve the badge as an 'unofficial' one, but many men attached the badge to their uniform breast pocket or wore it on their flying suit.

Often, where a bomber crew had ditched and been saved from their dinghy, the crew emblazoned the club badge on their next aircraft. Many aircrew carried their badges and membership cards with them as a lucky charm.

The crews of the air sea rescue launches were not eligible although they saved the lives of many aircrew. Carved crests were presented to them and they fixed them to the bridges of their craft.

Hundreds of aircrew were made members posthumously, their applications being forwarded by surviving crew members. Whenever applications came from men recovering in hospital, Charles Robertson never failed to send books with his replies to the patient.

The Goldfish Club still flourishes today, with a few new members qualifying each year. The club holds regular reunions and publishes a quarterly newsletter keeping this unique group of men in touch with each other.

Bibliography

OFFICIAL SOURCES AT THE NATIONAL ARCHIVES

ADM 1/11504	Royal Navy Awards
ADM 1/14578	Honours and Awards
ADM 1/29411	Award of DSC to Flt Lt D.A. Jones RAF
ADM 334/11	Air Sea Rescue
AIR 2/4733	Air Sea Rescue – Walrus Aircraft
AIR 2/4742	Sea Rescue Service – Formation
AIR 2/4745	Air Sea Rescue – Aircrew Training
AIR 2/5005	Air Sea Rescue Squadron – Formation
AIR 2/5267	Formation of Directorate of Sea Rescue
AIR 2/6257	Air Sea Rescue Services – Organization
AIR 2/8092	Experiences of Rescued Crews – Bomber
AIR 10/3457	The Airborne Lifeboat Mk I Instructions for Ditched Crew
AIR 10/3458	The Airborne Lifeboat Mk II Instructions
AIR 10/5553	Air Sea Rescue – Air Historical Branch Narrative
AIR 14/1617	Ditching Reports – Lancaster
AIR 14/1620	Ditching Reports – Halifax
AIR 14/1621	Ditching Reports – Wellington
AIR 15/676	Air Sea Rescue – 16 Group
AIR 20/214-8	Air Sea Rescue Historical Records
AIR 20/4320	Air Sea Rescue Reports
AIR 23/1143	Air Sea Rescue Service (Middle East) – General Policy

AIR 23/1492	Air Sea Rescue Narratives – NACAF
AIR 23/4492	Operational Rescues
AIR 23/5267	Air Sea Rescue Policy
AIR 23/5516	Operation 'Husky' – Air Sea Rescue
AIR 23/5627	Air Sea Rescue – 614 Squadron
AIR 23/6080	Air Sea Rescue Organization – Operations
AIR 23/7421	RAF Station Gambut – Air Sea Rescue Reports
AIR 27/ Numerous	RAF Squadron Operational Record Books
AIR 28/77	Operations Record Book – RAF Bircham Newton
AIR 28/409	Operations Record Book – RAF Kalafrana
AIR 28/506	Operations Record Book – RAF Luqa
AIR 29/444	Operations Record Book – 26 ASRU Felixstowe
AIR 29/449	Marine Craft Units
AIR 29/450	Air Sea Rescue and Marine Craft Units
AIR 29/451	No. 254 Air Sea Rescue Unit
AIR 51/1	Air Sea Rescue – Instructions
AIR 51/31	Air Sea Rescue – Investigations and Reports
WO 203/3638	Air Sea Rescue Operations and Airborne Operations

PUBLISHED SOURCES

Ashworth, Chris, *RAF Coastal Command 1936–1969* (Patrick Stephens, 1992)

Beardow, Keith, *Sailors in the RAF* (Patrick Stephens, 1993)

Bowyer, Chaz, *Men of Coastal Command* (William Kimber, 1985)

Burtt-Smith, Jim and French, John, *A Drop in the Ocean* (Leo Cooper, 1996)

Daniels, Stephen, *Rescue from the Skies* (HMSO, 1993)

Franks, Norman, *Another Kind of Courage* (Patrick Stephens, 1994)

Franks, Norman, *Beyond Courage* (Grub Street, 2003)

Franks, Norman, *Conflict over the Bay* (William Kimber, 1986)

Franks, Norman, *U-Boat versus Aircraft* (Grub Street, 1998)

Galea, Frederick, *Call-Out* (Malta at War Publications, 2002)

Low, Ronald and Harper, Frank, *83 Squadron* (Compaid Graphics, 1997)

Milberry, Larry, *The Royal Canadian Air Force at War* (Canav Books, 1990)

Nesbit, Roy Conyers, *The Strike Wings* (William Kimber, 1984)

Pilborough, Geoffrey, *History of RAF Marine Craft, Vol. 2* (Canimpex, 1987)

Rowe, Alan, *Air-Sea Rescue in World War Two* (Alan Sutton, 1995)

Sutherland-Brown, Athol, *Silently into the Midst of Things* (The Book Guild, 1997)

Van Hees, Arie-Jan, *Tugs and Gliders to Arnhem* (privately published)

Index

Italic page numbers refer to illustrations.

Aboukir 185
Abu Sueir 189
Aden 15, 18, 190
ADGB *see* Air Defence of
    Great Britain Command
Admiralty
    creation of Air Sea Rescue
        Service 20, 22
    rescue boats 24, 63, 64,
        109–10
Air Defence of Great Britain
    Command (ADGB) 62,
    169, 174
Air Headquarters Eastern
    Mediterranean 229
Air Headquarters Malta 220
Air Ministry 28, 44, 69
    air rescue boats 60
Air Sea Rescue Agency
    (United States) 114
Air Sea Rescue Flight 185–7,
    188–90, 208–9, 210, 226
Air Sea Rescue Marine Craft
    Units (ASRMCUs) 68
Air Sea Rescue Service 3
    badge 15, 115
    established 19–24
    organizational changes 169
air-to-surface vessel (ASV)
    radar 23, 44–5, 59, 117,
    126
airborne lifeboats 6, 69–85
    development 61
    Mediterranean 232, 235–40
    Northwest Europe 152–5,
        157, 178–9
    USAAF 114–15

aircrew losses
    1941 24
    1942 26, 28
    Battle of the Atlantic 118
    Battle of Britain 20
    bombing offensive against
        Germany 147
    creation of Air Sea Rescue
        Service 23
    USAAF 111–14
Ajaccio 220
Akyab 254, 259
Aldis lamp 71, 223
Alethangyaw 260
Alexandria 191
Alghero 232
Algiers 190, 192, 220
Amiriya 188
Anderson, Warrant Officer
    Don 256
Andrews, Lieutenant Andy
    77, 78
Anson aircraft 28, 60–2
anti-submarine patrols *see* U-
    boats
HMS *Antwerp* 234
Anzio 224
Apalon 268
Arakan Yomas 256
Archangel 118
Armstrong, Flight Lieutenant
    Howard 132–3
Army Co-operation
    Command 19, 52
Arnhem 175
Arnold, General 110
Arromanche 170

ASDIC 117
ASRMCUs *see* Air Sea
    Rescue Marine Craft
    Units
Assam 255
Aston, Sergeant 55
ASV *see* air-to-surface vessel
    radar
Atkins, Leading Airman R.
    166
Atlantic Gap 117
Augusta 216
Azores 142, 181

B17 Fortresses 110–12
    ditched 118–20, 151–5,
        163–4, 215
    as rescue craft 113–14
Baden-Powell, Lieutenant
    Colonel F. 272
Baker, Pilot Officer K. 193–5
Bally 253, 266, 267
Banana 243
Barca de Pesca 144
Bareham, Sergeant 129
Bari 224
Baril, Sergeant R. 263
Barnard, Commander G. 22
Barratt, Flight Lieutenant A.
    118
Bartels, Warrant Officer A.T.
    171
Basra 15, 18, 184
Bassingbourn 152
Bastia 225, 226, 233
Bateman, Warrant Officer
    Chas 258–61

Bathurst 241, 242, 243–4, 246
Battle of the Atlantic 116–44
Battle of the Bay 117–18
Battle of Berlin 146, 159–60
Battle of Britain 19, 20, 88–92
Battle of the Ruhr 146
Bay of Bengal 40, 253, 259
Bay of Biscay 78–82, 116–18, 122–7, 130–6, 140, 176
Beaufighters 200–1
  Burma 255–61
  ditched 177–80, 216–17, 227
  rescues using 102–3
Beauforts 47–9, 197–8
Beccles 177
Belford, Flight Lieutenant Noel 27, 155–9
Bembridge 89–90
Benbecula 118
Benghazi 189, 193
Benn, Squadron Leader W. 104
Beresford-Pierce, Flying Officer 188
Berka 189, 208
Berrett, Sergeant 244–5
Berry, Flying Officer 229
Betty 152–3
Bickle, Flight Sergeant, R. J. 236
Bicknell, Wing Commander R. 114
Bircham Barrel 41, 251–2, 257, 262–3, 266
Bircham Newton 41, 60, 62, 72
Birt, Flight Lieutenant 105
Bishop, Flight Sergeant D. 75
Bishop, Lieutenant Roger 210–11
Bisleys 216
Bizerte 192, 208–9, 210, 211, 216, 220
Bjarnason, Pilot Officer B. 263
Blackpool 28
Blenheims 188, 189
Blitzkrieg 145
Blomfield, Squadron Leader Peter 238
Blyth 18
Boddy, Warrant Officer 149–50

Boffin, Flight Sergeant C. 227–31
Bolton, Pilot Officer A. 132–3
Bombay 252
Bomber Command
  creation of Air Sea Rescue Service 22
  dinghies for heavy bombers 16
  emergency equipment 42
  offensive campaign against Germany 145–68
  pigeons 50
  rescue procedure 17–18
Bone 192, 216
Bordeaux 140
Borgo 224
Boston, Lincs 168
Bottomley, Air Vice-Marshal N. H. 21–2
Boulogne 53, 55
Boxted 114
Bradford, Flight Lieutenant Cecil 265–8
Bray, Wing Commander Norman 71–4
Brindisi 220
British Air Commission, Washington DC 64
British Expeditionary Force 86–7
British Power Boat Company 62–3
Brown, Sergeant Alex 197–200
Brown, Flight Lieutenant Jack 148–9, 150–1
Brown, Flight Lieutenant R. 237
Brown, Sergeant Thomas 152
Buchanan, Wing Commander J. K. 200
Buckie lifeboat 91–2
Bulley, Warrant Officer Gordon 24, 140–2
Burgess, Sergeant A. A. 160–1
Burke, Warrant Officer J. 266
Burma 252, 254, 255, 260–1
Burma-Siam railway railway 258–9, 268
Burnett, Flight Sergeant W. 236

Calais 57, 67, 102
Calcutta 262

Calvi 234
Campbell, Flight Lieutenant A. M. 53–4
Campbell, Sergeant E. 161
Canadian Pacific 89
Cant aircraft 198–9
Capraia 216–17
Capri 219
Carroll, Flight Sergeant J. E. 209
Carroll, Pilot Officer Tom 244
Carver, Squadron Leader John 98–101
Carver, Sergeant Peter 36, 206–7
Cassibile 215
Castle Archdale 130
Castletown 61
Catalinas 265–9
  India and the Far East 253
  Mediterranean 210–11, 214, 232
  Northwest Europe 17, 48, 116, 120–2, 128–9, 138–9
  West Africa 247
Catania 216, 220
Ceylon 15, 18, 252
Chamberlain, Warrant Officer R. E. 235–6
Chandler, Sergeant E. B. 12, 96–8
Channel Islands 8–9
Cheek, Sergeant B. 66
Cherbourg 174
Chesher, Flight Lieutenant George 80, 82–5, 179
Chipping Warden 72, 73
Chiringa 257
Chisnall, Flight Sergeant A. 119
Chittagong 251, 252, 254, 257
Chitty, Flying Officer A. 244
Christie, Flying Officer Dick 8, 75
Churchill, Winston 116
civil aircraft 17, 19
Civil Aviation Authority 87
Clark, Flying Officer J. 120–2, 163–4
HMS Clarkia 242–3
Cliff, Squadron Leader Headley 2, 47–9

HMAV *Clive* 191
Coastal Command
 anti-submarine squadrons
  176–7
 Battle of the Atlantic
  116–17, 122
 creation of Air Sea Rescue
  Service 20–1, 22–3
 ditching procedure 27
 emergency equipment 42
 Gibraltar 126
 high speed launches 15
 Overlord 169
 pigeons 50
 rescue procedure 17–18
 rescue sqadrons 61–2, 180–1
Coastal Command Review
 30–7
HM Coastguard 15, 19, 23
Cohen, Sergeant A. 160–3
Coleman, Flight Lieutenant
 G. B. S. 200–2
Collins, Pilot Officer W. 87,
 127–30
Cologne 93, 146
Coltishall 91
Conspicuous Gallantry Medal
 130
Contant, Flight Sergeant Cliff
 136–9
convoys 116–18, 241
Conway, Flying Officer Frank
 108–9
Cook, Flight Sergeant 162
Cooper, Corporal 191
Cooper, Flight Sergeant Mike
 4, 56–9
Corfu 198–9
Corsica 216, 220–1, 224–6,
 234
Cossey, Sergeant D. 137
Coulter, First Lieutenant
 266
Crawford, Flying Officer C.
 142–4
Crete 186, 226–32
Croke, Group Captain L. G.
 Le B 20
Cromer lifeboat *10*, 91, 153
Croydon aerodrome 15
Cruickshank, Flight
 Lieutenant John 7–8
Cuttack 261
Cyprus 191, 209
Cyrenaica 189
Czolowski, Pilot Officer 91

D–Day 68, 140, 172–4
 see also 'Overlord', Operation
Dakar 242, 244
Daly, Flight Sergeant W. 137
Dargue, Leading Aircraftman
 Albert 108–9
Davidstow Moor 62
Davies, Lieutenant W. J. 266
Dawson, Flight Lieutenant P.
 W. 186
de la Paulle, Flight Lieutenant
 Jacques 20, 130–3
Dean, Flight Sergeant 230–1
Dean, Flying Officer 175
Defiants 56, 60–1, 109
Denmark 153–4
Dennis, Flight Sergeant C. 67
Desert Air Force Sailing Club
 239
Desvres 55
Devlin, First Lieutenant Paul
 221–4
Dicken Award 49
Dieppe 67, 106–9
 see also 'Jubilee', Operation
Dilkes, Flight Sergeant N.
 127–30
dinghies 38–40
 'A' type 38
 ASV radar 44–5
 'C' type 16
 dinghy drill 15–37, *38*,
  110–12, 162, 194
 emergency packs 16–17, 27,
  29, 33, 40–3, 61, 100–1,
  211–12
 first aid kit 40
 flying boat 14
 Fortress crew *26*
 'H' type *1*, 16, 38, 40,
  131–3, 197–8, 217
 'J' type 16, 38, 40, 125–6
 'K' type
  design 39
  Dieppe 109
  location aids 44
  Mediterranean 200–1, 217,
   225
  Northwest Europe 53–4,
   75, 79–80, 99–101, 128,
   137–9, 141–4, 171,
   178–9
 'L' type 38, 62, 79–80,
  178–9
 'M' type 38, 53, 109, 114,
  225, 233

'Q' type 39–40, 123–5,
 143–4
 sails 39–40
 training in use of 25–37
 visual signals 44
 wing storage 14–15, 38,
  119–20
 wireless transmitters 44–50,
  112–13
 Youngman 38
 see also Bircham Barrel;
  Lindholme Gear;
  Thornaby Bag
Direction Finding (DF) 44
Directorate of Air Sea Rescue
 Services 20–4, 86
distress call procedure 15–16,
 19, 26–7, 28–9
distress flares *see* Verey pistol
ditching drill 25–9, 30–1,
 111–12, 160–2
Divers, Warrant Officer
 Arnold 209–10, 221–6
Dods, Flight Lieutenant W.
 125
Doenitz, Admiral Karl 116,
 117
Donley, Warrant Officer A.
 83–4
Douglas, Air Chief Marshal
 Sir W. Sholto 17, 169
Dover 57, 66–7, 102, 103,
 106–7, 109
'Dragoon', Operation
 233–4
Dudock, Lieutenant 132
Duke of York 138
Duncan, Brigadier General A.
 N. 111
Dunkirk 86–8
Dunsmore, Pilot Officer Bill
 197–200
Dyer, Flying Officer R. J.
 102–3
'Dynamo', Operation 86–8

Eaker, Brigadier General
 111–12
Eastern Air Command 190
Ebbage, Sergeant Clifford
 211–12
Edwards, Flight Sergeant John
 211, 244–5
Elba 216–17, 224–6
Engemoen, Flight Sergeant
 Lyle 165–7

Errington, Flight Sergeant 150
escape drill 25
escape kit 100, 217
Ester, Flying Officer 171
Euler, Flying Officer R. 227–31
Eyton-Jones, Flying Officer A. 8, 74–8

Faeroe Islands 118
Fairmile 'B' launches 24
Far East 250–71
Feather, Sergeant Desmond 175–6
Felixstowe 175
Feni 257
Fifield, Flight Lieutenant J. S. 57
Fighter Command 55
  creation of Air Sea Rescue Service 21, 23
  ditching procedure 27
  Lysander rescue craft 52–3
  rescue procedure 17–18, 19–20
  rescue squadrons 56, 60–2, 106–7, 180–1
Fitchett, Flight Sergeant Bernard 72
Fitchew, Flight Lieutenant 152
flares see Verey pistol
Fleetwood 28
Fletcher, Sergeant Tom 57–8
Flockhart, Sergeant Ron 246–8
Florence 232
flotation jackets see Mae West
Flower, Corporal Les 87–8
fluorescene 196, 205, 252
Flying Control 22
Foggia 232, 234, 237
Ford, Sergeant John W. C. 24, 141–2
Forigny, Squadron Leader Clive 93–5
Foss, Flight Sergeant Ron 126–30
Foster, Air Vice-Marshal 'Pussy' 239
Foster, Lieutenant K. 236–7
Foul Island 256–7
Foulness Control 102
Fox, Uffa 70

France
  Marie-Claire escape line 59
  reoccupation 184, 233–4
  see also D-Day; 'Overlord' Operation
Freer, Flying Officer Romeo 131–3
Freetown 241, 242
French, Squadron Leader Frank 138–40
Frisian Islands 74–5, 104, 177

Gadd, Warrant Officer W. 171
Gage, Pilot Officer D. H. 54
Gaidouronesi 228–31
The Gambia 241
Gambut 187, 189, 208, 227, 228, 231–2
Gaze, Flying Officer 157
George VI 115
Gerbini 221
Gibraltar 117, 126, 142–3
Glasgow 18
Glew, Sergeant 89
gliders 175–6, 181
Gneisenau 47, 95
Gold Coast 242
Goldfish Club 272–3
Goldspink, Flying Officer 237
Goldstein, Flight Sergeant A. S. 236
Goodyear, Flight Sergeant N. 235
Gorleston 175, 179–80
Graham, Flight Sergeant J. C. 161–2
Graham, Warrant Officer P. 224–6
Graham, Flying Sergeant Robert 79–82
Grave 175
Gray, Corporal 265
Gray, Flight Lieutenant Ken 137–9
Gray, Flying Officer Roderick Borden 23, 141, 142
Great Yarmouth 18, 105, 157, 163–4, 167, 175
Green, Flying Officer R. 164
Greenfield, Warrant Officer Bill 149–51
Gregory, Robert 22
Greulich, Lieutenant William 152–3
Griffiths, Sergeant M. 134

Grimsby 18
Grottaglie 232
Gulf of Martaban 258, 268

H. P. Bailey 10, 91
Hagg, Pilot Officer L. 84
Haines, Air Commodore H. A. 61
Hal Far 208, 210, 232
Halifax bombers
  anti-submarine patrols 117
  ditched 67, 133–4, 142–4, 148–9, 159–63, 164–7
  rescues using 123
Hamburg 146, 151–5
Hampden heavy bombers 16, 95–6, 97–8, 103–4
Harpur, Squadron Leader W. 84
Harris, Air Marshal Arthur T. 19–20, 25, 145–6, 164
Harrow heavy bombers 16
Hartley, Flying Officer Eric 21, 133–6
Harvey, Flying Officer L. 84, 179
Harvey, Flight Lieutenant Tom 246–8
Hatfield, Wing Commander Percy 242–3
Hatiali 254
Hawkinge 57–8, 89, 102, 106
Healey, Flying Officer Len 58–9, 171
Heimpal, Flight Lieutenant E. S. 165
Hemsworth, Flight Sergeant James 203–5
Henzarda 254
Herrick, Flight Lieutenant 164
Hesselyn, Flight Lieutenant Roy 149–50
Heyford heavy bombers 16
HF/DF fixes 117
high speed launches (HSLs)
  armament 109–10
  Dunkirk 86
  Fairmile 64, 69, 254
  Fairmile 'B' launches 24
  'Hants and Dorset' 193
  HSL 100 15, 192
  HSL 101 94
  HSL 102 94
  HSL 107 34, 191, 193–7, 199

HSL 110 184–5, 191
HSL 116 90, 97–8
HSL 121 185
HSL 122 108
HSL 123 54, 55, 108
HSL 127 66–7
HSL 129 191
HSL 131 162
HSL 141 185
HSL 158 163–4
HSL 166 192, 197
HSL 170 91–2
HSL 176 209–10
HSL 177 7, 14, 72–3,
 108–9
HSL 182 210
HSL 184 153, 163–4
HSL 190 72–3
HSL 341 261–3
HSL 2543 37, 225 6
HSL 2545 244
HSL 2551 153, 163–4
HSL 2595 211
HSL 2597 233
HSL 2622 230–1
HSL 2677 68
HSL 2679 32, 164, 180
HSL 2697 85, 175–6
India and the Far East 250
limitations 23
Mediterranean 220
Miami 193, 225–6, 251
Middle East 190–3
Overlord 172
production 15–16, 17–18,
 19, 62–5, 67–8, 185
Whaleback 63
wireless receivers 46
Hill, Flying Officer 121
Hillary, Pilot Officer Richard
 90
Hobbs, Staff Sergeant Bruce
 175–6
Hodson, Squadron Leader K.
 107
Holland 175–6, 178
Holmes, Squadron Leader
 Jack 17, 19, 121
Holmsley 133
Honey, Sergeant George
 148–51
Hong Kong 15
Hopkinson, Squadron Leader
 H. 225–6
Horlicks tablets 36, 43–4, 47,
 77, 96–7, 100, 134, 188

Horsa see gliders
Horwood, Pilot Officer Rupe
 258–61
Houtheusen, Flight
 Lieutenant Bert 247–8
'How to Survive in a Dinghy'
 30–7
Howe, Captain C. L. 20, 22
HSLs see high speed launches
Hucking, Flying Officer
 Philip 79–82
Hudsons 6, 23, 59–62, 70,
 72–4, 75–6, 157
Hughes, Squadron Leader S.
 W. R. 186
Huigli, Flying Officer Paul
 122–6
Humphreys, Flying Officer J.
 119–22
Hurghada 184–5
Hurricanes 102–3
Hurst, Sergeant 89
'Husky', Operation 208–16
Hyde, Sergeant 266

Ibsley 98
Iceland 118, 120
Identification Friend or Foe
 (IFF) 29, 66, 72, 163
India 250–71
Initial Training Wings 25–6
International Red Cross 205,
 213
Italy 184, 215–19, 220–6

Jackson, Flight Lieutenant A.
 138–9
Japan 254, 255, 270–1
Jesse Lumb 89–90
Jessore 252
'Jim Crow' squadrons
 106–7
Johnstone, Flying Officer D.
 126–30
Jones, Flight Sergeant B. 84
Jones, Flight Lieutenant David
 5, 65, 66–7
Joyce, Sergeant 131–3
'Jubilee', Operation 106–9
Jui 241, 246

Kabrit 186
Kairouan 206–7
Kalafrana 191, 192, 201
Kaminski, Lieutenant 238
Kammhuber, General 147

K.B.M. 91–2
Keeble, Flight Sergeant E. F.
 221–4, 233
Keelan, Lieutenant John
 152–3
Kennedy, Flight Sergeant Don
 32, 177–80
Kiel 164–5
Kittyhawks 206
knife, floating 42, 80, 123
Kopecky, Pilot Officer V.
 55–6
Krakowiak 230
Krendi 193

La Combattante 125
La Sebala 190
Ladds, Flight Sergeant Ken
 135–6
Lagos 243
Lancasters 28–9, 146–7,
 155–9
landing craft, LST 163
 262 3
Lane, Sergeant Cyril 175–6
Lang, Flight Lieutenant James
 211
Langdon, Lieutenant Noel
 28, 166–7
Langham 83, 177
Large, Pilot Officer Bob 57–9
Le Havre 72
Lecomber, Sergeant J. 74
Lee, Flight Sergeant Arthur
 156–9
Lee, Sergeant John 156–9
Lee, Flight Sergeant Peter
 246
Leigh Light 117
Leighton, Norman 149–51
Leonard, Sergeant R. 263
Leuchars 48, 49
Liberators
 anti-submarine patrols
 117
 ditched 126–7, 136–7,
 261–2
 as rescue craft 113–14, 132,
 253–4, 261–2
Liberia 242
lifeboats 6, 26, 88–92
 A-1 239
 see also airborne lifeboats
Limassol 209
Limavady 140
Lindholme 41–2

Lindholme Gear 41–2
aircraft 61, 113–14
India and the Far East
251–2, 262
Mediterranean 216, 220,
227
Northwest Europe 84, 112,
152, 157, 162, 165,
179–80
West Africa 242
Lindsay, Flight Sergeant
George 163–4
Lindsell, Flight Lieutenant
232
Lisbon 144
Lister, Flight Sergeant G. D.
227, 230
Ljubliana 237
Lloyd, Pilot Officer C. 266
Locke, Flying Officer Chas
268–70
Louw, Lieutenant Peter
232–3
LST see landing craft
Ludlow-Hewitt, Air Chief
Marshal Sir Edgar 17
Luqa 202, 203–4, 205
Lympne 107
Lyne-Hale, Sergeant L.
200–2
Lysanders 3, 19–20, 21, 23,
52–6, 60–1, 102–3

MacDonald, Pilot Officer 47
49
MacDonald, Flight Lieutenant
Alan 73
McGonigle, Second
Lieutenant Bill 221–4
McGown, Flying Officer Ian
29, 165
HMS Mackay 150–1
Mackay, Sergeant P. 12, 95–8
Mackintosh, Lieutenant Don
166–7
McLeary, Sergeant 265
McMurdio, Lieutenant 239
Mae West 39, 194
Battle of Britain 89
ditching procedure 31
improvised survival kits 41
rescues using 55, 101
USAAF 13, 115
visual signals 44
Mahn, Pilot Officer Holbrook
104–6

HMS Mahratta 21, 135–6
Mair, Francis 92
Maiskal Island 262
Maison Blanche 190, 209
Malaya 250, 254, 270–1
Maloney, Sergeant A. 127
Malta 184
marine rescue craft 15, 18,
185, 190–7, 210, 216,
220
rescue aircraft based on 199,
200, 202–5, 220, 232
Manak, Squadron Leader 149
Manchester bombers 102
Manchesters 167–8
Mandalay 268
Manfredonia 235
Mann, Warrant Officer
Douglas 32, 33, 177–80
Manston 15, 102–3
Margate, lifeboat 90
Maridor, Pilot Officer J. P.
103
Marie-Claire escape line 59
marine craft 62–85
see also high speed launches;
pinnaces; rescue motor
launches; seaplane tenders
'Market', Operation 175–6
Martin, Sergeant W. 66
Martlesham Heath 25, 106,
114–15, 148, 150, 164
Maryland aircraft 189
Mason, Flying Officer A. 85
Mastrodrasa, Tenente 199
Mathias, Pilot Officer W. B.
216–19
Mead, Group Captain Roger
133–6, 141
Mediterranean 184–207
Mediterranean Air Command
190, 215–16, 220–1
Mediterranean Allied Air
Forces 221, 232, 233–5
Mediterranean Allied Tactical
Air Forces 234
Mellaha 208
Mersa Matruh 185, 186, 189,
190, 209, 230
MGB see motor gun boats
MGBs see motor gun boats
Miami Ship Building
Corporation 64
Middle East 184
Middle East Command
17–18, 185

Middleton, Flight Sergeant
Ken 131–3
Miller, Flying Officer J. C.
127–9
mines 58–9, 163, 235–6
Misurata 208
Mitchell bombers 74–5, 114
Monte Corvino 220
Monte Cristo 218
Montrose 162
Moore, Flight Sergeant
Terence 35, 203–5
Moore, Sergeant Tommy 175
Moore-Brabazon, Right
Honourable J.T. 70
Morris, Corporal 265
Morrison, Pilot Officer Don
13, 14, 107–9
Mosquito 79
Motherwell, Flight Lieutenant
Vic 29, 164–7
Moths 250
motor anti-submarine boats
68
motor gun boats (MGBs)
104, 105–6
motor torpedo boats (MTBs)
86–8, 150, 219
Moulmein 261, 268
MTB see motor torpedo boats
Munro, Flying Officer J.W.
224–6
Murmansk 118

National Pigeon Service 46,
48
Nelms, Squadron Leader Reg
22, 136–9
Nelson, Lieutenant 237–8
Newall, Air Chief Marshal Sir
Cyril 20
Newhaven 72, 106, 109
Newman, Flight Sergeant L.
H. 215
Newsome, Flight Sergeant L.
237
Nicholls, Flying Officer
191
'Nickel' flights 72, 101–2
Nicolson, Warrant Officer
Nick 268–70
Nigeria 243
Nijmegen 174
Nixon, Flight Sergeant Harry
187–9
Norburn, Sergeant E. 75

Normandy landings *see* D-
    Day *and* 'Overlord',
    Operation
North Africa 184–93, 208
North Coates 104
North Sea 155–63
North West African Coastal
    Air Force 209
Northwest Europe 51–181
Norway 47, 118, 178

'Oboe' 146
Observer Corps 22
O'Dell, Flight Sergeant M.
    265
Ogilvie, Flying Officer C. A.
    209–10
Oliver, Pilot Officer B. J. 196
Operational Training Units
    (OTUs) 29, 72, 146
Oransay, SS 241–2
Ormiston, Warrant Officer
    Tom 149–51
Ostend 174
OTUs *see* Operational
    Training Units
Ouston 56
'Overlord', Operation 164,
    169–70, 172–4
Oyster Island 259

P. B. Cow & Co. 272
P47 Thunderbolts 114
HMS *Paladin* 207
Palermo 215, 216, 220, 221
Palestine 209
Pallett, Flight Lieutenant D.
    W. 244
Parham, Corporal Eric 37,
    225–6
Park, Air Vice-Marshal Keith
    19
Parkinson, Flying Officer G.
    72
Paterson, Warrant Officer C.
    233
Pathfinder Force 146
Peebles, Sergeant 104
Peel, Squadron Leader John
    9, 88–9
Peirse, Air Marshal Sir
    Richard 22
Penang 15, 18
Perkins, Sergeant Les 72
Persian Gulf 184–5
Peterhead 61

Philippeville 192
Phony War 116
pigeons 29, 44, 46–50, 131
pinnaces 63, 64–5, 68
    Middle East 191, 192
P 32 87
P 60 266
P 1304 39, 243–4
P 1311 244–5
    production 24, 64–5
Pirie, Gordon 257–8
Plymouth 169
Pocklington 148
Pointe Noire 242
Pomligliano 232
Ponza 217–18
Poole 169
Port Etienne 242, 243, 246
Port Said 184–5, 191
Portal, Air Chief Marshal Sir
    Charles 110
Portishead GPO radio station
    15
Portland 169
Portugal 142–4
Postgate, Flying Officer 85
Power, Rear Admiral 23
Predannack 79
Price, Flight Lieutenant Eric
    34, 196
prisoners of war 109, 198–9,
    207
Protville 211, 216, 219
'Prune', Pilot Officer 26
Pugh, Flight Sergeant D.
    159–62
Purkiss, Sergeant R. F.
    159–61

Ramree Island 259
Ramsbottom, Pilot Officer
    186
Ramsey, Vice-Admiral Sir
    Bertram 19, 87
Ramsgate 106, 175
Ramu 256
Rangoon 268–9
Rawlings, Flight Lieutenant
    A. 235–6, 237–8
Red Hills Lake 253, 263
Regensburg 215
Regional Control 22
rescue craft 52–85
rescue motor launches
    (RMLs) 68–9, 74–8
    production 64–5

RML 2 77
RML 498 157–9
RML 512 166–7
RML 526 82
RML 534 82
RML 547 77–8
RML 553 77–8
    wireless receivers 46
Reykjavik 120
Rhodes, Flying Officer E. 84
Richardson, Flight Sergeant
    Graham 22, 137
Rivaz, Pilot Officer 'Revs'
    . 11, 93–5
RML *see* rescue motor
    launches
RMLs, Overlord 170
RNLI *see* Royal National
    Lifeboat Institution
RNLI, Overlord 170
Robb, Lieutenant 69–70
Roberts, Flight Sergeant
    58–9
Robertson, Flight Lieutenant
    C. G. 171, 272–3
Robinson, Sub Lieutenant J.
    164
Roderick, Sergeant K. 65
Rogers, Flying Officer Jack
    37, 225–6
rope, floating 62
Ross, Flying Officer David
    138, 179–80
Ross, James 48, 49
'Rover' sorties 103–4
Royal Air Force (RAF)
    1 Squadron 54, 55
    32 Squadron 102
    39 Squadron 216–17
    47 Squadron 227–8
    49 Squadron 95
    83 Squadron 101–2
    102 Squadron 93, 159–62
    149 Squadron 65
    157 Squadron 79–81
    172 Squadron 125, 140–2
    177 Squadron 256–61
    190 Squadron 121
    198 Squadron 149
    200 Squadron 242
    203 Squadron 188
    206 Squadron 118
    210 Squadron 138–9
    217 Squadron 197
    221 Squadron 202–3
    224 Squadron 126

226 Squadron 74
228 Squadron 132
230 Squadron 186, 201, 210
235 Squadron 105
249 Squadron 196
253 Squadron 224
258 Squadron 53–4
260 Squadron 206–7
269 Squadron 62
272 Squadron 200
275 Squadron 53, 181
276 Squadron 53, 169, 171, 174
277 Squadron *3*, *25*, 53, 57–9, 102, 148–51, 170–2, 181
278 Squadron *28*, *31*, 53, 163–4, 166–7, 169, 181
279 Squadron 60, 61, 70–2, 74–6, 152, 157, 177, 180
280 Squadron 60, 61, 80, 83–5, 157, 177, 178–9
281 Squadron 56, 61, 177
282 Squadron 61, 177
283 Squadron 190, 208–9, 215, 220, 221–4, 232, 235
284 Squadron 208, 215, 232–3, 235
292 Squadron 252–3
293 Squadron 215–16, 224–6, 232, 235–6
294 Squadron 215–16, 220, 226–32, 235
305 Squadron 91
401 (RCAF) Squadron 107–8
415 (RCAF) Squadron 103–4
420 Squadron 164–5
422 (RCAF) Squadron 130
440 Squadron 170–2
486 (RNZAF) 72–3
489 Squadron 177–8
520 Squadron 142
603 Squadron 90
616 Squadron 57
meteorological squadrons 142–4
Pigeon Service 46–50
Royal National Lifeboat Institution (RNLI) 15, 23, 63, 88–92
Royal Navy, rescue motor launches 68–9
Royal Netherlands Naval Air Service 49
Royal Observer Corps 151

Rumbold, Squadron Leader P. 265–6

safety equipment workers 28
Saffron Walden 114–15, 163
St Eval 122, 177
St Omer 57
St Paul's Bay 191, 193, 195–6, 199
St Tropez 234
Salerno 216
Salina Island 215
Salmond, Sir John 22, 59–61, 91
Sardinia 210–11, 220–1, 234
Scampton 98
Scarpanto 227
Scatsa 61
Schamong, Oberleutnant zur See Clemens 243
Scharnhorst 47, 95
School of Air Sea Rescue 28
Sea Otters 61, 170–2, 252, 254, 270
SEAC *see* South East Asia Command
Seagull 34, 40
seaplane tenders 63, 64, 87
Selsey lifeboat 88
Seminole 223
Sfax 192
Shackel, Flight Lieutenant W. 263
Shetland Isles 47, 61, 122
Shields, Sergeant R. 65–6
Shnider, Flight Lieutenant Maurice 267–8
Shoreham 58, 106
Sicily 184, 192–4, 203, 208–16, 220–1
see also 'Husky', Operation
Sidi Barrani 187, 189
Sierra Leone 241
Silk, Flight Lieutenant F. H. 102
Singapore 18, 250
Singleton, Flying Officer G. 125
Sliema 192
Smith, Sergeant D. H. 256–8
smoke floats 16, 42, 49, 71, 114, 121, 139
Sommerville, 'Slim' *22*, 136–40
Sousse 192, 216
South East Asia Command (SEAC) 252–3, 271

Soviet Union 118
Spencer, Flight Sergeant Roy 211–15
Spitfires 61–2
ditched 57–9, 98–9, 107–8, 193–7, 206–7, 224–6
rescues involving 54, 57–9, 66–7, 97–8, 102–3, 149, 170–2, 201
Sproule, Pilot Officer M. A. 101–3
Squires Gate, Blackpool 28
ST *see* seaplane tenders
Stanley, Sergeant C. 266
Stark, Sergeant W. 196–7
station air sea rescue officers 26–8, 82, 110–11
Sterne, Squadron Leader W. 209
Stewart, Surgeon Lieutenant G. 129
'Stinkie' 48–9
Stirling, Flight Sergeant 104
Stirlings, ditched 64
Storey, Sergeant W. A. 256–8
Strever, Lieutenant Ted 197–200
Suez 184–5
Sullum Voe 122, 138, 139
Sumburgh 47
Sunderland flying boats
ditched 130–1, 246–8
Malta-based rescue aircraft 200–2
rescues involving *20*, *39*, 116, 121, 124–5, 128–9, 132–3, 141
West Africa 241
survival equipment 25, 28, 38–43, 113–14
survival suits 256, 268
Sutch, Flying Officer 163–4
Sutton harness 55
Swanton Morley 74
Swingate radar station 102–3

Tabarka 192
Taggart, Pilot Officer Robert 195–7
Tain 136
Takali 200
Takoradi 242, 243
Tangmere 57, 72, 88
Taranto 234
Taylor, Flight Lieutenant F. E. 261–3

Taylor, Flying Officer George 257–8
Tee Emm 26, 30
Tessier, Pilot Officer 47, 49
Tholthorpe 165–7
Thomas, Sergeant 104
Thomas, Squadron Leader G. D. M. 227–32
Thomson, Wing Commander Ron *16*, 118–22
Thornaby 41, 62, 177
Thornaby Bag 41, 49, 154, 186, 241
Thorneycroft 67
Thunderbolts 178
'Tiger Force' 271
Tilley, Flight Lieutenant W. B. 141–3
Tiree 62, 177
Tirpitz 47, 136
Tobruk 189
Todd, Flight Lieutenant 201–2
Toner, Sergeant Jock 137–9
Topcliffe 93
'Torch', Operation 117, 190, 192
training 25–37, 110–12
Training Command 17–18
trawlers 91, 94–5, 142–4, 153–4
Trigg, Flying Officer Lloyd 243
Triggol, Sergeant Bob 133–4
Trinder, Sergeant T. S. *27*, 156–9
Tripoli 193, 209
Trojer, Kapitanleutnant Hans 134
Trondheim 47
Tunis 190
Tunisia 184, 189, 202–3, 206–7, 208–10, 216
Turnhouse 56
turtles 264
HMS *Tynedale* 101
Type 'E' rescue gear 62
Typhoons 149, 170–2

U-boats
  Mediterranean 187
  Northwest Europe 116–19, 122–43, 176–7
  U-221 133–4
  U-417 119
  U-468 243
  U-534 140
U-968 137
West Africa 241, 243
Uffa Fox Boat 70–1
ULTRA 117
United States Army Air Force (USAAF) 110–15
  air sea rescue 153
  arrival in the UK 60, 67, 147
  Emergency Rescue Branch 114
  Far East 264
  Overlord 169–70
  training 28
Unkles, Flying Officer R. H. 244
Uptigrove, Sergeant W. E. 58

'Varsity', Operation 181
Vatican 205
Veitch, Lieutenant R. H. 235–40
Venn, Sergeant 47, 49
Verey pistol 42–3, 71, 94, 125, 157, 213, 217–18

Wallens, Squadron Leader R. W. 181
Walls, Second Lieutenant 266
Walruses *31*, 56–9
  creation of Air Sea Rescue Service 23
  India and the Far East 250–1
  Mediterranean 214–15, 216, 220–6, 232–4
  Middle East 186–7, 190
  North Africa 208–10
  Northwest Europe *25*, 49, 148–50, 164, 166–7, 181
  USAAF 114–15
'Walter' *see* air-to-surface vessel (ASV) radar
Waring, Group Captain E. F. 22, 41, 69–70
Warwicks 60–2, 114–15
  airborne lifeboat 70, 78, 80, 82–5
  India and the Far East 252–4
  Mediterranean 220–1, 232
  Middle East 190
  preparations for Overlord 169
  rescues by 162, 178–9
  water rations 16, 34–5, 42, 96–7, 134, 178, 214
Watkins, Flying Officer Allen *30*, 170–2
Watson, Sergeant B. A. 211–14
Watts, Pilot Officer 75
Weaver, Flying Officer F. G. 237
Wellingtons 116–17, 234–5, 252–3
  ditched 72–4, 140–1, 153, 187, 202–4, 212–13
  rescues by *38*, 125, 186–9, 226–31
  West Africa 241–8
  Western Desert 184–5, 186
Westphalen, Oberleutnant zur See Otto 137
Whahram, Flying Officer G. H. 126–7
Whalen, Sergeant L. 263–7
Whiteley, Flying Officer G. E. *24*, 140–2
Whitley heavy bombers 16, 93–4, 116–17, 122–3
Whitney, Flight Sergeant Eric 65–7
Wick 18
Wickenby 155
Wilcox, Pilot Officer J. 127–9
HMS *Wild Goose* 129–30
Wilkinson, Flight Sergeant C. H. 242–3
Wilkinson, Sergeant John 197–200
Williams, Sergeant C. 160–2
Williams, Sergeant Tony 202
Williamson, Flying Officer F. 85
Wilson, Flying Officer Lloyd 73
'Window' 146
'Winkie' 49
wireless transmitters 26–7, 44–50, 71, 157
Wood, Sergeant George 95–8
Woolston, Sergeant Bryan *12*, 95–8

Yorke, Flying Officer J. C. 216–19
Yoxon, Flight Lieutenant A. 261
Yugoslavia 235–40

'Zipper', Operation 270–1

Author's Acknowledgements

I have been given a great deal of assistance in researching, preparing and writing this book, a task I have found immensely stimulating and rewarding. My thanks go to many people.

First I want to thank Flight Lieutenant John Cruickshank VC, the last living airman holder of Britain's supreme award for gallantry, the Victoria Cross, for his most eloquent and appropriate Foreword. As a pilot who flew many anti-submarine patrols over the North Atlantic, he is uniquely qualified to understand the war at sea, and to appreciate the dangers and the demands placed on those who were forced to ditch or abandon their aircraft only to face a desperate fight for survival in such a hostile environment. I am most grateful to him.

The idea for this book stemmed from discussions with the staff of the Air Historical Branch. As on previous occasions, I have received a great deal of help from the Head of the Branch, Sebastian Cox, and his staff. In particular, I would like to thank Graham Day and Clive Richards. I also thank Stuart Hadaway of the RAF Museum and the staff of the photographic department of the Imperial War Museum. Jim Julian DFM, the President of the Goldfish Club, and Mike Dane, who edits the club's excellent newsletter, have been extremely helpful. Mike has been responsible for putting me in touch with a number of the members of the elite club, whose stories appear in later chapters.

I reserve a special thanks to the survivors and to those involved in rescuing them. Many have sent me details of their experiences and lent me valuable photographs. My thanks go to Peter Carver; Robert Gregory; Eric Harrison; Air Commodore Jack Holmes DFC★; Noel Langdon AFC; Peter Lee; David McPherson; Ken Middleton; Bill

AUTHOR'S ACKNOWLEDGEMENTS

ACKNOWLEDGEMENTS 287

Morris; Eric Parham DSM; Doug Todd; Bob Willis MBE, DFC; George Wood DFM; Bryan Woolston DFM; and Mrs Betty Thomson, the widow of Air Vice-Marshal Ron Thomson CB, DSO, DFC. From Canada I have received a great deal of support from Jack Logan; Ian McGown; Judge Terry Moore; Vic Motherwell DFC; and Mrs D Morrison, widow of Don Morrison DFC, DFM. Officials of the Air Sea Rescue and Marine Craft Sections Club, Jim Maton, John Mills, John Parsons and Ted Shute, also gave me valuable help.

I was very anxious to record the deeds of the men who manned the Royal National Lifeboat Institution's lifeboats and I thank in particular Barry Cox, the Honorary Librarian, and Paul Russell of the Cromer lifeboat. I also thank Group Captain Richard Bates AFC and Rob Glover of the Wickenby Register for their help.

I particularly want to thank two good friends and fellow authors, Norman Franks and Roy Nesbit, who have been most helpful in allowing me to use some of their own research material and photographs. I am also grateful to Larry Milberry of Canada and Arie-Jan van Hees from Holland, whose specialist books provided valuable information.

I have acknowledged all the photographs but, as always, I have a special thank you to friends Peter Green and Andy Thomas for supplying those that I found so elusive.

Finally, I want to thank the staff of the National Archives. Initially Jane Crompton encouraged me to write this book and her successor, Catherine Bradley, has given me a great deal of support and help. They have shown great patience in arranging for me to see a very large selection of documents held at Kew and for gaining the necessary permissions to use the material and the photographs from the National Archives. As usual, William Spencer has unearthed priceless information that managed to escape my efforts. Paul Johnson and Hugh Alexander have been tremendously helpful with photographs and have made all the arrangements for reproducing photographs and getting appropriate permissions to use them. Alf Symons oversaw production. Once again, it has been a pleasure to work with all of them and I am grateful for all their help and advice.

Picture Acknowledgements

The source of each picture is given in its caption. Every care has been taken to trace copyright holders. However, if we have omitted anyone we apologize and will, if informed, make corrections in any future edition.

IMPERIAL WAR MUSEUM COLLECTIONS

Many of the photos in this book come from the Imperial War Museum's huge collections which cover all aspects of conflict involving Britain and the Commonwealth since the start of the twentieth century. These rich resources are available online to search, browse and buy at *www.iwmcollections.org.uk*. In addition to Collections Online, you can visit the Visitor Rooms where you can explore over 8 million photographs, thousands of hours of moving images, the largest sound archive of its kind in the world, thousands of diaries and letters written by people in wartime, and a huge reference library. To make an appointment, call (020) 7416 5320, or e-mail mail@iwm.org.uk.

Imperial War Museum *www.iwm.org.uk*

IMPERIAL WAR MUSEUM